SELFISH LIBERTARIANS AND
SOCIALIST CONSERVATIVES?

SELFISH LIBERTARIANS AND SOCIALIST CONSERVATIVES?

The Foundations of the Libertarian–Conservative Debate

NATHAN W. SCHLUETER AND
NIKOLAI G. WENZEL

Stanford Economics and Finance
An Imprint of Stanford University Press
Stanford, California

Stanford University Press
Stanford, California

Special discounts for bulk quantities of titles in the Stanford Economics and Finance imprint are available to corporations, professional associations, and other organizations. For details and discount information, contact the special sales department of Stanford University Press. Tel: (650) 725-0820, Fax: (650) 725-3457

Printed in the United States of America on acid-free, archival-quality paper

Library of Congress Cataloging-in-Publication Data
Names: Schlueter, Nathan W., author. | Wenzel, Nikolai G., author.
Title: Selfish libertarians and socialist conservatives? : the foundations of the libertarian-conservative debate / Nathan W. Schlueter and Nikolai G. Wenzel.
Description: Stanford, California : Stanford Economics and Finance, an imprint of Stanford University Press, 2017. | Includes bibliographical references and index.
Identifiers: LCCN 2016024045 (print) | LCCN 2016025605 (ebook) | ISBN 9780804792912 (cloth : alk. paper) | ISBN 9781503600287 (pbk. : alk. paper) | ISBN 9781503600294 (e-book)
Subjects: LCSH: Libertarianism. | Conservatism.
Classification: LCC JC585 .S337 2016 (print) | LCC JC585 (ebook) | DDC 320.51/2—dc23
LC record available at https://lccn.loc.gov/2016024045

Typeset by Thompson Type in 10.5/15 Adobe Garamond

To my teacher and mentor, Jack Paynter (1938–2005)
—Nathan W. Schlueter

To my teacher and Brother Chime, James P. M.
Walsh, SJ, PhD, CXIX (1938–2015)
—Nikolai G. Wenzel

Contents

Acknowledgments

We wish to thank Hillsdale College for fostering an intellectual environment in which serious debates about ideas can flourish. We especially thank President Larry P. Arnn and former Provost Bob Blackstock for supporting us in the infancy of this project, by allowing us to coteach two classes on the libertarian–conservative debate in spring 2010 and spring 2011.

We thank our students at Hillsdale College (especially those in the libertarian–conservative debate classes), Florida Gulf Coast University, and Flagler College, from whom we have learned so much and for whom we had to sharpen our arguments.

We pay tribute to the late George Carey, whose superb collection of essays, *Freedom and Virtue: The Conservative-Libertarian Debate*, prompted us to write this more systematic book.

We thank Ryan Anderson at *Public Discourse* for publishing an early version of our exchange.

Special thanks to Leo, Helen, Emil, Karol, Mary, William, Margaret, and Judith Schlueter for generously allowing us to take over their household with long conversations by the fire. May they grow up virtuous and free.

Last but not least, we thank Margo Beth Fleming, our *editrix extraordinaire* at Stanford University Press, for her initial faith and for unflagging guidance and support. We also thank two anonymous reviewers for feedback, as well as Chris Coyne for reviewing three versions of the manuscript. Thanks to James Holt and the Stanford University Press production team.

Nathan dedicates this book to Dr. Jack Paynter (1938–2005), a model teacher, scholar, husband, and father, and above all a heroic example of courage in the face of suffering. Without his inspiration, encouragement, and support Nathan would not be who he is today. He thanks Liberty Fund for their many excellent conferences over the years and especially for a post-doctoral fellowship in 2000–2001 that first brought him into contact with the serious philosophical challenges of libertarianism. He also thanks Robby George and Brad Wilson for a marvelous year in the James Madison Program at Princeton University in 2011–2012, which helped bring to fruition a decade of reflection on the libertarian–conservative debate in the form of this book. For helpful feedback on portions of this manuscript, he thanks Ryan Anderson, Samuel Gregg, Thomas G. West, Paul A. Rahe, Sherif Girgis, and Jon Fennell. Above all, he thanks his wife Elizabeth, for whom his gratitude and affection are beyond words.

Nikolai dedicates this book to his teacher, mentor, and Brother Chime, Father James P. M. Walsh, SJ, PhD, CXIX (1938–2015). Although he was skeptical of many of the tenets of libertarianism, Father Walsh instilled in Nikolai the Ignatian tradition of imagination. And, if libertarianism is a theory of individual rights, it is also a theory of social cooperation and human flourishing (in fact, the two are mutually indispensable). Father Walsh was fond of Cicero's wisdom (Cicero, *De Officiis*, 22): "We are not born for ourselves alone . . . We . . . are born for the sake of other human beings, that we might be able mutually to help one another. We ought therefore to [contribute] to the common good of humankind by reciprocal acts of kindness, by giving and receiving from one another, and thus by our skill, our industry, and our talents work to bind human society together in peace and harmony." Objectivists will worry that Cicero contradicts Ayn Rand's oath (Rand 1957): "I swear by my life and my love of it that I will never live for the sake of another man, nor ask another man to live for mine." But the two sentiments find reconciliation in a narrow definition of the common good: a social order based on individual rights, which allows for mutually productive exchange and cooperation with others in a market order with a strong civil society. Thus the Jesuit teacher would not be too horrified that Nikolai cites, among others, the atheist Ayn Rand.

Nikolai also wishes to thank those without whose support this book would not have been possible. He thanks his family for their patience with his routine distraction and unavailability as he was thinking about this book. He thanks his father, Jack, for the ethic of inquiry; his late mother, Dominique, for instilling in him the ethic of justice; and his sister Sophie for pretty much everything. He especially thanks his aunt, Dr. Isabelle Glavany Godet, who started him thinking about the state when he was a teenager. The same goes for cousin, shadow philosopher, and satirist Cyril Bosc and his loving *compagne* Séverine Chevallier. Nikolai would have spent more time with his nieces, Solette Dominique Priest and Lila Margaux Priest, but for this book; he can only hope that they will grow up in a free(r) world.

He thanks David Boaz for the early and crucial guidance that set him on this path; in many ways, this book is the fruition of his generous advice. Thanks to the late Professor Leonard P. Liggio, Jo Kwong, Alex Chafuen, Brad Lips, Véronique de Rugy, and colleagues at the Atlas Economic Research Foundation for early nurturing of his philosophy of liberty. Deep gratitude goes to George Mason University's Walter Williams, Bryan Caplan, Russ Roberts, Pete Boettke, Don Boudreaux, Dragos Aligica, and Richard Wagner. Special thanks to Nathaniel Paxson for his loyal and warm friendship.

Thanks to Hillsdale College, and its administration, students, and colleagues, especially Ivan Pongracic, Charles Steele, and Gary Wolfram, for the best first academic job a fellow could want.

Many thanks to the Association of Private Enterprise, and especially J. R. Clark, Ashley Harrison, Ed Stringham, Bob Lawson, and Ed Lopez, for nurturing Nikolai's scholarship. Special thanks to Ben Powell, for being a mentor.

Nikolai thanks Ben Chang for friendship, support, and insight over the decades and his particular friend Chris Martin for his wisdom.

Jim Loveland and Geoffrey Lea kindly reviewed key portions of this book, providing difficult, but needed, feedback. Any errors remain our own, of course.

Thanks to Nikolai's colleagues at Florida Gulf Coast University and especially Brad Hobbs and Steve Scheff (the Mr. Gallagher to his Mr. Shean) for providing a home in the sun, away from Hillsdale's intellectually nurturing but frigid environment. Brad and Christy Hobbs, and the Weeks family (Shelton, Annemarie, Jessica, and Charlie) opened their homes more generously than could ever be expected. Nikolai also thanks the intrepid seekers with whom he shared over 100 different champagnes over four years in Fort

Myers, under the able leadership of Heather Smith and Cheryl Robinson. Hannah Grandy offered warm and intelligent support and the best spontaneous exposition of Mises. Allie Daniel was a relentless cheerleader. Mike and Lori Yashko, Jim Smith and Kathryn Eickhoff-Smith, Elsa Martinez and Jared Grifoni provided material and spiritual support in southwest Florida.

Nikolai thanks Flagler College, his colleagues, and especially Dean Alan Woolfolk, Allison Roberts, Alex Schibuola, Gary Hoover, Jill Miller, Jessica Howell, Vida Bajc, the Proctor Library staff, and the 2015–2016 new-hire cohort for a warm and supportive new home. Barbara Ottaviani Jones offered a surprising, refreshing, and deep well of culture and intelligent friendship. Special thanks to the purveyors of old-school cocktails at the Ice Plant and the welcoming staff of the Blue Hen and the Floridian for providing an office when he had none.

Mark Patton, George Peacock, Mark Grannis, John Sheridan, and Don Colleton were distant sounding boards (more than they knew).

Financial support from the Charles Koch Foundation and the Anthem Foundation is gratefully acknowledged.

Geoffrey Lea was the indispensable anvil against which Nikolai was able slowly to forge ideas, over many late nights at Johnny T's in Hillsdale, Michigan. The same goes for Charles Fornaciari, the devil's advocate during Nikolai's Fort Myers years, who patiently and ceaselessly forced him to question everything over fine wines at Bistro 41. Thanks, as always, to the Henry C. Simons Circle and especially its brilliant and affable leader, Anthony Evans.

Finally, Nikolai thanks Elizabeth Schlueter for her loving support of Nathan and this project, and for daring to let a crazy libertarian borrow her husband periodically.

SELFISH LIBERTARIANS AND SOCIALIST CONSERVATIVES?

Introduction

NATHAN W. SCHLUETER AND NIKOLAI G. WENZEL

The Book

For much of the last century, political argument and action in America have been organized around two competing movements, progressivism and conservatism. Progressivism (also called modern liberalism)[1] first emerged in the early part of the twentieth century. It is animated by sustained philosophical arguments about equality, justice, and the common good. Although the philosophy of progressivism is not monolithic, we would argue that the arguments of progressivism find their most mature and sophisticated expression in the writings of John Rawls (for an overview, see Tomasi 2012).

Conservatism too is animated by serious philosophical arguments about equality, justice, and the common good. But conservatism has no John Rawls. Instead it has a Russell Kirk, a Richard Weaver, a William F. Buckley, an F. A. Hayek (if indeed Hayek is a conservative), a Harry V. Jaffa, and so on. Because conservatism in America first appeared as a reaction to progressivism, it has been more commonly and easily defined by what it is *against* than what it is *for*. Indeed, as George Nash observes in his definitive history of American conservatism, "The very quest for self-definition has been one of the most notable motifs of [conservative] thought since World War II" (Nash 2006 [1976], xv). As a result, although conservatives have effectively challenged the arguments of progressivism, they have often failed to offer a clear, unified, and attractive alternative.

This failure is partly the result of a deep tension within the conservative movement between libertarianism and traditionalist conservatism (if indeed, both belong in the same family!). Although there have been notable efforts to resolve that tension through a kind of "fusionism" (see Meyer 1996) or, more recently, "conservatarianism" (see Cooke 2015), those efforts have not succeeded.[2] The reason is that the issues dividing libertarians and conservatives are not merely pragmatic; they are fundamental. Although fusionist libertarians find common ground with small-government conservatives, many libertarians are quite unhappy to be lumped in with a conservatism that (to them) has more in common with progressivism in its eager use of the state. Unfortunately, those issues have not been explored with the care they deserve. The debate between libertarians and conservatives has more often been characterized by journalistic polemics than careful inquiry. Hence the title and purpose of our book.

We hope to offer in this book a serious exploration of the philosophical, political, and economic issues underlying the libertarian–conservative debate. At the same time, we believe that a civil, informed, and energetic argument between a libertarian trained in economics (Wenzel) and a conservative trained in political philosophy (Schlueter) offers a more interesting, illuminating, and engaging format for readers than an impartial survey of the issues. There are many great books on libertarianism and many on conservatism. We have learned much from those conservative and libertarian books. However, these books often seem to be talking past one another, sometimes in unhelpful ways, and we are not aware of any book in which libertarians and conservatives engage one another in sustained argument.[3] Indeed, the field of debate between libertarians and conservatives is littered with straw men. To be sure, the subtitle of our book is intentionally tongue-in-cheek: Libertarians do not necessarily promote selfishness, as conservatives sometimes suggest. Indeed, it is precisely their preoccupation with justice and human flourishing that causes them to be so skeptical of the state. Nor does libertarianism necessarily rest on reductive materialism or libertine atheism. And if conservatives see a positive role for political authority in providing for things like education and care for the poor, this does not necessarily make them socialists, any more than support for a healthy moral ecology makes them theocratic puritans.

Our goal in this book is to get past the ad hominem and straw man arguments one often finds in the debate between libertarians and conservatives and to engage the ideas and arguments on their own terms. We are not interested in scoring debater's points. Although we have not avoided frank and direct speech, we have sought to avoid the kind of inflammatory polemic that generates more heat than light. Likewise, although we survey the various schools of thought within libertarianism and conservatism, we are primarily interested in seeking to identify and defend those that we find to be the best foundational arguments within libertarianism and conservatism. We leave it to politicians, policy analysts, and poets to convert these arguments into the currency of political practice.

A Bit about Us

The authors first met at a Hillsdale College faculty meeting in the winter of 2007. Schlueter, a philosophy professor, learning that Wenzel was new to the economics faculty, inquired into Wenzel's academic interests. "Constitutional economics," Wenzel replied—to which Schlueter impishly retorted, "Isn't that a contradiction in terms?" A heated discussion ensued, and a friendship was born that carried us through two popular courses on the libertarian–conservative debate and eventually to this book. In the meantime, Wenzel gave Schlueter his first bow tie, and Schlueter taught Wenzel how to mix a martini. We even enjoy periodic performances of American folk, bluegrass, and roots music (but those who have had the privilege of hearing "The Low Down Dirty Docs" will understand why we kept our day jobs).

Wenzel has said that if all conservatives were like Schlueter, he might be one too, a sentiment Schlueter gladly reciprocates with respect to Wenzel and libertarianism.

This book is not about its authors, but our readers may want to know something about what brought us to our respective positions. Schlueter's first interest in politics came as a young activist, participating in marches, protests, debates, and election campaigns. He paid his way through college working for the city, collecting trash and recyclable materials, paving roads, and flushing fire hydrants. The inefficiency he saw during his time there made a lasting impression on him.

After graduating from Miami University of Ohio (his time there over-lapped with that of Rep. Paul Ryan), Schlueter went on to pursue a PhD in politics at the University of Dallas, where he studied in depth the principles of the American founding. This study was reflected in his first book, *One Dream or Two? Justice in America and in the Thought of Martin Luther King, Jr.*

Schlueter first encountered libertarian ideas during a postdoctoral fellowship at Liberty Fund in 2000, where he read the works of James Buchanan, Murray Rothbard, Friedrich Hayek, and Wilhelm Roepke. He next turned to the works of Wendell Berry, where he found an interesting and attractive combination of traditionalist, localist, communitarian, and libertarian ideas. This interest resulted in his next book, *The Humane Vision of Wendell Berry*, edited with Mark Mitchell.

But perhaps the most decisive moment in Schlueter's intellectual development came with his move to Hillsdale College in 2005. There he found a rich, diverse, and energetic culture of debate and inquiry among faculty and students on the nature of free government and a free society. He was able to write most of this book in 2011–2012 while he was a Fellow at Princeton University's James Madison Program in American Institutions and Ideals, for which he is immeasurably grateful. There he also immersed himself in the writings of Alasdair MacIntyre and John Finnis, who provided him with the most important philosophical foundations and framework for organizing and synthesizing his ideas. Schlueter lives in Hillsdale with his wife, Elizabeth, and their eight children.

Wenzel was initially a bright-eyed Wilsonian institutionalist and social democrat. After graduating from the School of Foreign Service at Georgetown University, he was convinced that the U.S. government could solve all the world's problems . . . except those that required multilateral cooperation. A brief stint in the U.S. Foreign Service quickly disabused him of this view. He realized that his professional frustrations were not accidental but matched the theory of bureaucracy and politics he was reading at night (see Sowell 1996). After just one tour (in Mexico City), Wenzel left the State Department. The following two years were an exciting whirlwind of TV appearances and congressional testimony about the State Department's negligence in issuing visas to the 9/11 terrorists.

But Wenzel was drawn to the intellectual life, rather than the policy circles of Washington, DC. In the State Department, he had discovered conservative thought as the only obvious alternative to the social democracy of his youth. But conservatism was dissatisfying, as it was still too willing to use the state to advance its own purposes. So further reading led Wenzel first to libertarianism, then to the Atlas Network—and a PhD in economics at George Mason University. Originally concerned with the lot of the poorest in society (a lingering preoccupation), Wenzel was drawn to public choice theory and the intellectual humility of the Austrian school, both of which have an institutional home at George Mason University. He is now involved in several libertarian academic groups, including the Society for the Development of Austrian Economics, the Association of Private Enterprise Education, and the Mont Pelerin Society. On a lark, Wenzel was a delegate to the 2013 Florida Libertarian Party convention; illuminated, inspired, and energized, he nonetheless returned to his comparative advantage in the world of ideas.

Where We Agree

Before we develop our disagreements, it will be helpful to the reader to know where we agree. Although some people will find some of these areas of agreement questionable, we will not spend much time defending them here. (That will have to wait for another book.)

First, we agree with Richard Weaver that ideas have consequences (see Weaver 1984). Human action is not simply behavioral responses to external stimuli. It is profoundly shaped, conditioned, and motivated by our ideas about reality. The great conflicts among fascism, national socialism, communism, and liberalism in the twentieth century—as among Islamism, communism, progressivism, libertarianism, and conservatism in our own—point, for good or ill, to the powerful causal influence of ideas on human action.

Moreover, in these pages, we are not simply engaged in a power game of competing ideas; rather, we are both interested in the truth of our ideas. Aeschylus reminds us that we suffer into truth. In that spirit, we have sought through our conversations and the writing of this book to learn from each other, just as we hope that the poet William Butler Yeats was correct when he wrote that "truth flourishes where the student's lamp has shone." Although we each find strong reasons for holding our respective positions on the libertarian–conservative debate, we agree there is no "silver bullet" deductive argument that conclusively determines the debate one way or another. Moreover, we are each aware of weaknesses in our own positions that we do our best to acknowledge. This is not the first book on political authority, and it certainly will not be the last. There is much work that remains to be done, but we hope at least to have cast some light forward.

Second, we reject modern liberalism (or what we shall call here progressivism). We believe that progressivism involves an unreasonable distrust in the ability of human beings to cooperate and coordinate voluntarily to meet their needs in civil society and an unreasonable trust in the capacity of government experts to solve complex social problems. Moreover, progressivism is animated by an "ideal theory" (see Rawls 1971) that overemphasizes the importance of good intentions and underemphasizes practical feasibility (see Tomasi 2012, 197–225). As a result, we think that progressives have a pattern of protecting or promoting well-intentioned institutions and programs that are demonstrable failures. Although (like ideal theorists) we are concerned with identifying and defending principles of justice, we believe that feasibility is a constituent part of justice and not merely a secondary consideration. A sound public philosophy must take people as they are and not as we want or imagine them to be.

Third, we regard the modern administrative state as both unconstitutional and unjust. The administrative state is unconstitutional in at least three ways: First, it exceeds the powers delegated to the national government by the Constitution; second, it creates an unconstitutional, unelected fourth branch of government (the "administrative branch"); and third, it involves the unconstitutional delegation of legislative, executive, and judicial powers to that fourth branch (see Lawson 1994). Of course, these constitutional defects could be formally remedied by amending the Constitution, but this would not remedy the fact that the administrative state is also *unjust* insofar as it profoundly undermines what we see as one of the most basic principles of political justice, the rule of law (see Epstein 2011), and saps the energy and initiative of individuals within civil society.

Fourth, we affirm the basic moral equality of persons. Persons, as centers of intelligence, value, and action, are the fundamental principles of moral and political analysis. Every legitimate association, including the political association, exists for the good of persons. No person may be mistreated, abused, or sacrificed for the good of others, whether according to the "greatest happiness of the greatest number," the "general utility," or any other consequentialist reason. We deny, however, that this moral equality requires material, economic, or social equality, though we differ somewhat on what that moral equality allows and requires.

Fifth, we agree that virtue is a necessary, though not a sufficient, condition for free government. That is, we disagree with Immanuel Kant's assertion that "the problem of organizing a state . . . can be solved even for a race of devils, if only they are intelligent" (Kant 1992, 112). Although well-designed institutions matter, not even the best-designed institutions can save a race of devils from tyranny. We disagree, however, on which virtues are necessary and how they are acquired and maintained.

Sixth, we agree that economic freedom is a matter of basic justice and a necessary component of human flourishing. Thus we not only oppose the administrative state, we also oppose crony capitalism, which cloaks its statism with the language of the free market. Our convictions about the value of economic liberty are strongly influenced by the writings of Nobel Prize–winning economist F. A. Hayek. Hayek's defense of the free market rests not in the celebration of egoistic individualism but in the humble acknowledgment of the limits of human knowledge and action. Given those limits, Hayek pointed out the singular ability of the free market to coordinate widely dispersed information for the benefit of individuals and associations, and he showed why central economic planning must eventually lead to central social planning. We both object to certain aspects of Hayek's thought (Wenzel thinks Hayek still allowed for too much government intervention; Schlueter objects to Hayek's evolutionary account of moral knowledge). We also differ with one another on the extent to which social and political realities can be understood through the lens of economic assumptions. Nevertheless, we are indebted to Hayek's profound insights into the nature of social orders and his courageous defense of liberty.

In short, both Wenzel and Schlueter believe they are defending some version of classical liberalism. But classical liberalism, like conservatism, is a tradition with a history (see Frohnen et al. 2006, 498–502). It includes such diverse thinkers as Montesquieu, John Locke, David Hume, Edmund Burke, and Adam Smith. Classical liberalism, again like conservatism, is therefore disputed territory. One can identify areas of agreement within classical liberalism (such as those previously listed) but also highlight and develop strains within that tradition that are incompatible with one another. It would not be inaccurate to say that the libertarian–conservative debate is, in many ways, an extended argument on the meaning of classical liberalism.

The Order of this Book

The format of this book consists of parallel chapters in which each of us lays forward his arguments and responds to counterarguments.

In the first chapter Schlueter gives an account of conservatism that integrates the best insights of traditionalist conservatism, neoconservatism, and libertarianism, while correcting what he regards as erroneous tendencies in each. This form of conservatism might simply be called "American conservatism," because it seeks to preserve and promote the basic principles of the American founding, which conservatives regard as the highest development of the Western tradition of law and liberty. Those principles include limited constitutional government dedicated to securing both individual rights and the conditions for human flourishing; the rule of law; subsidiarity (especially in the form of federalism but also with respect to public policy at the state and local levels); and a commitment to public reason and deliberation. In short, American conservatism is a form of classical liberalism. The American founders drew heavily on the principal thinkers of classical liberalism, especially the Baron de Montesquieu, John Locke, David Hume, and Adam Smith, but they brought to this tradition deep reflection on the insights of history, experience, and premodern political philosophy. Following Christopher Wolfe, American conservatism might also be called "natural law liberalism" (see Wolfe 2009).

Like classical liberalism more generally, natural law liberalism affirms natural rights, the free market, limited government, the rule of law, and a commitment to public reason as the ground for law and public policy, and it repudiates principles of the ancien régime like religious intolerance, laws of entail and primogeniture, titles of nobility, and mercantilist economics. Unlike some forms of classical liberalism, which rest on philosophical skepticism (as one finds in David Hume and F. A. Hayek), natural law liberalism affirms the capacity of reason to discover natural principles of justice while also holding that reason depends on, grows from, and is limited by experience, history, and tradition. In other words, natural law liberalism rests on a conception of reason (or epistemology) that is neither Humean skepticism nor Cartesian rationalism but moderately realist, oriented toward truth, yet conditioned and limited by experience and tradition. This conception of reason informs the conservative conviction that politics (and with it citizenship, patriotism, and statesmanship) is both a necessary and a permanently problematic feature of human existence. In this book, unless otherwise noted, the words *conservative* and *conservatism* will always refer to this form of American conservatism or natural law liberalism.

In Chapter Two, Wenzel makes the case for libertarianism. Although he agrees with the philosophical foundations for libertarianism (in terms of rights and autonomy), Wenzel is a professional political economist. In this chapter, he will summarize the rights-based case for libertarianism and then emphasize the alternate case for libertarianism based on "robust political economy." Robust political economy integrates the insights from public choice theory and Austrian economics; it recognizes that economic and political actors cannot reasonably be assumed to be benevolent or omniscient, and it seeks to adopt political and social institutions accordingly. After establishing his methodology, Wenzel will identify and examine the three principal schools of libertarianism and their respective roles for government: classical liberalism (defense of rights and solutions to market failure), minarchy (defense of rights only), and anarcho-capitalism (defense of markets and civil society only, as government is not only inherently coercive but also unnecessary). He will ultimately make the case for minarchy: Legitimate government is limited to the protection of rights (life, liberty, and property)—and stops there. As he will make clear in subsequent chapters, unless he adds a qualifying disclaimer, Wenzel will use "libertarianism" to mean "minarchy."

Any attempt by the state to go beyond this limited role is both immoral and self-defeating, as it will necessarily violate the rights of some to advance the preferences of others. Fortunately, markets and civil society, based on a foundation of individual rights protected by a limited government, offer the greatest opportunity for human flourishing, without the dangers of interventionism by the state.

In Chapter Three, Wenzel will give his arguments against conservatism and respond to Schlueter's primary objections to libertarianism. In Chapter

Four, Schlueter will offer his arguments against libertarianism and respond to objections.

Because one important measure of a public philosophy is how it plays out in practice, the last two chapters will be dedicated to three cases studies: immigration, education, and marriage. We have chosen these particular case studies not only because they are persistent points of disagreement between libertarians and conservatives but because they bear directly and fundamentally on the disagreement between libertarians and conservatives on the nature of the political association and political authority. For each case study, we will explain the response from the competing strains within our school while emphasizing our primary case.

We close this introduction with a note of warning, and encouragement, to the reader: When we first undertook this debate, each of us had confidence that his respective position could rather easily defeat the other. Having now surveyed the territory in depth, we have both lost the naïve confidence of those early days. Like Plato's treatment of justice in *The Republic*, the libertarian–conservative debate touches on every subject of human interest and concern: metaphysics, epistemology, ethics, politics, even poetry. We are both much more profoundly aware of the limits of our own knowledge and thus also of the arguments in this book. As a warning, then, the reader should not expect to find the last word on the subject here, any more than Plato was the last word in philosophy. Careful readers will doubtless find many places here where the arguments require further support and development. In most cases we are all too aware of those places. But this should also be a source of encouragement for curious readers to take on themselves an exploration of the rich ideas that inform the libertarian–conservative debate. It is material worthy of a lifetime, and more, of study. For those readers, we have included a short list of suggested readings at the end of each chapter. Full citations can be found in the bibliography at the back of the book.

For Further Reading

George Carey's edited volume, *Freedom and Virtue: The Conservative/Libertarian Debate*, offers a superb introduction to this debate, in the form of point–counterpoint short essays. Bruce Frohnen, Jeremy Beer, and Jeffrey O. Nelson offer an encyclopedic overview of the different strains of conservatism in *American Conservatism: An Encyclopedia*, while George Nash offers a history of conservatism in *The Conservative Intellectual Movement in America since 1945*. Frank Meyer, the father of "fusionism" between conservatism and libertarianism, describes the differences between the two schools, while arguing that they are ultimately complementary, in his book *In Defense of Freedom*.

CHAPTER ONE

What Is Conservatism?

NATHAN SCHLUETER

THE QUESTION OF THIS TITLE presents formidable difficulties. Unlike libertarianism, conservatism is not a specific philosophy of government but a generic term that can have a wide range of specific meanings, depending on context. A Muslim conservative is not the same as a Catholic conservative or a Chinese conservative; a European conservative is not the same thing as an American conservative, and, within America, a paleoconservative is not the same as a neoconservative. Conservatism, whatever its form, is bound up with historical particularity.

But this does not necessarily mean that conservatism is completely *bound by* historical particularity, for there are moments in history when human beings seek to discover and protect transhistorical principles of right. Such moments characterize the history of the West, from the discovery of philosophy in ancient Greece, to Roman republicanism, to patristic and scholastic Christianity, to classical liberalism. Although these moments did not unfold into one another in any smooth, organic, and uncomplicated way, there is an undeniable continuity between them such that one may legitimately speak of a Western philosophical and political tradition.[1] Conservatism seeks to "conserve" the best elements of that tradition.

But while this is true of the conservatism I wish to defend here, the account is far too broad to be of much use in the conservative–libertarian debate. We must begin by narrowing the lens to the specific historical context in which the libertarian–conservative debate originated. That context is post–World War II America. This is not to deny that the debate has much deeper historical roots than this period or that elements of the debate transcend historical particularities (both of these propositions are evidently true, and I will say more about them in what follows), but focusing on this period will help highlight the issues in this debate. In doing so, I am largely following George H. Nash's strategy in his magisterial *The Conservative Intellectual Movement in America*. But whereas Nash doubts that there is "any single, satisfactory, all-encompassing definition of the complex phenomenon called conservatism," and even suggests that "conservatism is inherently resistant to precise definition" (Nash 2006 [1996], xiii–xiv), I am more hopeful that a unified account of American conservatism can be formulated. As Nash concedes, despite his own doubts, "The very quest for self-definition has been one of the most notable motifs of [conservative] thought since World War II" (Nash 2006 [1996], xv). And indeed one may even learn something from Nash's doubt: Any adequate definition of conservatism will have to make principled (and not merely pragmatic) room for some difference and disagreement while avoiding a lowest common denominator "mere conservatism." Such, at any rate, is the kind of conservatism I intend to define and defend here.

In the following sections I will elaborate on this form of conservatism. First, in the following section, I will argue that conservatism rests on a recognition of the mutual interdependence of liberty, tradition, and reason, what I call the "equilibrium of liberty." The principles of the American founding, I assert, rest on the singular achievement of just such an equilibrium, and the conservatism I wish to defend, therefore, looks to the principles of the American founding. Next, in the section after that, I argue that the principles of the American founding are a form of classical liberalism, which I call natural law liberalism. In the following three sections I give an outline of natural law liberalism with respect to limited government, natural rights, and consent. I next show how the principles of the American founding can be said to be an expression of natural law liberalism, giving special attention to constitutional design and statesmanship. I end my discussion by giving a brief summary of the conclusions of the chapter.

The Equilibrium of Liberty: Libertarianism, Traditionalist Conservatism, Neoconservatism

The case for a unified conservatism can be built from the three primary strains within the conservative intellectual "movement": Libertarianism, traditionalist conservatism, and neoconservatism. Of course, this is a simplified

Error in notes

picture. There are "liberaltarian" libertarians who positively repudiate conservatism and seek alliances with progressivism (see, for example, Lindsey 2010), and the Christian right and Tea Party movements don't fit neatly into any of these categories. But the Christian right and Tea Party can to some extent be characterized as grassroots populist movements in search of clarification about their own identity, rather than separate strains within conservatism. Or so I shall argue here.

Each of the strains within conservatism can be said to represent a principle. For libertarianism, that principle is *liberty*; for traditionalist conservatism, *tradition*; and for neoconservatism, *reason*. It is interesting, and perhaps not surprising, that each of these strains also tends to be associated with an academic discipline: Libertarians tend to the field of economics, paleoconservatives to history and literature, and neoconservatives to the social sciences, especially sociology and political science.

The fundamental insight to a sound account of conservatism is that all three of these principles are necessary for human flourishing and that, although they are in some tension with one another, the three principles are interdependent. Taken in isolation, each of these principles not only fails to achieve its *own* end; it also tends toward monstrous consequences.[2] Set in careful equilibrium, like the constitutional system of checks and balances, each principle not only *prevents* the perverse tendencies of the others but also *provides* best for their most wholesome influence and development.[3] We might call this the equilibrium of liberty. Frank Meyer offered something like this principle in his defense of "fusionism," but as Murray Rothbard rightly pointed out, Meyer's fusionism was really libertarianism.[4] Because the equilibrium of liberty is the underlying principle in everything that I have to say about conservatism, it will be useful to say more here about the separate strands of which it is comprised.

Begin with libertarianism. According to Wenzel, "Libertarianism considers liberty the highest political good." In the words of David Boaz, "Libertarians believe respect for individual liberty is the central requirement of justice" (Boaz 1997a, 1). I will of course have much more to say about libertarianism in the following pages, but for now it can be said, in agreement with libertarianism, that liberty, both civil and political, is indeed one of the most important principles of justice. By *civil liberty* I mean freedom to pursue one's own flourishing without requiring the permission of coercive government. It includes the freedom to pray, speak, give, buy, sell, trade, and cooperate with others on common projects, according to one's best judgments. Political liberty is the right to participate in the decision making of government, through advocacy of issues and candidates, voting, and participation in public office.

Explaining the value of civil and political liberty should not require much space. Civil liberty rests on the equal dignity of human persons, who can achieve their flourishing only through their own self-constituting choices. Civil liberty also unleashes the greatest human potential for discovery, knowledge, and invention, resulting in benefits for all human beings.[5] Political liberty not only serves as an important check on government power, it also reflects human equality. As Thomas Jefferson put it in a letter to Roger Weightman, "The mass of mankind has not been born with saddles on their backs, nor a favored few booted and spurred, ready to ride them legitimately" (Jefferson 1975, 585).

But it is worth pointing out here that these two forms of liberty are not identical and can indeed be in great tension with one another. Over sixty years before John Stuart Mill highlighted this tension in *On Liberty* (1978 [1959]), Thomas Jefferson, criticizing the first post-Revolution constitution of Virginia, wrote that "173 despots would surely be as oppressive as one" and that "an *elective despotism* is not the government we fought for" (Jefferson 1975, 164). The founders of America regarded the reconciliation of civil and political liberty as one of the most important and difficult political tasks. As James Madison put it in *Federalist 10*: "To secure both the public good and private rights against the danger of [a majority faction], and at the same time to preserve the spirit and form of popular government, is then the great object to which our inquiries are directed" (Hamilton, Jay, and Madison 2001, 45). The entire architecture of the U.S. Constitution (that is, a written constitution of enumerated powers, bicameralism, federalism, separation of powers, checks and balances, and so on), what Madison called its "auxiliary precautions" and "inventions of prudence" (*Federalist 51*; Hamilton, Jay, and Madison 2001, 269), are designed to address this difficulty.[6]

Moreover, if it is true that civil and political liberty are great goods, it is also true that they depend on conditions that are a rare and always fragile achievement. Liberal democracy is more circumscribed and threatened today than at the end of the Cold War, despite Francis Fukuyama's famous (or infamous) prediction of its global triumph (see Fukuyama 2006). Those conditions include not only the security provided by well-designed political institutions but also opinions, sentiments, and habits favorable to liberty in the members of the political association. In making liberty the highest political good, libertarians inadvertently undermine those conditions.

I shall support this claim with one example relevant to today's political climate. It is obvious that liberty requires an effective defense against domestic and international terrorism. It is also obvious (at least to nonlibertarians) that effective defense requires powers in the government adequate to the threat, powers of secrecy, investigation, preemption, and quick action, that not only circumscribe the strict boundaries of individual liberty but are also liable to great abuse. Although the use of these powers demands vigilance on the part of citizens, that vigilance must rest on a reasonable recognition of the complex and delicate trade-offs necessary to protect a free society. Libertarians, in promoting an abstract and absolute conception of liberty as the highest political good, undermine the institutions necessary to protect liberty as well as the opinions on which those institutions rest.

Unlike libertarianism, traditionalist conservatism is rooted in a sober awareness of the conditions of human flourishing.[7] Traditionalist conservatives trace their roots to Edmund Burke, who with prophetic insight and eloquence predicted the bloody tyranny that would result from the "*liberté*" of the French Revolution. Russell Kirk, the father of traditionalist conservatism, saw in Burke the remedy to modern rationalism, whether in the form of progressivism or libertarianism. Against rationalism, Kirk promoted "custom, convention, and old prescription" as "checks both upon man's anarchic impulse and upon the innovator's lust for power" (Kirk 1986, 9).

F. A. Hayek, too, although not a traditionalist conservative, contested rationalist and constructivist theories of liberty, observing that "freedom is not a state of nature but an artifact of civilization" (Hayek 2011 [1960], 107). Sounding much like Kirk, and Burke, Hayek asserted that "there probably never has existed a genuine belief in freedom, and there has certainly been no successful attempt to operate a free society, without a genuine reverence for grown institutions, for customs and habits and 'all those securities of liberty which arise from regulation of long prescription and ancient ways.'"[8] Hayek concluded: "Paradoxical as it may seem, it is probably true that a successful free society will always in large measure be a tradition-bound society" (Hayek 2011 [1960], 122).

But Hayek also exposed a weakness in traditionalist conservatism: Although tradition is a necessary condition for a free society, it is not a sufficient condition. The sting in Hayek's criticism of traditionalist conservatism, which is worth quoting at length, should not conceal its kernel of truth:

> . . . conservatism fears new ideas because it has no distinctive principles of its own to oppose to them; and, by its distrust of theory and its lack of imagination concerning anything except that which experience has already proved, it deprives itself of the weapons needed in the struggle of ideas. Unlike [classical] liberalism with its fundamental belief in the long-range power of ideas, conservatism is bound by the stock of ideas inherited at a given time. And since it does not really believe in the power of argument, its last resort is generally to claim a superior wisdom, based on some self-arrogated superior quality. (Hayek 2011 [1960], 526)

Neoconservatism seeks to address this weakness in traditionalist conservatism by supplying reasoned arguments in defense of conservative principles. Irving Kristol, sometimes called the intellectual godfather of neoconservatism, is often credited with the quip that a neoconservative is "a liberal who has been mugged by reality."[9] The early neoconservatives were modern liberal intellectuals who became disillusioned by what they perceived as failures of progressive social and economic programs. But, rather than abandon government policy altogether, neoconservatives sought to improve it, in part "by taking administrative authority from federal agencies and placing it in local hands wherever possible and by maximizing the choices of individuals" (John Ehrman in Frohnen et al., 2006, 612).

Without question, neoconservatism has helped energize the conservative movement and to give it credibility in the wider culture, but traditionalist conservatives and libertarians question the extent to which neoconservatives have shed their progressivism. In domestic affairs, neoconservatives continued to support the New Deal, the beachhead of modern progressivism. Neoconservatives have also been strong proponents of a muscular foreign policy and of interventionist efforts to plant liberal democracy in troubled regions of the world by toppling despots and engaging in prolonged nation building. Trillions of dollars and thousands of lives later, those regions are more unstable than before intervention. Traditionalist conservatives and libertarians are right to worry that neoconservatism has not entirely shed the rationalist constructivism of progressivism.

In short, libertarianism, traditionalist conservatism, and neoconservatism each rest on an important principle, yet each of them has a tendency to exaggerate that principle at the expense of the others. Liberty, tradition, and reason each require the others for their completion. The equilibrium of liberty is a rare and always fragile achievement that must be won anew in every generation. The American founding was such an achievement, but that achievement is more threatened today than ever before by the strains of rationalism and traditionalism. (Indeed, as I will suggest in my next chapter, there is a rationalist strain in Hayek's own thought that significantly undermines his otherwise formidable system of liberty.) The task of American conservatism is the recovery of the founders' understanding of the equilibrium of liberty, and that recovery requires prudence, the one cardinal virtue explicitly appealed to in the Declaration of Independence.

Put most simply, then, American conservatism is committed to conserving the principles of the American founding, and to renewing the models of political leadership that gave those principles life.[10] It does not regard the American founding as perfect. None of the founders thought it was, and all acknowledged that practical compromises had to be made that were in conflict with those principles.[11] But they believed it to be the least imperfect political regime the world has yet known, able to provide the conditions for human flourishing while at the same time preventing tyranny.

Hayek himself approved of this form of conservatism. Although he famously distanced himself from the label "conservative," Hayek, a native of Austro-Hungary, had in mind the European or Continental form of traditionalist conservatism that existed as a reactionary and rearguard defense of the ancien régime against classical liberalism. But Hayek observed that "liberalism" (by which he means classical liberalism, the tradition of Montesquieu, Locke, Burke, Smith, and Tocqueville) is "the common tradition on which the American polity had been built" (2011 [1960], 519), and thus that conservatives in America can "defend individual liberty by defending long-established institutions" (521).

Classical Liberalism and the American Founding

In short, the principles of the American founding that conservatives defend are a form of classical liberalism. Conservatives today are rightly suspicious of the term *liberal*, for two reasons. On the one hand, liberalism has come to be associated exclusively with progressivism, an ideology that repudiates the principles of the American founding and promotes in its place the centralized administrative state. Those conservatives should remember that the traditionalist Edmund Burke was a classical liberal in the Whig reform tradition. He was also "the man whom [Adam] Smith [the founder of free market economics] described as the only person who he [Smith] ever knew who thought on economic subjects exactly as he did without any previous communication having passed between them."[12] It was not until the twentieth century, when progressives like Franklin Delano Roosevelt claimed for themselves the mantle of liberalism, that American liberals opposed to the New Deal became known as "conservatives." The semantic change was a seismic shift, and, although it is perhaps too late now for conservatives to recover their rightful title, they must not forget that positive system of liberty that conservatism exists to defend.

But then a second and more powerful conservative objection appears: Even in its classical form, so the argument of some traditionalist conservatives goes, liberalism rests on a corrosive anthropology of individualism and radical autonomy that eventually undermines the nonliberal conditions necessary for free government. As Patrick Deneen puts it in a much-discussed *First Things* article:

> Liberalism is a bold political and social experiment that is far from certain to succeed. Its very apparent strengths rest upon a large number of pre-, non-, and even antiliberal institutions and resources that it has not replenished, and in recent years has actively sought to undermine. This "drawing down" on its preliberal inheritance is not contingent or accidental but in fact an inherent feature of liberalism. (Deneen 2012b)

In Deneen's reading, classical liberalism rests on a radical break with the premodern tradition that, consistently followed, must eventually lead to progressivism. In my reply to Deneen I wrote the following:

> Deneen writes as though the truly liberal reforms of the American founding—the institution of republican forms of government, the prohibition of titles of nobility, the elimination of religious establishments and primogeniture, the abolition of slavery, the admission of truth as a defense in cases of libel, and so on—put America on the sure path to abortion on demand and redefining marriage. But this is absurd. No signer of the Declaration of Independence thought that in affirming equality and natural rights he was also affirming a voluntarist moral philosophy, and every one of them would be as troubled by the state of modern America as is Deneen. (Schlueter 2012)

In other words, Deneen's case rests on an unreasonably narrow account of liberalism that traces its genealogy to Thomas Hobbes. It does not mention that liberals writing after Hobbes explicitly repudiated his moral and political philosophy and would have expressed full agreement with Alexander Hamilton's description of it as an "absurd and impious doctrine" ("The Farmer Refuted," in Frisch 1985, 19). More important, it overlooks the possibility of a form of liberalism more continuous with the premodern tradition and rooted in a more positive view of nature, reason, and morality. One finds such a form of liberalism in the American founding.

The American founders simultaneously and seamlessly affirmed traditional ideas like the natural law, public morality, and the common good and more modern ideas like natural rights, limited government, property rights, and consent. And in support of such affirmations they appealed to both classical and modern sources. As Thomas Jefferson said of the Declaration of Independence, "All of its authority rests on the harmonizing sentiments of the day, whether expressed in conversation, in letters, printed essays, or in the elementary books of public right, as Aristotle, Cicero, Locke, Sidney, &c" (Jefferson 1979, 11–12). And as Donald Lutz points out, in "Sydney's *Discourses Concerning Government*, published the year before Locke's *Second Treatise*, Sidney quotes liberally from Aristotle, Plato, the Bible, and the Jesuits Bellarmine and Suarez" (Lutz 1988, 118). The mention of these last two, both leading Thomists and natural law thinkers of the Catholic Counter-Reformation, is particularly interesting. As an abundance of recent scholarship has persuasively argued, many of the leading ideas of classical liberalism, including human equality, natural rights, government by consent, the free market, and limited government, are not new inventions of John Locke and Adam Smith but are anticipated by scholastic and early Renaissance theologians.[13] And this should not be surprising when one considers that the deepest roots of classical liberalism lie in Christianity, which not only severs the ancient unity of theology and politics but lowers the ends of political authority by locating the highest human citizenship in a transpolitical community, the City of God.[14]

Deneen and others assume without argument that this appeal to traditional and modern ideas and sources (the Bible, classical philosophy, Protestant theology, the English common law, Whig political theory, the Enlightenment, and so on) in the founding period is eclectic and ultimately incoherent. But surely both justice and prudence dictate that an argument is required before the wholesale dismissal of the principles of the American founding.

Although the founders drew from such a public philosophy, they were too preoccupied with the practical tasks of establishing and governing a new nation to reduce it to a systematic philosophical treatise. And indeed, such a treatise would have been superfluous at the time. Although there were practical disputes about particular matters of constitutional design (for example, should the executive office be unitary or plural?) and constitutional interpretation (such as, does Congress have the power to incorporate a bank?), there were in general few, if any, disputes about the moral and political foundations of free government.[15] The principles of the American founding, therefore, were undertheorized. For the most part their foundations were held tacitly, rather than explicitly and deliberately.

It is only later, when those foundations were challenged, first by progressive ideas imported from continental Europe in the mid- to late nineteenth century and later by progressivism in the 1960s, that the demand for a more systematic explication and defense of those principles became pressing. It is clear that the defense of conservatism can no longer depend on the mere assertion of tacit pieties. Conservatism must offer a *better* public philosophy if it is to compete in the marketplace of ideas.

That effort requires saying something *more* than what the founders said, inferring and establishing connections they did not explicitly make, in a way that persuasively accounts for what they did say, and in a way American conservatives would recognize as their own. The key idea here is John Henry Newman's concept of the development of doctrine as applied to public philosophy (see Newman 1989). Just as the Nicene Creed of the fourth century, formulated under the pressures of heterodoxy, did not state anything that orthodox Christians did not already tacitly believe, so the public philosophy of American conservatism should only make clear, consistent, coherent, and defensible the beliefs that conservatives already tacitly hold.

To highlight the fact that the principles of American conservatism rest on a coherent public philosophy, one can use a more principled, less partial, term for it. Various names might be used—classical liberalism, commercial republicanism, natural rights liberalism—but the term that I believe captures best, or most comprehensively, what the founders said, and did, is *natural law liberalism,* a term I take from Christopher Wolfe (Wolfe 2009).[16] The natural law is the oldest tradition of moral inquiry in the West, and the American founders appealed to it ubiquitously in their public speeches and writings.[17] And, although the natural law has been strongly challenged by modern thinkers like David Hume, Immanuel Kant, and John Stuart Mill, it has proven itself capable of competing with, and defeating, those challenges.[18] In this book I use the terms *natural law liberalism* and *conservatism* interchangeably. And although it is not always explicitly highlighted in my treatment, the reader should notice how natural law liberalism incorporates all three principles of American conservatism—liberty, tradition, and reason—in a way that will (I hope) appeal, in different ways, to traditionalist conservatives, neoconservatives, and libertarians.

Why Natural Law Liberalism?

The natural law is rooted in a basic, practical orientation toward reality, a conviction that there exist objective moral norms that are discovered, not fabricated, by reason. It is what C. S. Lewis called "the Tao," or "the doctrine of objective value" (Lewis 1944, 18). In this sense, the natural law is nothing esoteric. It is merely a reflection and extension of the commonsense understanding of what all people ordinarily do: Pursue good and avoid evil.[19]

But that pursuit, as Lewis acknowledges, necessarily takes place within a tradition. In this sense, the natural law is a tradition of rational inquiry into the means and ends of human flourishing. It embodies therefore the conservative belief already mentioned that tradition and reason are interdependent. Today tradition and reason are often set in opposition to one another, but this separation reflects unwarranted Romantic and Enlightenment prejudices. As recent thinkers like Michael Polanyi, F. A. Hayek and Alasdair MacIntyre, each in his own way, have shown, reason necessarily requires and grows from a tradition of inquiry.[20] In this view, traditions are not irrational prejudices but forms of knowledge directed to truth.

This view of reason as generated through tradition yet aimed beyond tradition avoids the Scylla and Charybdis of rationalism and historicism. With rationalism it affirms that reason is capable of arriving at certain knowledge about reality, but it denies that reason rests on and is built on an indubitable foundation or method for knowledge, clear and certain to all rational persons. With historicism it recognizes that knowledge vitally grows from and depends on particularities of history, language, and culture, but it denies that knowledge *itself* is relative to history, language, and culture, or that there is no knowledge as such, only competing and incommensurable claims to knowledge. What historicists critically miss is the way in which rival traditions of inquiry can (and sometimes do) learn from one another, correct one another, and (sometimes) even defeat one another.

As MacIntyre puts it, "All reasoning takes place within the context of some traditional mode of thought, transcending through criticism and invention the limitations of what had hitherto been reasoned in that tradition; this is as true of modern physics as of medieval logic" (MacIntyre 2007, 222). And, one might add, it is also true of morality and politics. Like natural science, the natural law is a living tradition, growing through time and experience, in which the insights of previous thinkers are adopted, modified, developed, abandoned, and (sometimes) recovered.[21]

Three very important points follow from this account of the natural law: First, as with natural science, knowledge of the natural law can be expected to change and develop in light of better evidence and arguments. Second, the natural law is not identical to the claims of any one thinker and therefore not a monolithic doctrine. The argument, "Augustine said that the natural law means *x*, but we now know that *x* is clearly wrong, therefore the natural law is wrong," is no more valid than the claim that "Newton said that nature means *x*, but we now know that *x* is clearly wrong, therefore nature is wrong." Sound appeals to natural law thinkers are primarily appeals to arguments, not to authorities. Third, although the natural law provides true insights into the means and ends of human flourishing, it does not provide an a priori blueprint for morality, much less for social and political order.

Natural law liberalism, then, is a genuine *development* of the natural law tradition, one that affirms many of the basic commitments of liberalism while rooting them in a positive notion of human knowledge and the human good that avoids the corrosive pitfalls of individualism and moral relativism. To see how this is possible, I will outline in the next three sections a basic account of natural law liberalism. My account will rely principally on the work of John Finnis.[22] I rely on Finnis not because he is the final or most authoritative voice on the natural law but because his argument illustrates in a compelling way how a traditional account of the natural law can support many of the basic claims of classical liberalism. In particular, Finnis shows how the natural law can be known independently of, but is compatible with, metaphysical or theological claims; affirms a pluralistic account of the human good and human happiness; and promotes an instrumental view of the political common good. My summary will focus on three features of natural law liberalism: limited government, natural rights, and political authority. In the final section, I will show how the principles of the American founding are a prudential expression of natural law liberalism.

Natural Law Liberalism: Limited Government

Classical liberalism, whatever its form, rests on a belief in limited government. In its most general sense, this means that participation in politics is not itself an *end* of human flourishing, as Aristotle and the classical republican tradition held, but is only a *means* to human flourishing. Although the case for limited government is partly rooted in a distrust of the human tendency to abuse power, this alone cannot justify limited government. The distrust of power doesn't say what power is *for*, and an excessive distrust of power can even make the abuse of power more likely. This is the lesson of the earliest American constitutions, which, taking to heart David Hume's "just *political* maxim, *that every man must be supposed a knave*" (Hume 1985, 42), circum-scribed political (and especially executive) power to such an extent that rights were increasingly subject to invasion and abuse (see Rahe 1994). It was pre-cisely this emergency that led to the constitutional convention of 1787 and the maturity of experience expressed by Alexander Hamilton in *Federalist 70* that "a feeble executive implies a feeble execution of government. A feeble execution is but another phrase for a bad execution; and a government ill ex-ecuted, whatever it may be in theory, must be, in practice, a bad government" (Hamilton, Jay, and Madison 2001, 362–363).

A sound case for limited government therefore ultimately rests on a posi-tive view of human flourishing and of the legitimate though limited role government plays in that flourishing. The primary object of the natural law is to identify the ends and means of human flourishing, which can also be called happiness, understood not as a temporary emotional satisfaction but as a complete life. Natural law theory, therefore, is eudaimonistic rather than deontological or utilitarian. Human beings can distinguish intrinsic goods, which people have reason to pursue for their own sake, from instrumental goods that are pursued only as a means to other ends. Intrinsic goods provide self-evident (that is, indemonstrable) and noninstrumental reasons for action, as well as reasons for avoiding certain actions. Who can reasonably deny that knowledge and friendship are good and worthy of pursuit for their own sake or that ignorance and friendlessness are bad and to be avoided? (And what demonstrative argument could be given to persuade them?) Moreover, be-cause each of the basic goods is equally, intrinsically good, and because there are an infinite number of ways to participate in those goods, there is no fixed hierarchy of goods or way of life based on those goods.[23]

The natural law is also concerned with the means of human flourish-ing. Although fiction often relates the grim absurdity of people like King Midas or Ebenezer Scrooge who pursue instrumental goods as if they were intrinsic goods, instrumental goods do indeed provide reasons for action. Freedom from coercion is an instrumental good because it is only through self-constituting choices of goods that human beings can fully flourish. But freedom from coercion, though it does provide a reason for action, is not it-self an intrinsic good, nor is it an end of human action. Any person who has acquired freedom from coercion inevitably asks, what shall I *do now*?

Human beings also require social life for their flourishing. That human beings are social, if not political, animals by nature is affirmed as forcefully by modern liberals like John Locke and Thomas Jefferson as by Aristotle and Thomas Aquinas.[24] As every economist knows, the Robinson Crusoe theory of human action is radically incomplete. From the time they enter the world, utterly helplessness and needy, to the dependencies of illness and old age, human beings rely on the cooperation and assistance of others not only for their nourishment, care, and protection but also for the higher goods of art, play, knowledge, and friendship. The most basic and important human association is the family, which is rooted in the sexual complementarity and mutual fidelity of spouses and is ordered to the unconditional care and rearing of children.

But if the Robinson Crusoe theory of human nature is incomplete, so is that of the Swiss Family Robinson.[25] The family is not self-sufficient. As Finnis points out, a family "cannot even properly provide for the unimpaired transmission of its own genetic basis; a family that breeds within itself is headed for physical self-destruction" (Finnis 2011, 147). The family also depends on an inherited stock of language, technology, and culture built up by the efforts of others, as well as cooperation and trade with other individuals and families.

And so the social order grows, within which human beings, individually and in cooperation with others, pursue a wide range of particular projects and goods. At this point the nature of the political association and its common good begins to appear. In the words of Finnis:

> So there emerges the desirability of a "complete community," an all-round association in which would be co-ordinated the initiatives and activities of individuals, of families, and of the vast network of intermediate associations. The point of this all-around association would be to secure the whole ensemble of material and other conditions, including forms of collaboration, that tend to favour, facilitate, and foster the realization by each individual of his or her personal development. (Finnis 2011, 147)

There are several things to notice about Finnis's account. First, when Finnis speaks of the "co-ordination" of the members of the civil association, he is *not* referring to an integrated organization and direction of those members by a central authority to a single unified end, like a coach directing a football team. To be sure, there are occasions when *positive* coordination of at least some members of the political association to a common end is required, as with defense or other collective goods that cannot reasonably be supplied without the assistance of government. Most often, however, the coordination required by the political association will be *negative*, more like a referee impartially enforcing the rules of the game.

Second, the point of the political association is to favor the realization of *each* individual's *personal* development. Finnis, with the natural law tradition more generally, repeatedly and forcefully repudiates all utilitarian or "greatest good of the greatest number" accounts of the common good. (See, for example, Finnis 2011, 154). "*Each* and everyone's well-being," he writes, "in each of its basic aspects, must be considered and favoured at *all* times by those responsible for co-ordinating the common life" (Finnis, 2011, 214; italics in original).

Finally, the common good of the political association, as Finnis describes it, is an *instrumental* good. It consists in an "ensemble of *conditions*" for the achievement of human flourishing and not the ends of flourishing itself. The end of political authority therefore is not perfectionist; it cannot provide knowledge, friendship, religion, or any other basic good. These are the objects of individuals and associations within civil society. But this does not mean that government must be antiperfectionist. Modern liberals and libertarians believe with John Rawls that liberalism requires government to be neutral with respect to competing conceptions of the good (see Rawls 2005 [1993]). However, this belief is subject to formidable objections, the most significant of which is that it is not itself neutral. Despite its pretentions to neutrality, antiperfectionism actually favors and promotes a nonneutral and questionable view of the self and its relationship to the good and unjustly prevents persons from acting on reasonable competing views (see Sandel 1998 and Finnis 2011).

Against antiperfectionists, natural law liberals argue that true neutrality requires a public form and legal structure in which competing arguments based in reason are offered for deliberation. Natural law liberals therefore can be called "soft perfectionists," insofar as they maintain that government plays a legitimate but indirect or subsidiary role in fostering and protecting *the conditions* in which individuals pursue their own perfection ("the pursuit of happiness," as the Declaration puts it), rather than perfection as an end in itself.

As we have already seen, the natural law recognizes a wide variety of basic goods that lead to human flourishing (for example, knowledge, friendship, marriage, worship, play, and the like), and *each* of these basic goods can be realized to different degrees and in an infinite number of ways. Moreover, these basic goods can be fully realized only through the free choices of persons, individually and in cooperation with others. For this reason, natural law liberalism requires a wide scope for free choice, and this wide scope can be expected to result in a richly diverse social order. John Paul II expresses the basic insight of natural law liberalism when he writes the following:

> The social nature of man is not completely fulfilled in the State, but
> is realized in various intermediary groups, beginning with the family
> and including economic, social, political and cultural groups which stem
> from human nature itself and have their own autonomy, always with a
> view to the common good. (John Paul II 1991, sec. 13)

This affirmation undergirds the moral and political principle of *subsidiarity* (from the Latin word for "help"), according to which "a community of a higher order should not interfere in the internal life of a community of a lower order, depriving the latter of its functions, but rather should support it in case of need and help to co-ordinate its activity with the activities of the rest of society, always with a view to the common good" (Catholic Church 1995, sec. 1883). The principle of subsidiarity is a profoundly conservative principle and more useful than "decentralization," which is only negative in form and does not distinguish those cases when decentralization is a threat to liberty and human flourishing. (As the founders saw clearly, smaller communities are not always more just than larger ones).

The natural law, therefore, affirms the primacy of civil society, with its plurality of nonstate associations, including the free market, which sets fixed limits to the rightful exercise of political authority. (I say more about the limits of economic analysis in my reply to Wenzel.) But although reason supports a legitimate pluralism, it does not support antiperfectionism. There are some actions that directly damage intrinsic goods or indirectly undermine the conditions for the achievement of intrinsic goods. This is most obvious with respect to wrongful actions that harm the physical persons and property of others, such as assault, murder, rape, and theft. But it also includes wrongful actions that cause moral harm to others. It is unjust to present human beings (especially weaker human beings like children) with powerful temptations to actions that undermine or corrupt basic goods. In the worst case, human beings seek to exploit such strong temptations in others for personal profit, as with drug pushers, prostitutes, pimps, and pornographers. Such activity is a source of moral harm to the character and integrity of other persons and to the social conditions that support good human choices and thus an injustice that may be prohibited by law. This is especially clear in the case of children, who require for their mature development not only the loving attention, assistance, encouragement, and discipline of their parents but also a social order that at the very least does not undermine the difficult work of parents. In the words of Robert George, the law cannot make human beings moral, but it can effect the conditions in which human beings make themselves moral (George 1995).

Notice I said "*may be prohibited by law.*" The purpose of human law, according to the natural law, is not simply or exclusively to prohibit immorality but to promote the conditions for human flourishing. Actions that are purely private and have no effect on public morality are beyond the scope of human law, but immoral actions that cause moral harm to others are a matter of justice and are rightly subject to proscription. Even so, the legal prohibition of the action must not result in worse harms (such as public expense, corruption of authority, corruption of persons through black market, and the like) than toleration of the action. As Thomas Aquinas puts it, "In human government . . . those who are in authority, rightly tolerate certain evils, lest certain goods be lost, or certain greater evils be incurred: thus Augustine says [*De Ordine* ii, 4]: 'If you do away with harlots, the world will be convulsed with lust.'"[26]

To the surprise of modern liberals and to the dismay of some conservatives, both Aquinas and Augustine suggested that prostitution should be tolerated. Whatever one happens to think of their views on this matter, one should notice that their argument does not rest on a supposed moral "right" to engage in prostitution but on a prudential prediction about the relative costs and benefits to the common good of prohibiting prostitution. Natural law liberalism can thus ground limited government in a robust moral theory, rather than the corrosive moral skepticism that informs much of progressivism and libertarianism.

Natural Law Liberalism: Natural Rights

The argument is sometime made that the soft perfectionism of natural law liberalism conflicts with natural rights, especially the natural right to liberty. The notion of natural rights makes some conservatives nervous, however. It was, after all, Thomas Hobbes, a philosophical materialist and political absolutist, who first introduced a distinctive conception of prepolitical natural rights into popular Western philosophical discourse.[27] Classical writers (including Aristotle, Cicero, Augustine, Aquinas) most often wrote about what is *right* (singular) by nature; rarely if ever did they write about natural right in terms of individual natural *rights* (plural) inhering in individuals prior to and independent of their participation in the political association.[28] Moreover, in France, the "rights of man" resulted in the reign of terror; in America, "rights talk" has not only enabled activist government but it has also resulted in a radical individualism that has undermined the social capital that a free society requires (see Glendon 1993).

Those conservatives who have defended natural rights have not always made clear how those rights fit into the larger moral and political framework they also support. Nor have they explained how such an ostensibly fundamental moral truth as natural rights was not discovered until relatively late in human history. Natural law liberalism can respond to all of these objections by showing how the idea of natural rights makes sense only within a larger theory of human flourishing.

Recall that the natural law, in its most general sense, refers not to a particular theory about morality but to a basic orientation of practical reason toward the basic goods that constitute human flourishing. Recall also that human beings learn about reality, including the natural law, through particular traditions of inquiry. Thus, although the natural law is evident in human experience and history, it can be (and is) *expressed* in a diversity of ways, according to the particularities of language, history, and culture. Further, those expressions are subject to development and can be more or less adequate to the truth.

Natural *rights*, as the term implies, are (or can be) an expression of the natural law. Although the expression is late, it corresponds to an affirmation that has always been implicit in the natural law, the dignity of the human person. It is hardly a strain on natural law reasoning, indeed it is a genuine development of such reasoning, to make explicit that the *reason* murder or slavery are wrong is *because* they violate some moral quality *in* innocent human beings. I can see no serious objection to calling that quality (or set of qualities) "natural rights" and to declaring that slavery is wrong because it violates the natural right to liberty.

But this declaration also points to the weakness in natural rights discourse. What does the natural right to liberty mean? Does it prohibit incarcerating criminals? Does it prohibit parents from restraining their children? There is no way to answer these questions without going beyond natural rights language to a larger moral theory. Natural rights language is an attractive but blunt moral instrument because its absolute and peremptory expression overlooks the reasonable scope and limits that determine the true meaning of the right in question. In fact, natural rights only make sense within the context of the larger framework of the natural law *because only the natural law identifies the goods that natural rights exist to protect.* To see how this works in practice, consider two rights that are often subjects of political dispute, private property and freedom of speech.

The right to private property is so fundamental to liberalism that John Locke even used it as a synecdoche for all rights (see chapter IX of Locke's *Second Treatise*; Locke 1988). Surely human beings have such a right, but what is its ground, and how far does it extend? Locke himself offers a "labor theory" of ownership: Because persons own their own labor, they also own those things (not previously owned) with which they have mixed their labor.

There is surely something right in the labor theory of ownership. If persons do not have a primary natural right to their own labor, and thus to the fruits of their own labor, then who does? But Locke's labor theory of ownership, and, indeed, *all* labor theories of ownership, have fatal problems. Consider the following dilemmas: If one puts a fence around a piece of land, does one own only the land beneath the fence or all of the land enclosed by the fence? If the former, can someone else jump over the fence and claim the uncultivated land within it? If the latter, how can one gain rights to land that one has not mixed with one's labor? And if one rightfully owns the land one has enclosed with a fence, may another person enclose *that* land with a fence, locking him in and refusing him entrance or exit? May one rightfully acquire a monopoly over a necessary resource like water? Locke says no, but it is difficult to see how he does so without significantly undermining his own theory.[29] Finally, assuming one does rightfully own land, does one have the right to build a nuclear reactor on it?

Natural law liberalism provides a way of responding to these dilemmas. The natural law account of property is already present in Aristotle and has been developed over centuries of experience and argument. According to the natural law, the right to private property is rooted in three goods: The first good is the matter, scope, and relative autonomy it gives human beings to exercise responsible freedom and to develop their capacities; the second good is the powerful incentive private property gives to human beings to care for and develop the things they own and to benefit others through such care and development; the third good of private property is the cushion it provides persons against the domination of others, including the government.

These justifications establish a strong presumption in favor of private property and economic liberty; however, they can be defeated by more compelling reasons, such as prior ownership, the severe need of others, the threat of harm or actual harm to others, and the duty to pay one's fair share for the institutions that support the common good (defense, the justice system, and the like).[30] Thus one finds in the Western legal tradition (including the common law, state governments, and the U.S. Constitution) legal limits on the acquisition and use of private property and provisions for such things as taxation, government takings of private property for public use (the takings clause), and takings as punishment for crime (the due process clauses).

Consider also the right to free speech. The right to free speech is explicitly protected in the U.S. Constitution and in every state constitution. At the same time, these same governments prohibit speech that is seditious, libelous, slanderous, and obscene. Is this a contradiction? No. Speech, as Aristotle remarks in the first book of his *Politics* (Chapter 2, 1253a5–10), is the mark of what is distinctively human. It is a reflection of human intelligence and the necessary means for the goods of knowledge of the truth, social cooperation, and friendship. But speech is abused when it is used to contradict these goods. Slander, for example, is speech that makes false, defamatory claims about others. It thus causes unjust harm to reputation, which is a personal and social good that promotes both cooperation and friendship. The prohibition of slander, therefore, does not violate the right to freedom of speech.[31]

These remarks are intended to illustrate how natural rights can be said to be an expression of the natural law and make no sense apart from the full context of that law, which determines the specific content of the right in question according to the nature of the basic goods and the requirements of justice. In many cases these determinations are obvious, but in some cases they are quite difficult and complex. This is especially the case with the natural right to liberty as it relates to political authority. The assertion of the Declaration of Independence that human beings have a natural right to liberty and that governments derive "their just powers from the consent of the governed" is a recurring theme in the public speeches and sermons of the founding era and is repeated almost verbatim in six of the new state constitutions.[32] To see what the founders meant by this assertion takes us to the very heart of the libertarian–conservative debate.

Natural Law Liberalism: Political Authority

The justification of political authority is one of the thorniest problems for political philosophy. The various claims to rule, such as noble birth, wealth, and power, all seem arbitrary from a moral point of view. Social contract theory (sometimes called "transfer theory") was invented to address this problem by grounding political authority in the consent of sovereign, prepolitical individuals. As with natural rights, which in most forms arose concurrently with social contract theory, there is both a salutary and a pernicious way to understand social contract theory. In the salutary sense, social contract theory is a powerful reminder that political authority is limited to and exists for the good of each and every individual member of the political association. In its pernicious sense, social contract theory requires the *actual consent* (explicit or tacit) of every individual over whom legitimate political authority exercises power. This strict understanding, however, faces insuperable logical, historical, and practical problems.

First there is a logical problem. Political authority requires either unanimous consent or less than unanimous consent. If it requires unanimous consent, then in fact there *is* no political authority because each individual simply does what he or she wants to do. If it requires less than unanimous consent, then some individuals are empowered to rule others against their consent, and thus consent theory violates its own moral requirement (see Finnis 2011, 248).

But perhaps social contract theory only requires unanimous consent at the beginning of the social contract to form a political association that will be ruled thereafter by less than unanimity? But then two historical problems appear. First, what political authority can point to such a moment of unanimous consent at its foundation? (And is every existing political authority that cannot do so therefore unjust?)[33] Second, how could the unanimous consent of one generation (assuming this is possible) bind another without once again violating its own moral requirement?

John Locke's response to the first problem seems to entail a subtle but significant shift in his argument, in which the legitimacy of government is made to depend not on its *origins* in consent but on its action toward rightful *ends*.[34] This shift strikes me as correct, and I will say more about it in a moment. Locke's response to the second problem is that any person who has not given his express consent to a government but "hath any Possession, or Enjoyment, of any part of the Dominions of any Government, doth thereby give his *tacit Consent*, and is as far forth obliged to Obedience to the Laws of that Government, during such Enjoyment, as any one under it."[35] But although tacit consent has the advantage of addressing the generation problem, it is by no means clear that someone who merely *acquiesces* to political authority is thereby morally *obliged* to obey it, especially when the costs of emigration—one's family, friends, language, property, life—are high, as they usually are. We may acquiesce to a robber at gunpoint when the cost of resistance is high, but this does not mean we acknowledge his authority. This kind of reasoning in effect would make any de facto government, however tyrannical, just. Moreover, it is difficult to see how tacit consent can be understood to include those individuals who explicitly repudiate the political authority and refuse its advantages.[36]

Finally, there are the practical problems: Whose consent is required? Children? Eighteen-year-olds? The mentally ill? Criminals? Lines must be drawn, yet every line will seem to be in some sense arbitrary. Inevitably the doctrine of consent must be subject to political considerations.

In sum, social contract theory, strictly and consistently interpreted, ends in anarchism (or anarcho-capitalism). As Murray Rothbard puts it, "*What* distinguishes the edicts of the State [for those who have not consented to it] from the commands of a bandit gang?" (Rothbard 2006, 63). For Rothbard, the answer to this question is obvious. And it is not only the authority of the state that is in question:

> Regardless of his age, we must grant to every child the absolute right to run away and to find new foster parents who will voluntarily adopt him, or to try to exist on his own. Parents may try to persuade the runaway child to return, but it is totally impermissible enslavement and an aggression upon his right of self-ownership for them to use force to compel him to return. The absolute right to run away is the child's ultimate expression of his right of self-ownership, regardless of age. (Rothbard 2006, 102)

Rothbard exemplifies the remorseless logic of strict contractarianism. Unless we are prepared to regard all parental authority as slavery, we must acknowledge that at least some forms of authority are legitimate independent of consent. How can this be?

Rather than looking to the *origins* of authority in consenting, sovereign individuals, one might (following Locke's subtle shift above) look to the *end* or *purpose* of authority for social and dependent persons. Most people do not object to parents exercising reasonable coercive authority with their own children, whether the children have consented to that authority or not. Why not? First, because children obviously *need* coercive authority for their security and development; and second, because parents bear a *special relationship* to their children that makes them uniquely suited to satisfy this need. This second principle is of course defeasible: Parents who neglect and abuse their children forfeit their authority (but to whom?).[37]

Like parental authority, political authority is justified and limited by *need* and a *special relationship*. Human beings, to live and flourish in society, *need*

an overall authority to coordinate their actions for the security, peace, and justice of all, and legitimate political authority is that overall authority that bears a *special relationship* to the members of that society such that it can and does provide the need for coordination.

The nature of that special relationship is necessarily both practical and historical. The reason (most) Americans recognize the legitimacy of American political authority over them and not, say, French political authority, is because (1) it is effective (more or less) in securing their "safety and happiness" (to quote the Declaration of Independence) and (2) because it is theirs by history, tradition, and fact. Both of these together are the reason for citizenship. As with parental authority, however, political authority is defeasible. To be legitimate, it must be both effective and justly limited to its proper objects.

Effective political authority requires at least the *acquiescence* of the ruled. And it can generally be said that government by consent gives persons a say in the direction of the political association of which they are members, provides a salutary check on the abuse of political power, and is an important source of social and political stability. But it is also clear that these goods critically depend on the condition and quality of the consenting persons. Political liberty can occur only when fierce ethnic, tribal, and religious rivalries have been moderated by the recognition of common citizenship and where citizens have acquired sufficient habits of restraint, toleration, trust, intellectual development, and respect for the rule of law. These are the fragile achievement of decades, even centuries, of gradual change under steady pressure. Citizens of such regimes should be grateful when they inherit such an achievement and must be vigilant not to squander it.

Roger Scruton expresses the underlying truth of contract theory well: "Theorists of the social contract write as though it presupposes only the first-person singular of free rational choice. In fact it presupposes a first-person plural, in which the burdens of belonging have already been assured" (Scruton 2006, 8). Although "membership" is more fundamental than "contract" to the political association, the political membership does not have to be the all-consuming membership of the classical polis, in which all private affairs are ordered to the public good. As I have already pointed out, natural law liberalism acknowledges a plurality of associations and thus "memberships," through which human beings flourish. But liberal democracy requires "a

genuine 'we' of membership: not as visceral as that of kinship; nor as uplift-
ing as that of worship" (Scruton 2006, 13) but one that "involves a discipline
of neighborliness, a respect for privacy and a desire for citizenship, in which
people maintain sovereignty over their own lives and the kind of distance
that makes such sovereignty possible" (15).

Natural Law Liberalism and the American Founding

The point of the preceding remarks is to trace the basic outline of a form
of classical liberalism, natural law liberalism, and to show how it is able to
ground limited government while also accounting for the complex realities of
social and political life. Political life is complex because politics can never be
neutral with respect to competing conceptions of the good. This means that
politics can never be merely a technique for discovering the best means to the
achievement of given ends, as modern liberals and libertarians often suggest.
Even where there is general agreement on political principles, politics will
always involve philosophical and practical disputes over the precise meaning
and application of those principles.

The American founders accepted the fact that political life is both necessary and problematic, and they designed their political institutions to account for this fact. The most impressive outcome of their efforts was the
Constitution of the United States, the oldest written constitution still in use
in the world today. Although James Madison, who is sometimes called the father of the Constitution, frankly confessed that the Constitution lacks "that
artificial symmetry which an abstract view of the subject might lead an in-
genious theorist to bestow on a Constitution planned in his closet or in his
imagination" (*Federalist* 37; Hamilton, Jay, and Madison 2001, 184), *The
Federalist Papers* overall reveal the extent to which the Constitution was the
result of profound reflection on human nature and the permanent problems
of political life. It will be useful to recover some elements of that reflection, if
only to show the scope of the political problem and the impressive attempts
the Constitution makes to deal with that problem.[38]

I will focus my attention in this last section on four claims: First, although the founders used the language of natural rights, they understood
those rights within the context of a larger moral order, the natural law. Second, although the founders believed that the primary task of government is

to secure rights, they did not believe this was the only legitimate purpose of government. They were informed by a larger conception of the political common good. Third, the founders believed in the necessity of strong, though limited, government. They were well aware of how difficult it would be to establish such a government and to preserve it through time. Indeed, they believed this would be a permanent task for American citizens and would require from them moral and intellectual virtue as well as statesmanship. Finally, I will consider the founders' understanding of political authority in light of natural law liberalism.

I have already pointed to a peculiar feature (at least to modern liberals and some traditionalist conservatives) of the American founding: It appeals to *both* individual natural rights and to a natural moral law. This is most evident in the Declaration of Independence, which refers in its first paragraph to "the Laws of Nature and Nature's God," and in its second paragraph to "certain inalienable rights, among which are Life, Liberty and the Pursuit of Happiness." A majority of the new states included almost identical language in their first constitutions.

One might argue that the founders understood the moral law to be nothing more than respect for natural rights, but this argument is belied by the evidence. Although the Declaration states that "to secure these rights governments are instituted among men," it also states that a people may "establish new government, laying its foundation on such principles, and organizing its powers in such form, *as to them shall seem most likely to effect their safety and happiness*" (italics mine). Although securing rights is a primary purpose of government, it is not the only purpose.

To see this better, one must keep in mind the fact that the American constitutional order includes an intricate relationship between the national and state governments. As Donald Lutz points out, "There were thirteen state constitutions in existence in 1787, and they were part of the national document. Referred to directly or by implication more than fifty times in forty-two sections of the U.S. Constitution, these state constitutions had to be read in order to understand what the document said" (Lutz 1988, 2). The reason there are no provisions in the U.S. Constitution for criminal law, education, marriage, registration of property titles, and the like, is not because the founders thought such things are beyond the rightful powers of government, per se, but because they thought these things were best provided for by the states. And indeed the states did (and do) provide for them.

The Declaration of Independence's double allusion to both natural rights and happiness as the proper end of government is imitated in the six revolutionary state constitutions that adopted declarations of rights. The constitution of Virginia (1776), for example, states "that government is, or ought to be, instituted for the common benefit, protection, and security of the people, nation, or community; of all the various modes and forms of government, that is best which is capable of producing the greatest degree of happiness and safety" (Section 3).

It is important to see that such appeals to these ends were not merely expressive. As a part of the common good, this moral order was also regarded as a fit subject for legislation. Notably, unlike the U.S. Constitution, none of the state constitutions enumerated government powers. It was universally assumed, and never questioned, that state governments, unlike the national government, had the power to pass reasonable legislation to protect the health, safety, welfare, and morals of their citizens. These state powers are explicitly protected in the tenth amendment of the U.S. Constitution and have been repeatedly acknowledged—if often truncated—by the Supreme Court.[39]

My point here is twofold: First, although the founders believed in limited government, they were not libertarians but soft perfectionists. Second, although they were soft perfectionists, they believed this power was best exercised at the local level, where governments could be responsive to the particular and diverse needs and circumstances of individual communities. This last point is particularly important: Federalism allows for something like Robert Nozick's "framework for utopia," wherein the U.S. Constitution provides a general legal framework within which local communities (within just limits provided by the Constitution) can promote what they believe to be the best conditions for human flourishing (see chapter 10 of Nozick 1974) and where the diversity of local communities that emerge can really generate information about the best conditions for human flourishing.

Federalism corresponds better to the truth about humanity's social and political nature than the individualism of libertarianism, and it mitigates, though it does not eliminate, the threat of government abuse. *But there is no perfect solution to the threat of government abuse.* Human beings need political authority for their flourishing, yet human beings are liable to abuse political authority. As the Roman poet Juvenal famously put the problem, *Quis custodiet ipsos custodies? (Satires,* Satire VI, 347–348), That is, "Who will guard the guardians themselves"? James Madison, the "father of the Constitution," put the challenge this way in *Federalist* 51: "In framing a government which is to be administered by men over men, the great difficulty lies in this: you must first enable the government to control the governed; and in the next place oblige it to control itself" (Hamilton, Jay and Madison 2001, 269).

Government by consent can provide an important check on government abuse, but, as I have already noted, consent can also be a *source* of government abuse. It was the great achievement of the American founders to recognize this permanent need and danger with deep insight and sobriety and to draw on the best resources of nature and history for a good, if imperfect, solution.

What was their remedy? First, a well-designed constitution. The entire architecture of the U.S. Constitution (that is, a written constitution of enumerated powers, bicameralism, federalism, separation of powers, checks and balances, a difficult amendment process to remedy imperfections, and so on), what Madison called its "auxiliary precautions" and "inventions of prudence" (*Federalist 51;* Hamilton, Jay, and Madison 2001, 269), is designed to prevent bad government *and* to provide for good government.[40]

But the founders were well aware that neither consent alone nor "parchment barriers" would be sufficient to this task (see *Federalist* 48). Their own experience confirmed that just government requires the constant assistance, and sacrifice, of the most wise and virtuous citizens. It is in the language of statesmen that the Declaration concludes: "We mutually pledge to each other our Lives, our Fortunes, and our sacred Honor." The establishment of the American political order would have been impossible without the likes of Madison, Hamilton, Jefferson, Adams, and above all Washington, and it cannot be preserved without such human beings stepping forward in every generation.

But this demand also presents a difficulty that is neatly summarized by James Madison in *Federalist* 57: "The aim of every political constitution is, or ought to be, first to obtain for rulers men who possess most wisdom to discern, and most virtue to pursue, the common good of the society; and in the next place, to take the most effectual precautions for keeping them virtuous whilst they continue to hold their public trust" (Hamilton, Jay, and Madison 2001, 295). The various devices of the Constitution (for example, different election requirements and terms of office for the different branches) can be understood as a series of filtering devices to promote this end.

The founders' second remedy was political education. On the last day of the constitutional convention, Benjamin Franklin declared: "Much of the strength & efficiency of any Government in procuring and securing happiness to the people, depends on the general opinion of the goodness of the Government, as well as of the wisdom and integrity of its Governors" (Farrand 1967, 643). Franklin's point was echoed years later by Abraham Lincoln:

> In this and like communities, public sentiment is everything. With public sentiment, nothing can fail; without it nothing can succeed. Consequently, he who moulds public sentiment, goes deeper than he who enacts statutes or pronounces decisions. He makes statutes and decisions possible or impossible to be executed. (Lincoln 1989, 524–525)

In reminding Americans of this uncomfortable truth, Lincoln was imitating the statesmanship of the founders by educating citizens on the conditions of liberty. Political education is not only the task of political leaders, it is primarily the task of citizens, especially parents, teachers, pastors, and other persons in positions of authority and leadership. But government can play an important *subsidiary* role in assisting in this task. Section III of The Northwest Ordinance, arguably the most important piece of legislation passed by the Continental Congress in 1787 and unanimously affirmed by the first Congress of the United States in 1789, stipulated: "Religion, morality, and knowledge, being necessary to good government and the happiness of mankind, schools and the means of education shall forever be encouraged." The view that government has a positive but subsidiary role to play in citizen education was shared by even the most ardent defenders of limited government, including Thomas Jefferson and Adam Smith. I will return to this subject in my last chapter.

Finally, we come to the problem of political authority. The contract theory of government (or what the founders, with greater theological and communitarian sensitivity, called the *compact* theory of government) is one of the most universally and explicitly held principles of the American founding.[41] As we have already seen, in the strictest sense, the compact theory of government requires the unanimous consent of every individual who is subject to it. I have shown why this requirement is implausible. But the founders understood social contract theory in its salutary, not its pernicious, sense. In every case, the theory was affirmed by representatives of "the people" who had been selected by far less than a majority of the individuals they claimed to represent, apparently without objection.[42]

The founders believed that government by consent is the highest reflection of the basic equality and dignity of human beings, but they did not make the consent of every individual an unconditional requirement of justice. Government exists to protect rights and secure the common good, and popular consent cannot be required (or even reasonably desired) in those cases where it would result in instability, lawlessness, disorder, and despotism. On the other hand, to deny consent to a people who have the capacity and desire for it is unjust.[43] But even in those cases, there always are, and necessarily will be, reasonable restrictions on suffrage, subject to the conditions, circumstances, and deliberations of that political association. The compact theory of government is an important part of the American political tradition, and its affirmation reflects a high level of human political development. But unless that theory is understood within the larger context of the natural law, it can be, and is, a source of considerable mischief and harm.

Conclusion

The foregoing remarks make it possible to give a more condensed account of the conservatism I wish to defend here. Whether one calls it American conservatism or natural law liberalism, it will be characterized by the following affirmations:

1. Political liberty depends on the mutual interdependence of liberty, tradition, and reason. This equilibrium of liberty must be rooted in moral character and provided for in political institutions.

2. A concept of reason working *through* tradition (and not rationalism or historicism), is the only reliable ground for knowledge.

3. The most developed expression of the Western political tradition is natural law liberalism, which grounds the basic commitments of classical liberalism in a positive view of the human good and human flourishing.

4. The principles of the American founding are a unique and valuable historical expression of natural law liberalism. Those principles, if not perfect, have provided for human flourishing to a higher degree than any alternative principles we know of. Those principles include government by consent limited to the conditions for human flourishing; a written constitution, carefully designed to prevent bad government and to promote good government; federalism; political education; and statesmanship.

Most happy are the people who have inherited through the statesmanship and sacrifice of others a set of political principles and institutions that limit political authority to its rightful ends. Most wise are the people who regard themselves as stewards of that inheritance. And most foolish are those people who under a false dream of liberty would treat that inheritance like mere scaffolding that can now be pulled down.

For Further Reading

The account of conservatism given here is strongly indebted to four books. For an energetic and compelling critique of the Enlightenment and postmodern separation of reason from tradition, see Alasdair MacIntyre, *After Virtue*. For a defense of conservatism that is rooted in both reason and tradition, see Roger Scruton, *A Political Philosophy: Arguments for Conservatism*. For a comprehensive account of the natural law as it relates to human law, ambitious readers will want to read John Finnis's *Natural Law and Natural Rights*. (Less ambitious readers may want to start with J. Budziszewski, *Written on the Heart: The Case for Natural Law*.) On the principles of the American founding, there is perhaps no better historical account than Paul Rahe, *Republics Ancient & Modern, Volume III: Inventions of Prudence: Constituting the American Regime*.

CHAPTER TWO

What Is Libertarianism?

NIKOLAI G. WENZEL

IT IS USEFUL FOR ME TO PAINT A PICTURE of the contemporary American political landscape before I define libertarianism.

Years ago, I examined a chart of presidents under Mexico's one-party dictatorship of the Institutional Revolutionary Party (Partido Revolucionario Institucional, or PRI), which ruled the country for roughly seventy years. The presidents in this chart veered from left to right and back, all within one party. From the libertarian perspective, the United States has lapsed into similar political seesawing within one de facto party, the "Republicrats." George W. Bush, who rode into the White House as a free-market–leaning "compassionate conservative," gave us the biggest nonmilitary increase in spending since Lyndon Johnson's Great Society. Jimmy Carter, a "man of the people," has also been dubbed the greatest free-market economist in the twentieth century, for leading (or allowing) the successful deregulation of trucking, airlines, and telecommunications. Barack Obama has blithely continued with the corporate welfare and failed drug war he inherited from his predecessor. Deficits and unfunded mandates soar.

A back-of-the envelope calculation indicates that at least 60 percent of federal spending today is not authorized by the Constitution (if you have any doubt about this, compare the enumerated powers of Article 1, Section 8, with actual spending). Instead of constitutional constraint, we have big government. The national debt now stands at more than 100 percent of annual production (as Margaret Thatcher famously (if perhaps apocryphally) quipped, "The problem with socialism is that, eventually, you run out of other people's money to spend"). Governments at all levels directly control about half of national economic activity (if we consider that 40 percent of gross domestic product (GDP) is made up of government spending at all levels, to which we can add another estimated 10 percent of GDP in compliance costs or stifled economic activity due to the tens of thousands of pages of regulations that are churned out every year).[1] Beyond economics, civil rights attorney Harvey Silvergate estimates that the average American unwittingly commits three felonies a day (see Silvergate 2011). About half of the prison population in the United States is locked up for using, possessing, or selling drugs—nonviolent offenses that did not involve violating the property rights of others.

The size and scope of the state leads to fundamental questions about the proper role of government. Enter libertarianism.

The Libertarian Alternative

Fortunately, there is an alternative to rampant interventionism: libertarianism. Readers should not expect a comprehensive action plan for every contingency because there cannot be a complete ex ante set of instructions for every foreseeable problem. I offer here a summary, which I hope will whet my readers' interest, lead them to more thorough assays, and cause them to scrutinize any form of interventionism more carefully.

Libertarianism is a political philosophy about the protection of individual rights. Instead of seeking liberty as one of many ends, libertarianism considers liberty the highest political good. As Lord Acton wrote, "Liberty is not a means to a higher political end. It is itself the highest political end" (Acton 1907 [1877]). Likewise, economist F. A. Hayek explains that "we must show that liberty is not merely one particular value but that it is the source and condition of most moral values" (Hayek 2011 [1960], 6).

From this flows a philosophy of limited government and the protection of individual rights. Libertarianism relies on government as protector of rights, to provide an umbrella within which individuals can peacefully go about their business, interact, and thrive. Libertarianism thus relies heavily on markets and civil society to supplement that which individuals cannot complete on their own and that which government cannot deliver without violating individual rights.

Libertarianism is a *political* philosophy; it does not make claims beyond politics. Although other matters are very important to human flourishing, they are outside the realm of politics and thus outside the realm of libertarianism. Social relations and interpersonal virtue (the way we treat each other) are political problems. Questions of intrapersonal virtue (the way we cultivate and treat ourselves), salvation, art, or beauty, are important to individual libertarians, but they are not of the political, and thus not of libertarianism. To accuse libertarianism of lacking an overall soteriology, eschatology, aesthetic theory, or life-encompassing metaphysics is akin to accusing biology of lacking a theory of opera. This does not mean that biologists deny the existence or importance of opera but that they lack anything meaningful to say about it from the standpoint of their discipline. The problem with ethics-driven communitarianism (as in the case of conservatism's attempts to regulate morality) is that it justifies intervention in the personal sphere to the point where everything could become political.

Chapter Outline

In this chapter, I will make the case for libertarianism. As I will explain in the following discussion, I have immense respect for rights-based justifications for libertarianism, but I am not a philosopher, and I am concerned about the epistemological foundations of natural rights. So I use the language that I know. I should thus make it clear that I agree with rights-based libertarianism without relying on it for my argument. Instead of natural rights, I use the simpler approach of robust political economy: People are not omniscient and cannot be assumed to be benevolent (see Pennington 2011 or Ikeda 2003). Which institutions will be robust enough to cope with these two problems? That is, which institutions will minimize harm and maximize the opportunities for human flourishing? I will argue that those institutions are the institutions of libertarianism.

As I will explain in my reply to Schlueter, conservatism has many valid concerns. Most conservatives are concerned with liberty and individual rights (if not unconditionally); they recognize the efficiency of markets over central planning for the production of most economic goods; and they emphasize the virtues necessary in citizens of a free society under limited government (even if they would have government attempt to impose them). Alas, conservatives would violate many of their own terms by implementing their program through the state. Libertarianism, instead of violating individual rights and the basic lessons of political economy, calls for problems to be addressed through markets and civil society.

Rothbard (2006, 26) explains that there are three bases for libertarianism: emotivism, utilitarianism, and natural rights. I drop the first as irrelevant for these purposes; however, I note that there is indeed strong support in the United States today for the nonintellectual, gut-feeling, protolibertarianism that Grover Norquist, president of Americans for Tax Reform, has dubbed the "leave me alone coalition." In the second section of this chapter, I will treat the intellectual foundations of libertarianism. First, I will outline the position that individuals have certain rights that nobody may violate, and the state is tasked with protecting those rights. I will then turn from the right-based argument to a more consequentialist approach, moving from philosophy to political economy. To avoid disaster, political economy calls for institutions robust enough to cope with the reality of nonomniscient and nonbenevolent agents. Although human beings are capable of greatness, they are also capable of evil. Which institutions will minimize evil and maximize the opportunity for flourishing? Likewise, which institutions will maximize opportunities for the creation and transmission of knowledge, both within time and over time?

In the third section, I will discuss the three principal strains within libertarianism. At one extreme within libertarianism, the classical liberals advocate a state that protects individual rights but also solves market failures. In economic terms, classical liberals are also known as theorists of the "productive state"—that is, the state should solve collective action problems, decreasing overproduction of bads (such as environmental harm) and increasing underproduction of goods (such as education, roads, or mosquito control) when the market has failed—without, however, lapsing into the "redistributive" state of progressivism.[2] At the other extreme, the anarcho-capitalists reject the state completely. The state is inherently violent and thus immoral—but it is also not necessary because markets and civil society can solve problems of governance and collective action, without the state's violence or unintended consequences. In between the two, the minarchist libertarians call for a "protective state" devoted to the protection of individual rights—nothing less and nothing more, for if the state attempts anything more, it will violate rights. But if it attempts anything less, it will fail at protecting rights.

In the fourth section, I will preempt some criticisms of libertarianism, as I address some popular misconceptions.

In the fifth section, I will conclude. I will also explain why, in the rest of the book, I adopt political economy over a rights-based approach and why I am advocating minarchist libertarianism over anarcho-capitalism or classical liberalism.

The Intellectual Foundations of Libertarianism

RIGHTS AND LIBERTY

One of the two principal justifications for libertarianism comes from individual rights. According to rights-based libertarians, individuals have natural rights that nobody—not even the state—may violate. In fact, the purpose of the state is the protection of individual rights. To quote from the Declaration of Independence, "We hold these truths to be self-evident, that all men are created equal, that they are endowed by their creator with certain unalienable Rights, that among these are Life, Liberty and the pursuit of Happiness— That to secure these rights, Governments are instituted among Men . . ."

Although there exist earlier seeds, the quintessential articulation of rights comes from philosopher John Locke. Locke argues that individuals have a natural right (antecedent to government) to their life, liberty, and property. Civil government is then established to protect those rights, in a manner more efficient than the state of nature—but government's power is limited to the defense of rights, and government remains subject to the laws of nature (see Locke's *Second Treatise on Government*, Locke 1988, especially chapters 2, 9, and 11). Murray Rothbard makes a derivative argument, based on the individual's right to self-ownership. From this right to self-ownership comes a right to property, a right to exchange, and a right to contract. However, instead of deducing from this a need for government, Rothbard relies on the "non-aggression axiom," which rejects any aggression against the property rights of an individual (including life, liberty, and property). Thus, Rothbard rejects the creation of a state, for it, too, is subject to the nonaggression axiom. Any state, argues Rothbard, will violate individual rights, because (a) it receives its income from coercion, thus violating the nonaggression axiom; (b) it is allowed to use violence, which violates the nonaggression axiom; and (c) there are no real safeguards against the state because it enjoys

State of Nature v. State of Civility?

a monopoly of protective services and thus a monopoly on legitimate (or legitimized) violence. Hence Rothbard's argument for reliance exclusively on civil society and markets to protect rights (see Rothbard 2006, especially chapters 2, 3, and 12, for a more developed argument; see also Nozick 1974).

In more instrumental terms, political economist Frédéric Bastiat offers an argument for property rights that is based on human nature, if not quite on natural law: Labor is indispensable for survival, and the individual "will not perform any labor if he is not *sure* of applying the fruit of his labor to the satisfaction of his wants." Therefore, property is a right, and the proper object of the laws is protection of property (Bastiat 1995a [1848]). In a similar vein, philosopher Ayn Rand offers the following argument for "man's rights":

> There is only one fundamental right (all the others are its consequences or corollaries): a man's right to his own life. Life is a process of self-sustaining and self-generated action; the right to life means the right to engage in self-sustaining and self-generated action—which means: the freedom to take all the actions required by the nature of a rational being for the support, the furtherance, the fulfillment and the enjoyment of his own life. (Such is the meaning of the right to life, liberty and the pursuit of happiness.) . . . Thus, for every individual, a right is the moral sanction of a positive—of his freedom to act on his own judgment, for his own goals, by his own voluntary, uncoerced choice. As to his neighbors, his rights impose no obligations on them except of a negative kind: to abstain from violating his rights . . . The right to life is the source of all rights—and the right to property is their only implementation. Without property rights, no other rights are possible. Since man has to sustain his life by his own effort, the man who has no right to the product of his effort has no means to sustain his life. The man who produces while others dispose of his product, is a slave. (Rand 1967a)

Several thinkers have been bothered by the concept of rights, a point to which I return in my critique of Schlueter's conservatism. After all, if we can assert a right to life, liberty, and property, why not assert a right not to be offended, a right to impose one's vision of truth on others, and so on? And rights talk can quickly run up against epistemological problems—indeed, how do we really *know*? Economist James Buchanan offers a solution, in what might be dubbed a minimalist, or robust, theory of rights:

> That is "good" which "tends to emerge" from the free choices of the individuals who are involved. It is impossible for an external observer to lay down criteria for "goodness" independent of the process through which results or outcomes are attained. The evaluation is applied to the means of attaining outcomes, not to outcomes as such. And to the extent that individuals are observed to be responding freely within the minimally required conditions of mutual tolerance and respect, any outcome that emerges merits classification as "good," regardless of its precise descriptive content. (Buchanan 2000a [1975], 19)

In similar terms, legal scholar John Hasnas beautifully proposes a movement "toward a theory of empirical natural rights" (Hasnas 2005). Hasnas points to weaknesses in natural law theories (basically, they rely on theological or epistemological assertion for their premises). He responds with "an alternate conception of natural rights that is not beset by the foundational problems [discussed in the preceding paragraphs], but is nevertheless philosophically useful." In sum, "In place of the traditional conception of natural rights as rights that human beings are inherently *endowed with* in the state of nature, [he offers] a conception of natural rights that *evolve* in the state of nature." In a very Hayekian fashion, he points to rules of conduct that have evolved to maximize human cooperation and minimize conflict:

> To the extent that these incipient rules entitle individuals to act entirely in their own interests, individuals may come to speak in terms of their right to do so (e.g. of their right to the quiet enjoyment of property) . . . Over time, these rules become invested with normative significance and the members of the community come to regard the ways in which the rules permit them to act at their pleasure as their rights. Thus, in the state of nature, rights evolve out of human beings' efforts to address the inconveniences of that state. In the state of nature, rights are solved problems.

Although Hasnas lacks the tidiness of Locke, his theory works quite well as a basis for government:

Individual empirical natural rights, then, are theoretically imperfect, exception-laden, fuzzy-edged entities. Yet, taken together, they form a remarkably good approximation of Lockean natural rights. This is not coincidence, but is due to the empirical fact that Locke's set of broad negative rights to life, liberty, and property consists in precisely those rights that are most likely to produce peaceful relationships among human beings in the absence of civil government.

We thus have a rights-based argument for liberty that does not face the epistemological problems of natural law. One final point on the subject of rights bears mentioning here. Among rights-based libertarians, there is divergence in the importance of rights. For some, like Murray Rothbard, Ayn Rand, or the philosopher Robert Nozick, individual rights are absolute and may never be trumped; this will be reflected in the anarcho-capitalist and minarchist strains of libertarianism. For classical liberals, rights are not absolute, which means they can be bent in the name of resolving market failures or overall efficiency. Although they are not absolute, individual rights are "thick" to classical liberals; this means that individual rights cannot be violated willy-nilly but must be carefully balanced with other objectives, according to strict rules. For example, the takings clause in the Fifth Amendment to the U.S. Constitution states: "Nor shall private property be taken for public use, without just compensation." By contrast, a "thin" conception of individual rights would give something approaching carte blanche to the state in its designs, in the name of raison d'état or the public good; this is the case with progressivism and (I will argue) often with conservatism. I return to these distinctions in my discussion of the three strains of libertarianism.

ROBUST POLITICAL ECONOMY

The Incentive Problem: Institutions for Nonbenevolent Agents

Before the revolution in so-called public choice economics—the public choice of collective action, as opposed to the private choice of individuals acting in the market—political analysis was romantically divorced from reality, as public "servants" were assumed to be selfless executors of "the common good." Likewise, market actors were also assumed to be benevolent, if narrowly self-interested. As a result of these assumptions, markets were seen as yielding suboptimal results that could be corrected by selfless government agents.[3]

For public choice theory, people are people. The traditional dichotomy of people acting one way in market situations and another way entirely in government is cast aside. Gone are individuals acting selfishly in markets and selflessly in government, acting for private gain in the market and for public interest in government. In government, just as in markets, people will consider a number of different things that give them satisfaction: pleasure, profit, service to others, leisure . . . But there is no longer a heroic assumption that individuals, on election to political office or ascension to bureaucratic position, magically grow angel's wings. Instead, people respond to incentives. They seek to maximize their satisfaction within constraints, such as budgets, scarcity of time, laws and other rules of the game, social norms and other informal institutions, ethical and religious considerations, and so on. It is ironic to see statist romantics of the left and the right assume that virtuous leaders will overcome the people's shortcomings—especially after the public choice revolution. Only through proper institutions can people properly orient their selfish interests to the service of others; libertarianism, as we will see, involves a quest for such institutions.[4]

This symmetry applies at the institutional level, as the individual level. The "Nirvana fallacy" comes from the work of economist Harold Demsetz, who enjoins us to compare apples with apples and not oranges with Nirvana (Demsetz 1969). It is unfair and unsound to compare one institutional mechanism (the market) with an idealized perfection (Nirvana), while comparing its alternative (the state) with . . . nothing at all. To use an eschatological analogy, we cannot compare a fallen world with heaven, when heaven is not an option for a fallen world. Far too often, the market is seen to yield an imperfect outcome, so the government is called in to regulate without anybody asking the question whether the government will do a better job. Examples of the fallacy abound, from Social Security to health care and from public education to nationalized money.

Beyond assumptions, public choice theory explains how the political process distorts incentives, leading to irrational and inefficient policies, and yielding incoherent information about voter preferences (for general background, see Gwartney et al. 2005, chapter 6).

In a market system, incentives are mostly well aligned: Consumers must pay for what they want, so they face the consequences of their actions. Likewise, a business faces the harsh reality of the profit test. The government lacks such a test. If I don't like the Florida Division of Motor Vehicles, I can't simply take my business to the competing DMV. Politicians can be changed but only after their term is completed and only through a very inefficient voting mechanism. And bureaucrats are near impossible to fire. Likewise, it is very difficult to shut down a government agency, even if its stated purpose has passed. The feedback mechanism for governmental activity is weak to nonexistent, leading to inefficient outcomes and bad policies in ways that would not exist within the market's mechanism of information and discipline.

The political process also breaks the individual consumption-payment link. In the market, a consumer who wants more of something will have to pay for it: one beer, $5; two beers, $10. In collective action, some people can pay much for little or little for much. One need only look at the fact that roughly half of Americans do not pay federal income taxes—but have a say, through the polls, on how tax revenue is spent. As of 2009, the top 50 percent of taxpayers paid 98 percent of tax revenue; in other words, the bottom 50 percent of taxpayers enjoyed 25 percent of the votes but paid only 2 percent of the tax revenue. The top 5 percent of taxpayers paid more (59 percent) than the bottom 95 percent. And the top 1 percent paid 37 percent of tax revenue yet enjoyed only 0.5 percent of the votes that allocated that spending.[5] We see the skewed incentives for additional public spending at somebody else's expense.

Through the political process, policies will tend to emerge that concentrate benefits and diffuse costs, transferring wealth from the politically unorganized and invisible many to the politically organized and visible few, while increasing the size and power of the redistributive state. As an example, each American adult pays an estimated $15 per year to subsidize an inefficient U.S. sugar industry that cannot compete in a free market but relies instead on trade protections and subsidies.[6] Although it is in the interest of the sugar industry to preserve its estimated $3 billion in annual subsidies, it is not in the interest of any individual voter to fight for a $15 refund. Nor will elected officials tend to listen to individual voters over an organized lobby. In fact, most Americans don't even know they are paying this subsidy. An estimated five-sixths of U.S. wealth transfers (not government purchases but transfers of wealth through the political process) do not flow from wealthier Americans to poorer Americans. Rather, these wealth transfers flow from the disorganized many to the organized few (see Gwartney et al. 2005, 139 and chapter 6 generally). In sum, the political process amounts to "rent seeking," the use of government to take, rather than create, wealth. Such rent seeking amounts to legalized plunder, as Frédéric Bastiat so eloquently explains in his essay "The Law" (Bastiat 2012 [1850]). In the words of journalist H. L. Mencken, "Government is a broker in pillage, and every election is a sort of advance auction in stolen goods" (Mencken 1996, 331).

A corollary problem involves information. In a market, entrepreneurs require information about the goods and services consumers wish them to produce. This information is generated and transmitted through the price mechanism (for a delightful illustration, see Read 1958). What of decisions that require collective action? How are the preferences of individuals, in their roles as citizens (rather than consumers) to be revealed, so elected officials can make decisions on public spending and public laws? The distorted incentives of politics will lead to inefficient outcomes because it is possible to advance private preferences through public means: Voters can lie about their preferences because they can pass the cost to others. In addition, because of concentrated benefits and diffuse costs, the political process will tend to emphasize the preferences of organized interests rather than yielding correct information.

Public choice theory does not imply that government will never work. It does provide a strong enjoiner to analyze government realistically and to engage in honest comparative analysis of the market versus the state.

To be sure, a romantic vision can elevate our hearts and lift our imaginations.[7] Economist Dan Klein, for example, writes about the beauty and danger of the "people's romance" (Klein 2005). Klein describes situations where people irrationally attribute special powers to their groups. Cheering for one's preferred sports team, flaunting a political bumper sticker, or flying a flag will usually have no effect whatsoever. But it makes people feel good to refer to a team as "mine," boast that "we" won today, or feel pride in a victory to which they contributed in no way. This sort of irrational groupthink is harmless and can build affective bonds in civil society. Moving to the level of government, however, such romance can be downright pernicious. We thus see wars stirred by patriotic fervor or massive government redistribution programs that con people into thinking they are participating in a large-scale effort of national solidarity when they are really engaged in inefficient but legalized plunder.

In sum, if government is a necessary evil, it is nonetheless an evil. The eloquent words of political scientist Vincent Ostrom serve as a reminder:

> The very nature of government involves the legitimate use of force in ordering human relationships. The use of force in human relationships is of the nature of an evil. The use of instruments of evil as a necessary means to realize the advantage of ordered social relationships creates a fundamental moral dilemma that can be appropriately characterized as a Faustian bargain. A reasonable expectation, given the Faustian bargain, is that governments will fail. (Ostrom 1984, 422)

In the similar words of George Washington, "Government is not reason; it is not eloquence. It is force. Like fire, a troublesome servant and a fearful master."[8] Although Alexander Hamilton, in *Federalist 70*, called for vigorous government, there is much more prudence in Thomas Jefferson's concern: "I own I am not a friend to a very energetic government. It is always oppressive" (Thomas Jefferson to James Madison, December 20, 1787, in Kurland and Lerner 1986, chapter 18, document 21).

Where does this leave us? Which institutions are most likely to align the incentives of bureaucrats and politicians with the interests of those they represent? Which institutions will tend to mitigate the redistributive tendencies of politics?

Postromantic analysis of government pushes us to seek institutional designs that will be robust in the face of actors who cannot be assumed to act toward some "common good." Instead, the political problem comes down to adopting institutions that will constrain bad behavior and provide incentives for good behavior. A postromantic analysis calls for rule of law and constitutional constraints on the state. It also calls for limited government, to minimize the opportunities for government capture, wealth redistribution, and advancement of private preferences through public means. Voluntary mechanisms (the market and civil society) align incentives properly and thus vastly outperform the ballot box in aggregating and revealing preferences. I return to concrete examples in the following pages.

The Knowledge Problem: Institutions for Nonomniscient Agents

Two intellectual movements fundamentally affected economic, political, and social analysis, and thus public policy, in the twentieth century. First, positivism encouraged social scientists to analyze the social sphere as they would the natural sphere, with ensuing attempts to engineer society as if it were mere clay in an omniscient potter's hands (see Hayek 1979 [1952]). Second, the midcentury mathematization of economics led economists to eschew individual choice in favor of tidy mathematical models; differential equations and econometric regressions allowed the economist to counsel the prince about allegedly optimal social outcomes. This methodology evolved into the dominant "neoclassical" school of economics. This school holds that (a) markets do well in most small settings involving individuals and isolated business firms, but (b) market failure is prevalent and can be fixed by government intervention, and (c) the macroeconomy is inherently volatile and needs management along the lines initiated by John Maynard Keynes (basically, countercyclical fiscal policy and manipulation of interest rates). See Leighton and Lopez (2012) for a superb intellectual history.

Against this new methodology, there emerged dissenting voices. As early as 1920, Austrian economist Ludwig von Mises explained that communism—as the reductio ad absurdum of central planning—could not, by its very nature, function (Mises 1990 [1920]). Because communism lacks private property, it lacks prices and thus competition. Without the profit and loss system to convert individual choices into efficient outcomes, according to division of labor and knowledge, there cannot be efficient allocation of scarce resources, and communism must fail.[9] Mises was ultimately right, although it took another seventy years and more than 100 million deaths before communism crumbled (Courtois and Kramer 1999)—even if it was not completely discredited, as evinced by the lack of decommunization in Eastern Europe (after a century of crimes), the abundance of Che Guevara T-shirts, and lingering proclivities to engage in central planning.

More broadly, Mises's student F. A. Hayek also rebelled against what he perceived to be an "abuse of reason" or the (inappropriate) use of the methods of the natural sciences in the analysis of social phenomena (see Hayek 1979a [1952]). Hayek and his fellow Austrian economists demonstrated why the neoclassical paradigm was fallacious from its assumptions to its methodology. A complex, rich literature can be summed up into a fundamental problem: In a world without omniscient agents, how can economic activity take place, and how can social cooperation happen? The quest for robust institutions to cope with the problem of nonomniscient people, constitutes the second part of robust political economy. It is associated with the Austrian school of economics.[10] Although it started with economics, this counterrevolution has implications for knowledge and thus social choice.

The so-called knowledge problem comes down to the simple fact of human ignorance. Indeed, there is much that we, as individuals, do not know. But there is also much that we do not know that we do not know. If we know that we are ignorant of something, we can acquire the knowledge, through books, conversations, teachers—or Google. But if we don't know that we don't know something, we cannot even begin the process of remedying our ignorance. What is more, much of the knowledge that we have is tacit: We cannot even articulate it but know it implicitly, from gut feelings, rules of thumb, market signals, or tradition and custom. Likewise, most knowledge does not exist in any centralized repository but must be generated and discovered through the daily interactions of millions of individuals (see also Sowell 1980).

To illustrate this rather abstract concept, let us turn to *I, Pencil*, Leonard Read's clever autobiography of a pencil (Read 1958). A pencil is actually quite complex, as it involves multiple inputs from multiple different countries: miners for the ore, smelters for the metal, lumberjacks for the wood, bankers to facilitate the international transactions, a merchant marine and navigational systems to bring all the elements together, and so on. In sum, "not a single person on the face of the earth knows how to make" a pencil. Yet pencils, for all their complexity, are cheap and abundant . . . and this without any single person being in charge. What makes this production possible? What brings together these "millions of tiny know-hows"? In a world of radically limited knowledge, how is economic activity, the economic cooperation of the market, or trade based on division of labor, even possible? The answer is the price mechanism, which gives information about the relative scarcity of resources, provides individual participants an incentive to cooperate, and generally coordinates activity.

As a further illustration, suppose we are considering the construction of a bridge. Technical knowledge will be required: the strength of steel or concrete, the appropriate structural design of the bridge, and the like. However, this is not the end of the story, as economic knowledge is also required: how much the different kinds or sizes of bridges will cost, how much people expect to use the bridge, how much people will be willing to pay (directly or indirectly), how much people would value the alternate uses of the resources used for the bridge, what financing mechanism is most appropriate (bonds to be repaid by users or taxpayers, user financing), and so on. We can set aside technical knowledge as readily available. The more difficult questions involve economic knowledge. How is this knowledge best acquired? How is it best transmitted? And what criteria should be used for resolving competing knowledge claims? These questions come down to processes of information aggregation and rules for making decisions under collective action; in sum, these questions come down to social choice.

Analytically, individual choice is easy. Individuals lack complete knowledge about themselves, but they are still in a position to make life decisions, doing the best they can given the available information. But we still have a fundamental problem: How is information to be generated and used for collective decision making?

We have already seen that the political process skews incentives, thus leading to incoherent outcomes. We now have a second part of the story: Skewed incentives lead to skewed knowledge.

Many economists claim a special knowledge about socially optimal results. This is the hallmark of the orthodox neoclassical theory against which the Austrian school rebelled. Social planners claim to know the optimal number of competitors in a market, the optimal minimum wage for workers, the optimal level of imports in an economy, or the optimal price of money—hence the public provision of welfare, education, monetary policy, agricultural subsidies, rent controls, minimum wages, antitrust laws, and a whole slew of other interventions in the economy. Similarly, social theorists often claim to know socially optimal outcomes—hence laws about maximum numbers of children (for the environment) or incentives to have more children (to offset decreasing fertility rates), restrictions on the sale of alcohol or other substances, the restriction of pornography or prostitution, Sunday closing laws, bans on Walmart or Starbucks or other businesses, or immigration quotas. All of these amount to an imposition of knowledge by some on others. The same applies to religious knowledge. Indeed, there have historically been conflicts over interpretation and understanding of the truth, among and within religions. Although some try peacefully to persuade others of the truth of their beliefs, others attempt to impose it through state coercion. This imposition can be relatively gentle (in the form of bans on alcohol or Sunday closings) or outright violent (such as the Inquisition, the stoning of infidels, or the lack of property rights for women). As the philosopher Voltaire wrote, "If there were only one religion in England, there would be danger of tyranny; if there were two, they would cut each other's throats; but there are thirty and they live happily together in peace" (Voltaire 1733).

In a world of limited knowledge, imposition presents two problems. First, no individual has sufficient knowledge to determine ends for others (Hayek 1960, 88).[11] It is thus little more than an arbitrary exercise of force to attempt to do so. Second, interventionism will lead to unintended consequences. Two political economists illustrate this problem.

Frédéric Bastiat writes of "what is seen, and what is not seen" (Bastiat 1995b [1848]). In his seminal example, Bastiat writes of the "broken window fallacy." A mischievous child breaks a window; the surrounding crowd applauds the child's actions, as he has just created economic activity, in the form of a job for the glazier. This is what is seen. What is not seen is that the owner of the window must forgo the new suit he was going to buy with the money now designated for the window repair. The (seen) glazier's gain is offset by the (not seen) tailor's loss, and there is no net economic activity created from destruction. Those who commit the broken window fallacy rejoice in destruction or government investment, as they see an opportunity for reconstruction or economic stimulus while ignoring what is not seen. We see this fallacy committed time and again when the success of a government policy is trumpeted and the costs and unintended consequences are ignored. As a simple example, mandatory airbag laws in the United States save an estimated 400 lives each year. However, before we get too excited about government's ability to save lives through coercion, we should ask ourselves if the estimated cost of $50 billion could have been more effectively deployed elsewhere (Gwartney et al. 2005, 11).

Ludwig von Mises writes of the dynamics of intervention, whereby intervention in one market disrupts information flows and market equilibria, thus leading to a distortion in another market and another call for intervention, ad infinitum, in a domino effect (see Mises 2007 [1955)]). In his example, if the government wishes to facilitate poor children's access to milk by placing a price ceiling on it, this will cause a disruption. Dairy farmers have the same input costs but are suddenly faced with diminished revenue. Many will leave the market, sell their capital, and start producing goods that do not suffer from price controls. This means that the shelves are empty and children don't get their milk. So the government approaches the dairy farmers, who complain of the price of cattle feed. No problem! The government will now place a price ceiling on cattle feed. And the cycle continues, on and on. As examples of the unintended consequences of imposing knowledge on others by the sword, we can think of the failed and costly U.S. drug war, the devastating European Wars of Religion, the modern welfare state, or the housing bubble and bust (on the latter, see Horwitz and Boettke 2010).

This brings us to F. A. Hayek's principal institutional exposé, *The Constitution of Liberty* (Hayek 1960; for links between Hayek's epistemology and his politics, see Wenzel 2010b). Hayek begins by emphasizing the desirability of liberty, "the creative powers of a free civilization," and the observation that civilization advances by the number of important operations we can perform without thinking about them (Hayek 1960, 22). "Civilization enables us constantly to profit from knowledge which we individually do not possess" (Ibid., 24). In a world of limited knowledge, individuals must rely on "signs or symbols, such as prices offered for their products or expressions of moral or aesthetic esteem for their having observed standards of conduct—in short, of their using the results of the experience of others" (Ibid., 29). Based on the critical fact of limited human knowledge, Hayek emphasizes the importance of institutions in creating and communicating knowledge—over time of accumulated stocks (via traditions, cultural heritage, or teaching) but also among contemporaries. This includes the communication of economic knowledge through prices and of social knowledge through approbation or custom (Ibid., 27). Our limited knowledge implies a faith in accidental learning because we don't know what we don't know. "Humiliating to human pride as it may be, we must recognize that the advances and even the preservation of civilization are dependent upon a maximum of opportunity for accidents to happen" (Ibid., 29). In sum, "Man learns from the disappointment of his expectations" (Ibid., 30). The case for freedom—in maximizing the opportunities for learning, accidental learning, and recovering from our mistakes—rests on an argument for knowledge: "Our faith in freedom does not rest on the foreseeable results in particular circumstances, but on the belief that it will, on balance, release more forces for the good than for the bad" (Ibid., 31). I illustrate this theoretical claim with specific examples in the following discussion.

Beyond institutions (formal and informal) that facilitate and encourage generation and transmission of knowledge, our ignorance also calls for a free framework of institutional correction. To be sure, mistakes will happen: "Liberty is an opportunity for doing good, but also an opportunity for doing wrong" (Ibid., 79). Some bad institutions, morals, and customs will emerge with bad results. But if the society is free, the institutions will correct themselves in a feedback process of learning (Ibid., 67). Whole lotta faith ...

On the other hand, if the society is not free, if it thwarts (intentionally or unintentionally) the process of knowledge creation and transmission by imposing the knowledge that some claim over others, unintended consequences will occur. Many of today's economic and social ills stem from interventionist tinkering. As Hayek writes, "It is indeed probable that more harm and misery have been caused by men determined to use coercion to stamp out a moral evil than by men intent on doing evil" (Ibid., 146). The cost of avoiding mistakes is often far greater than the cost of mistakes. Likewise, even if there is no outright imposition of personal preferences on others, the political process ossifies decisions and blocks the process of institutional learning: Its "coercive, monopolistic character destroys the self-correcting forces which bring it about in a free society that mistaken efforts will be abandoned and the successful ones prevail" (Ibid., 110).

Our limited knowledge calls for a prudent and principled rejection of social engineering, as we simply lack the knowledge to impose better outcomes.[12] This translates into specific institutional characteristics.

First, a limited scope of government, as very few tasks allow for coercive, government action. Hayek explains that "coercion occurs when one man's actions are made to serve another man's will, not for his own but for the other's purpose" (Hayek 1960, 133). There is thus no sense that we are "entitled to prevent [others] from pursuing ends which we disapprove so long as [they do] not infringe the equally protected sphere of others" (Ibid., 79). In a world without omniscient agents, robust political economy does not allow for public imposition of private preferences.

Second, the state must be constitutionally constrained, with clear rules set forth ex ante for the acceptable process of information aggregation and public powers, lest the state become an instrument to impose coercively the will and knowledge of some on others.

Three Strains of Libertarianism

Within the great family of liberty, there is dissent. This dissent can be condensed into three schools of thought: classical liberalism, anarcho-capitalism, and minarchy.

CLASSICAL LIBERALISM

Many thinkers who fit squarely within the philosophy of liberty have espoused a broader role for government than merely the protection of individual rights. These are the so-called classical liberals. As Schlueter explains in the previous chapter, the current nomenclature is frustratingly inaccurate. Indeed, classical liberals are liberal (in the original and true sense of the word) because they are skeptical of heavy-handed governmental intervention and give prima facie precedence to individual liberty.

In philosophical terms, classical liberals espouse a "thick" but not absolute conception of individual rights—that is, individual rights are central, but they are not absolute. Rights may occasionally be trumped for public purposes, but the burden of proof will always rest with the collective, and the state does not have carte blanche to run roughshod over individual rights.

In economic terms, classical liberals espouse the concept of the "productive" state beyond the "protective" state—but not the "redistributive" state. Classical liberals believe that markets are, by and large, efficient. However, markets occasionally fail (by overproducing bads or underproducing goods or by strangling competition). In such cases, the state may step in to fix market failures. Again, though, the state does not have carte blanche to run the economy but is called on only in cases of market failure.

Adam Smith, who is largely considered the father of classical liberalism, provides a simple example that illustrates the problem. Smith painstakingly lays out what he calls the "obvious and simple system of natural liberty" against mercantilism and other forms of state intervention in the economy that were prevalent in his day. For Smith (1981 [1776], IV.9.51),

> All systems either of preference or of restraint, therefore, being thus completely taken away, the obvious and simple system of natural liberty establishes itself of its own accord. Every man, as long as he does not violate the laws of justice, is left perfectly free to pursue his own interest his own way, and to bring both his industry and capital into competition with those of any other man, or order of men. The sovereign is completely discharged from a duty, in the attempting to perform which he must always be exposed to innumerable delusions, and for the proper performance of which no human wisdom or knowledge could ever be sufficient; the duty of superintending the industry of private people, and of directing it towards the employments most suitable to the interest of the society.

From the philosophy flows a political structure:

> According to the system of natural liberty, the sovereign has only three duties to attend to . . . : first, the duty of protecting the society from violence and invasion of other independent societies; secondly, the duty of protecting, as far as possible, every member of the society from the injustice or oppression of every other member of it, or the duty of establishing an exact administration of justice.

The third function of the state is the most important for our purposes because it sheds light on the distinction between classical liberalism and minarchy. The state has a duty of "erecting and maintaining certain public works and certain public institutions." As Smith explains, the state should provide those public works and institutions "which it can never be for the interest of any individual, or small number of individuals, to erect and maintain; because the profit could never repay the expence to any individual or small number of individuals, though it may frequently do much more than repay it to a great society." Such goods include roads, a baseline of public education, and infrastructure and improvements that will facilitate trade and the proper functioning of a market society.

Starting in the 1930s, the economic mainstream lapsed into a full alarmist cry of market failure, with thousands of "economic engineers" called on to fix every little shortcoming, especially in the macroeconomy (see, especially, Samuelson 1954, and Keynesian macroeconomics generally; see also Leighton and Lopez 2012 for a superb overview). Twentieth-century classical liberal economists did not go quite that far; instead they operated on the assumption that markets are usually efficient but sometimes get gummed up and need a bit of a nudge. The three basic categories of market failure are overproduction, underproduction, and lack of competition.[13] In the case of overproduction, the social cost exceeds the private cost. For example, the Acme Company may produce anvils at a revenue of $10 million and a cost of $1 million, for a profit of $9 million. But, in the process, Acme causes $4 million of pollution to its neighbors (a "negative externality" that Acme does not take into account). Because the social cost exceeds the private cost, Acme is overproducing. Thus, classical liberals will call on the state to "internalize the externality" and decrease the overproduction, through taxation or regulation. In this sense, the state is merely enforcing property rights and increasing efficiency. The opposite occurs with underproduction, when the social benefit exceeds the personal benefit, so entrepreneurs do not produce as much as is needed by society (as in the case of education, welfare for the poor, or environmental protection). In this case, a classical liberal will call for state support (if not outright production), to increase the underproduction of the good. Finally, in the exemplary case of a monopoly, one company captures enough market share that competition (and thus the market process) fails. A classical liberal would call for cautious government regulation of the monopoly to allow markets to work.

Even public choice theory, with its skepticism about state action, suggests that the choice among individual, cooperative, and political action depends on a cost–benefit analysis (in terms of efficiency, externalities, and decision-making costs). If individual action is most efficient, a purely private solution will emerge. If voluntary cooperation is most efficient, market solutions will prevail, unless there are prohibitive bargaining costs. If governmental action is expected to be the most efficient, it will be chosen (see Buchanan and Tullock 1999). In the words of Hayek biographer Alan Ebenstein (2003, 126), the goal for classical liberalism is not to minimize government but to maximize competition. Thus, such stalwart defenders of liberty as Milton Friedman are associated not with complete privatization of education, but with school vouchers, and not with a full dismantling of the welfare state, but an emphasis on measures that are less distortionary than outright grants, such as the earned income credit. Even F. A. Hayek allows for a state role beyond preventing coercion. He proposes that the state should guarantee a minimum income and correct market failures. Like other classical liberals, Hayek does not offer free rein to state intervention but provides careful conditions, arguing that redistribution must occur according to the principles of rule of law and generality (that is, no favored groups).[14]

ANARCHO-CAPITALISM

At the other extreme within libertarianism, anarcho-capitalists would replace limited government with noncoercive, market-based governance (see Rothbard 2006 or Nozick 1974; for a comparative overview, see Tomasi 2012).

An etymological disclaimer is again in order. Indeed, it is a pity that anarcho-capitalism is so frequently dismissed simply because of its name (perhaps this is why Murray Rothbard and other anarcho-capitalist libertarians refer to anarcho-capitalism simply as "libertarianism"). Legal scholar John Hasnas (2008) defines this linguistic sleight of hand as follows:

> Anarchy refers to a society without a central planning authority. But it is also used to refer to disorder or chaos. This constitutes a textbook example of Orwellian newspeak in which assigning the same name to two different concepts effectively narrows the range of thought. For if lack of government is identified with the lack of order, no one will ask whether lack of government actually results in a lack of order. And an uninquisitive mental attitude is absolutely essential to the case for the state. For if people were ever to seriously question whether government is really

productive of order, popular support for government would almost instantly collapse.

We are back to Dan Klein's "people's romance," as described earlier. Rothbard (2006, 57) explains how the state makes itself seem inevitable, thus shutting down any inquiry into a stateless alternative. But if, with Rothbard, Hasnas, and others, we do indeed question the necessity of the state, we open a fruitful intellectual conversation.

First, anarcho-capitalism argues that limited government is a chimera. Let us pause for a moment and engage in a simple thought exercise. We give all the guns and the legitimacy of violence to a small group of people—then we are surprised that the small group somehow manages to break its paper chains, and institutional niceties like constitutions and bills of rights, and uses that power for its own purposes! As Rothbard (2006, 67) worries:

> In a profound sense, the idea of binding down power with the chains of a written constitution has proved to be a noble experiment that failed. The idea of a strictly limited government has proved to be utopian; some other, more radical means must be found to prevent the growth of the aggressive state.

Who will guard the guards if we assign a monopoly on the legitimate use of violence to the state? The simple case of the U.S. Constitution shows how a theoretically limited government cannot sustain itself. Within mere years of constitutional ratification, the federal government was violently quashing dissent, discouraging the American tradition of direct response to tyranny, raising taxes, and abridging free speech (Hummel and Marina 1981). Within seventy years, the federal government sent half a million men to their death, invading the Confederacy to preserve the Union without clear constitutional authority (Hummel 1996).[15] Today, about half of all economic activity in the United States is controlled, directly or indirectly, by the federal government. The Constitution was nice while it lasted, but politicians played the game to their advantage and successfully crushed the countervailing forces the founders had so carefully designed. For a detailed overview of judicial deference to the legislature, executive, and administrative agencies and the gradual erosion of constitutional constraints, see Neily 2013 or Levy and Mellor 2008.

Second, anarcho-capitalism argues that the "liberal paradox" (coercion to prevent coercion) is not only futile but unnecessary. Just as the market and civil society are the best providers of shoes, pencils, or education, the same is true for security. Just as government will abuse its power if it provides traditional goods and services, the same will happen with the provision of security and the protection of individual rights. The market and civil society can protect individual rights more effectively than the state. Limited government is a fool's errand, and the only defense of rights can be found in markets and civil society. As historian Ralph Raico (2006, 501) explains, "By extending the realm of civil society to the point of extinguishing the state, Rothbard's view appears as the limiting case of authentic [that is, classical] liberalism."

So, what would an anarcho-capitalist world look like in reality? In the words of anarcho-capitalist Roy Childs in his famous letter to Ayn Rand on the impossibility of limited government, "I am not a builder of utopias" (1969). It would be hubris to provide an exact blueprint of what institutions might emerge in an anarcho-capitalist society. In his "libertarian manifesto," Rothbard (2006) does give us an overview of a free society, with privately produced *governance*—as distinguished from coercive, monopolistic *government*. At the most fundamental level, the defense of individual rights would be provided by private security agencies, disputes would be adjudicated by private arbitrators, and national security would be handled by a combination of citizen militias and private collective action (voluntarily funded defense agencies). Beyond security, anarcho-capitalism rejects the very notion of public goods to be provided by the state or externalities to be remedied coercively. On this dimension, anarcho-capitalism and minarchy agree, so I will not expand here.

What are we to make of anarcho-capitalism? To be sure, it is a radical alternative to the statism that has captured the human imagination for several thousand years. But, as Rothbard (2006, 67) argues, instead of tinkering with a failed idea, we should seriously consider scrapping government and looking for an alternative. After all, the state has a dismal record of protecting property rights and life, and most governments are little more than organized bandits. Little less, perhaps—as the economist Gabriel Calzada (paraphrasing nineteenth-century anarchist and abolitionist Lysander Spooner) points out, the difference between the state and a bandit is that a bandit merely steals your money. The state, after stealing your money, tells you that it is for your own good.

The case against the state is straightforward. But what about the case for a stateless alternative? Is the state not a necessary evil? Perhaps. But perhaps not. Hasnas (2008) writes convincingly of "the obviousness of anarchy." As he writes, "I intend to show that a stable, successful society without government can exist by showing that it has, and to a large extent, still does." In short summary, Hasnas convincingly argues that the rule of law emerged spontaneously (at least in common law countries), as did property and tort law. Police services were private until the mid-nineteenth century, and a good portion is still privately provided today (up to three-quarters, according to some sources; generally, see Benson 1998).

At the extreme, the worst-case scenario of anarchy has historically come nowhere close to the abuses of the state; the twentieth century alone saw more than 100 million people systematically murdered by the state (a number that doubles if one includes wars waged among states).

Such a short description does not do justice to anarcho-capitalism, but it should be sufficient to whet the reader's appetite for the possibility of non-coercive governance. It also should provide the theoretical framework for my later discussions of anarcho-capitalist solutions to the three case studies we discuss later in the book and will hopefully encourage the reader to drink deeply from the "suggested readings" appendix to this chapter.

MINARCHY

Under minarchy, the purpose of the state is the protection of individual rights from the aggression of others; the state itself may not engage in any coercion, except to prevent coercion. This, of course, does not imply that the individual can do everything alone. Individuals operate within markets and civil society to achieve what they cannot on their own, in a movement from private choice to public choice or from individual action to collective action. Government provides an umbrella for the defense of rights, within which individuals can cooperate and thrive.

For the balance of this book, I will primarily emphasize robust political economy and minarchist libertarianism. In fact, unless I specify otherwise, I will use the term *libertarian* to mean minarchy.

Why political economy over rights, and why minarchy over classical liberalism or anarcho-capitalism?

I am very sympathetic to rights-based approaches to libertarianism. I agree with Rand (1967a,b,c) and Rothbard (2006) that rights cannot be ignored. Two theories of liberty from the Austrian school of economics illustrate the problem. The first is the utilitarianism of Ludwig von Mises. The second is the ethical agnosticism of F. A. Hayek. Both are helpful but incomplete, and they show why a theory of rights is necessary.

Ludwig von Mises, one of the greatest apologists of liberty in the twentieth century, was a utilitarian. For him, property rights and free markets with division of labor maximized social cooperation and were thus desirable. Just as freedom leads to harmony of interests, governmental intervention leads to conflict, as it pits different groups of society against each other.[16] Mises, as a radical subjectivist, refused to go any further than utilitarianism (Mises 1999 [1949]).

F. A. Hayek, as we have already seen, is primarily an epistemologist. Because of his radical uncertainty, he is reluctant to promote one vision of rights over others. But he is clearly preoccupied with liberty and individual rights. Likewise, Hayek writes extensively of emergent norms and the "general rules" that individuals in society must follow. Mises delightfully confines himself to the realm of economics. He does not attack the ends of interventionists but demonstrates that their proposed means must fail. He further shows that liberty, and only liberty, leads to human flourishing and harmony of interests. Hayek is deliciously honest in his use of the knowledge problem.

Both Mises and Hayek are valuable building blocks. But both are frustrating and incomplete. What if oppression of a small minority leads to flourishing for everybody else?[17] Is this acceptable? What if government intervention and violation of property rights were actually more efficient than markets? Would that be acceptable? What if efficient but unjust norms emerge in a Hayekian process—are there no criteria outside of efficiency by which to judge them? Clearly a theory of rights is necessary. But, as an economist who has drunk deeply from the cup of philosophy without becoming a professional philosopher, I am not prepared to make that argument. With Thomas Jefferson, I simply "hold these truths to be self-evident" and guide the interested reader to authors who can make a strong case for a rights-based libertarianism. As a political economist, I rely on political economy.

What, then, of my choice of minarchy over classical liberalism? Both are inspiring, and both present problems.

Classical liberalism is noble—initially as a foil against royal absolutism, then as a precursor to modern libertarianism. And far be it from me to downplay the contributions of such heroes of liberty as John Locke, Adam Smith, F. A. Hayek, or Milton Friedman. However, the classical liberals did not go far enough and were naïve about the possibility of controlling the state. There are fundamental problems with classical liberalism, whether Buchanan and Tullock's calculus, Hayek's generality principle, or the idea of government solving market failure. None of these can ultimately stand the test of robust political economy. After all, robust political economy casts fatal doubt on the very existence of socially optimal equilibria, the ability of specialists in political economy to identify them, and the state's ability to correct market failures without unintended consequences or political capture.

What is more, Mises (2007 [1955]) ably demonstrated that intervention in one market will lead to intervention in another, in a chain of interventions. For example, a minimum guaranteed income raises questions of citizenship and exclusion of peaceful travelers, leading to another set of regulations beyond the original intent; this will in turn place a burden on businesses to enforce immigration and labor laws. On the regulatory side, even minor interventions in the market will be distortionary and will lead to subsidy, further regulation, or busting monopolies that were created by state intervention in the first place. Epstein (1999) explains how "one pervasive theme of modern regulatory and constitutional work highlights the disparate impact of formally neutral rules. Let the same restriction apply to a large plant and to a small one, and the cost of compliance—or, more accurately, the cost of compliance per unit of good—could easily differ. The effect, therefore is to place a heavier tax on the one business than on its rival, which in turn retards entry or spurs exit, thereby increasing industrial concentration." Libertarianism protects liberty better than classical liberalism.

At the other end of the spectrum, anarcho-capitalism is appealing and in many cases obvious (with Hasnas 2008). Even such a detractor of anarcho-capitalism as Buchanan (2000a [1975], 7) agrees that "even if we acknowledge

that the principle fails as a universal basis for social order, we should recognize that is essential properties can be seen to operate over large areas of
human interaction." But anarcho-capitalism is not fully convincing as a general organizing principle. As Buchanan bluntly states, "The libertarian anar-
chists who dream of markets without states are romantic fools who have read
neither Hobbes nor history" (Buchanan 1964). Similarly, Ayn Rand discards
anarcho-capitalism as leading to civil war, for there is a need for disinterested
enforcement and keeping violence out of market relations (Rand 1967b). In
the end, minarchy offers a stronger case than anarchy—even if anarcho-
capitalism is deeply inspiring and even if the possibility of limited government turns out to be a chimera.

In this paean to minarchy, I also acknowledge significant challenges. Although I am addressing these issues in parallel research, I do not hope to
have a fully convincing answer anytime soon. But these areas of marginal
fuzziness are not fatal flaws, and they do not ultimately detract from minarchy's superiority over other systems.

First, even a minimal government must be funded. What, then, is the
justification for taxation? Is it not a violation of property rights, even if taxes
are minimal and fund only the defense of rights? This is a problem worth
exploring further; however, I agree with Ayn Rand that "a program of voluntary financing would be amply sufficient to pay for the legitimate functions of
a proper government" and that those with lesser financial ability could free-
ride on the voluntary payments of those who are able to pay (Rand 1964).

Second, minarchy does not squarely address the problem of political authority. Indeed, why should citizens be bound to obey the orders of the state?
And who decides if the state is truly legitimate? This problem is addressed by
Locke but not in an entirely convincing manner, as Pitkin (1965, 1966) deftly
explains. Although this warrants further investigation, I will leave aside the
issue for now, simply arguing that citizens are bound to respect the rights of
others and that a legitimate state will only enforce rights.

Third, the robust political economy critique that leads to the rejection of
conservatism, progressivism, and classical liberalism can also be applied to
minarchy. After all, how are we to know the optimal levels of spending on
the defense of individual rights? And how can we protect against rent seeking in the government provision of security and legal services? And is the

state not a legal monopoly, with all that monopoly entails? These are valid concerns, but I think they are outweighed by the ultimate advantages of minarchy over anarcho-capitalism.

Radically dismal view of human nature

On a simpler level, we can pare things down to the bare essentials. Government is violence; we can think of it as a man with a gun. Violent redistribution of wealth seems, plainly, to be undesirable, even for solving alleged market problems. On the other hand, violence does seem to be necessary for preventing violence and thwarting those who would impede the rights of others or remove the conditions necessary for social cooperation and productive exchange. As Mises (2007 [1955], 37) wrote, "Government ought to protect the individuals within the country against the violent and fraudulent attacks of gangsters, and it should defend the country against foreign enemies. These are the functions of government within a free system, within the system of the market economy." Or, in the (probably apocryphal) words of George Orwell, "We sleep safe in our beds because rough men stand ready in the night to visit violence on those who would do us harm." Of course, such guards must still be guarded, and minarchy is not without its challenges. Minarchy is not perfect; but it does not claim to be. Indeed, given nonomniscient and nonbenevolent human beings, the best we can do is provide the most robust institutions possible to cope with those facts. In the words of Algernon Sidney, "Our inquiry is not after that which is perfect, well knowing that no such thing is found among men; but we seek that human Constitution which is attended with the least, or the most pardonable inconveniences" (Hayek 1960, epigraph).

I have dedicated most of these pages to outlining a set of negatives. A libertarian government is forbidden from doing almost everything. In fact, a libertarian government is empowered to do only one thing: defend individual rights. So, what might a libertarian society look like? Far be it from me to engage in violation of the knowledge problem by putting forth an exact description of what a libertarian society would look like. As a foundation for vibrant civil society and markets, a framework of governmental protection of rights will allow individuals to flourish, but details will vary as they emerge in different situations. Repeating Roy Childs's disclaimer, "I am not a social planner and . . . do not spend my time inventing Utopias" (Childs 1969). In the words of Thomas Jefferson's first inaugural address, a libertarian government would be "a wise and frugal Government, which shall restrain men from injuring one another, shall leave them otherwise free to regulate their own pursuits of industry and improvement, and shall not take from the mouth of labor the bread it has earned. This is the sum of good government, and this is necessary to close the circle of our felicities" (Jefferson 1801).

It is impossible to foresee the details of a libertarian society. Problems will be solved through market innovation or cooperation, except for problems of coercion or violence, which will be resolved by the state. The common law will emerge to round out the edges of rights-claims (see Zywicki 2013).

Although we cannot foresee the detailed outcomes of the free interactions of millions of human beings, we can learn from history. Many authors have examined particular instances where, contrary to conventional wisdom, the market and civil society have done a better job than governmental coercion and central planning—when they are not prevented from doing so. See for example: Anderson and Leal (2001) on free-market environmentalism; Beito (1992) on nongovernmental provision of welfare; Tooley (2013) or Dixon (2013) on private education for poor children; or Rosenberg and Birdzell (1987) on institution-based economic growth. More generally, see the work of Coase (1960) on the resolution of conflict and negative externalities without coercion.[18]

Addressing Objections to Libertarianism

WHAT LIBERTARIANISM IS NOT

I now address some common misconceptions about libertarianism.

First, libertarianism is not an all-encompassing philosophy. Thus, libertarianism recognizes the importance of education for a self-governing polity—but rejects coerced education. Libertarianism recognizes the importance of voluntary compliance with social norms—but rejects coercive governmental imposition of those norms. And most libertarians engage enthusiastically in the self-improvement of intrapersonal virtue—while rejecting coercion of intrapersonal morality.

Second, libertarianism is not license or libertinism. Libertarianism certainly rejects governmental coercion of behavior that does not harm others. But this does not mean that libertarianism rejects rules and authority. Civil society and the market are rich with rules that guide behavior and punish transgressions: Markets punish with bankruptcy the inefficient entrepreneur who wastes scarce resources by not creating value for consumers, churches punish transgressors with penance or excommunication, boors and cheats are socially shunned, owners of private property can refuse admittance or service, and parents have authority over their children until adulthood.

Third, libertarianism is not moral relativism. Just because libertarianism refuses to unleash the coercive power of the state against failures in intrapersonal virtue does not mean that libertarianism has no moral component. Instead, libertarianism refuses to correct perceived shortcomings through violence. This is not the same as passively accepting shortcomings. Many libertarians act to correct those—but never through government coercion and always through voluntary mechanisms, such as entrepreneurship, persuasion, approbation, or charity.

Fourth, libertarianism is not atomistic individualism. Quite the contrary, libertarianism recognizes the importance of voluntary association, from civil society to markets, for human flourishing. Libertarianism is anything but anomic or atomistic, but, instead of coerced cooperation, it emphasizes voluntary association.

Fifth, libertarianism is not a utopia. Granted, a completely free society has never existed, even if a partial version of libertarianism (the Enlightenment and the Industrial Revolution) unleashed huge benefits for all of humanity. But just because most of human history has eschewed liberty in favor of domination of the many by the few does not mean that libertarianism is a utopia. Indeed, libertarianism is realistic about human nature. It recognizes the limits of fallible human beings, who are only too apt to abuse power. If anything, the state of life for most of humanity is an indictment of social engineering.[19]

Finally, libertarianism is not a naïve claim that people are good, so they don't need any boundaries. Instead, libertarianism fully realizes that people, given the chance, are capable of awful things. So, instead of hoping that wise, good, and virtuous statesmen will emerge, libertarianism seeks to restrain power. In the words of Thomas Jefferson, "In questions of power, then, let no more be heard of confidence in man, but bind him down from mischief by the chains of the Constitution" (Kurland and Lerner, chapter 8, doc. 41).

WHAT ABOUT VIRTUE?

*Inter*personal virtue (the way we treat each other), has an obvious and direct link to the political problem. *Intra*personal virtue is a problem of character that does not involve others—and thus lies outside the purview of politics. Nevertheless, it is of tantamount importance for politics and self-governance. Thus does Hayek remind us that there is an inverse relationship between virtue and coercion (Hayek 1960, 62). But this does not imply that the state should (or can) coerce virtue. The state has historically done more harm than good in its attempts to impose virtue, and it will always violate individual rights in its attempts to do so. Hayek explains that "it is indeed probable that more harm and misery have been caused by men determined to use coercion to stamp out evil than by men intent on doing evil" (Ibid., 146). C. S. Lewis likewise asserts that "of all tyrannies a tyranny sincerely exercised for the good of its victim may be the most oppressive. The robber baron's cruelty may sometimes sleep, his cupidity may at some point be satiated, but those who torment us for our own good will torment us without end for they do so with the approval of their own conscience" (Lewis 1972 [1948]). Similarly, James Buchanan warns us: "Let those who use the political process to impose their own preferences on the behaviors of others be wary of the threat to their own liberties, as described in the possible component of their own behavior that may be subjected to control and regulation. The apparent costlessness of restricting the liberties of others through politics is deceptive. The liberties of some cannot readily be restricted without limiting the liberties of all" (Buchanan 2000, 340).

Fortunately, markets and civil society are better at promoting intrapersonal virtue, with the added benefit of eschewing coercion, just as they are better at providing food, shelter, or art. One need look only at Montesquieu's artful phrasing of *"le doux commerce"* (gentle commerce) bringing people together. This is echoed by Alexis de Tocqueville (2000, Book III, Chapter XVIII):

> Trade is the natural enemy of all violent passions. Trade loves moderation, delights in compromise, and is most careful to avoid anger. It is patient, supple, and insinuating, only resorting to extreme measures in cases of absolute necessity. Trade makes men independent of one another and gives them a high idea of their personal importance: it leads them to

want to manage their own affairs and teaches them to succeed therein. Hence it makes them inclined to liberty but disinclined to revolution.

We also see this virtue of markets in Adam Smith's famous language:

> Every individual . . . generally, indeed, neither intends to promote the public interest, nor knows how much he is promoting it. By directing [an] industry in such a manner as its produce may be of the greatest value, he intends only his own gain, and he is in this, as in many other cases, led by an invisible hand to promote an end which was no part of his intention. (Smith 1981 [1776], Book IV.II)

Markets and civil society promote virtue, again without the unintended consequences of governmental intervention. In the words of economist Deirdre McCloskey:

> The leading bourgeois virtue is the Prudence to buy low and sell high. I admit it. There. But it is also the prudence to trade rather than to invade, to calculate the consequences, to pursue the good with competence . . .
>
> Another bourgeois virtue is the Temperance to save and accumulate, of course. But it is also the temperance to educate oneself in business and in life, to listen to the customer, to resist the temptations to cheat, to ask quietly whether there might be a compromise here . . .
>
> A third is the Justice to insist on private property honestly acquired. But it is also the justice to pay willingly for good work, to honor labor, to break down privilege, to value people for what they can do rather than for who they are, to view success without envy, making capitalism work since 1776.
>
> A fourth is the Courage to venture on new ways of business. But it is also the courage to overcome the fear of change, to bear defeat unto bankruptcy, to be courteous to new ideas, to wake up next morning and face fresh work with cheer . . .
>
> Beyond the pagan virtues is the Love to take care of one's own, yes. But it is also a bourgeois love to care for employees and partners and colleagues and customers and fellow citizens, to wish all of humankind well, to seek God, finding human and transcendent connection in the marketplace . . .

Another is the Faith to honor one's community of business. But it is also the faith to build monuments to the glorious past, to sustain traditions of commerce, of learning, of religion, finding identity in Amsterdam and Chicago and Osaka.

Another is the Hope to imagine a better machine. But it is also the hope to see the future as something other than stagnation or eternal recurrence, to infuse the day's work with a purpose, seeing one's labor as a glorious calling. (McCloskey 2006)

In closing, Adam Smith explains the benefits (to all) of individual self-interest, channeled by the right institutions into division of labor, cooperation, and ultimately, service to others: "It is not from the benevolence of the butcher, the brewer, or the baker, that we expect our dinner, but from their regard to their own interest. We address ourselves, not to their humanity but to their self-love, and never talk to them of our necessities but of their advantages" (Smith 1981 [1776], Book I.II).

WHAT ABOUT JUSTICE?

But what about justice? Libertarianism maximizes the opportunities for human flourishing because it maximizes the opportunity for learning, for material flourishing within the market, and for spiritual flourishing within civil society.

The history of the world and contemporary cross-country studies plainly show a strong positive correlation between economic liberty and per-capita income.[20] On average, politically open societies that respect rule of law and property rights grow three times faster than unfree societies (3 percent per year versus 1 percent per year). As a reminder about the magic of compound growth, a mere 2 percent difference in annual growth amounts to a small difference over one generation, but quadruple the growth over fifty years and seven times the growth over a century. What is more, economically and politically free countries have a more balanced distribution of wealth than countries that are unfree (Scully 1992, 1998). And markets and civil society have historically done a better job of taking care of the poor than the welfare state (and without the unintended consequences); see Beito 1992.

Naturally, material well-being is not the only criterion by which to judge a political system. But any system other than libertarianism is ipso facto unjust because the rights of some will be violated by others. As Bastiat so eloquently demonstrates, law is organized justice but only if it is limited to the defense of individual rights. Otherwise, the law is perverted into legalized plunder (Bastiat 2012 [1850]). As Ayn Rand explains, a free society, based on individual rights, is the only system that provides justice because it is the only system of moral-social-political organization that is based on voluntary interactions, that respects individual rights, and that bans violence from human interactions and social organization (Rand 1967a). And, returning to Hayek, libertarianism allows for a better discovery of appropriate norms of justice than any other system.

Conclusion

In her essay "What Is Capitalism?" Ayn Rand reminds us that "there are only two fundamental questions . . . that determine the nature of any social system: Does a social system recognize individual rights?—and Does a social system ban physical force from human relations? The answer to the second question is the practical implementation of the answer to the first." She concludes that "in mankind's history capitalism [that is, libertarianism] is the only system that answers: Yes" (Rand 1967a).[21] Likewise, I can only hope that the case for libertarianism (and against intervention by the state) would flow obviously from robust political economy or individual rights.[22] But I harbor no such illusions.

In this chapter, I hope to have whetted the reader's appetite to learn more about the beauty of cooperation, efficiency, and harmony of interests—and the ugliness of coercion to impose private ends through public means. Libertarianism is better at generating wealth, health, education, and leisure than any other system—but it is also better at providing virtue, justice, and the other nonmaterial goods that are crucial for human flourishing.

Political scientist Bill Allen cautions us about "the human—all too human—temptation to apply a collective scratch to what is a collective itch." When we apply a "governmental scratch to relieve each and every itch in a single sweep of the legislative pen, we succumb to the fallacy of overgeneralization, which accomplishes nothing more than the magnification of imperfections and hence the enlargement of our dangers." There is the problem: "Where each of us could handle his own itch with a timely applied personal scratch, none of us individually can shrink the blistering that results from the collective scratch." He closes with the warning that "by applying power where liberty would serve, we render ourselves helpless, whether to salve our own itching or to resist the excesses of power." In conclusion, "Liberty does not promise that we will not itch; liberty promises that we can manage the itches we ordinarily experience. Society, political society, ideally, would be an association in virtuous effort, not an association in power" (Allen 2000).

Liberty produces more material wealth, more opportunity, more virtue, stronger communities, more order, more widespread justice, deeper affective ties, and more human flourishing than the coercion of central planning— even if central planning is motivated by a desire to encourage human flourishing and virtue. Or perhaps especially so.

For Further Reading:

The single best, comprehensive, magisterial source on libertarianism is David Boaz's *Libertarianism: A Primer.* For a simple, hard-hitting, and clear exposition of individual rights and minarchy, nothing beats Ayn Rand's two essays on "Man's Rights" and "The Nature of Government." On the methodology of robust political economy, Mark Pennington's aptly titled *Robust Political Economy* offers a superb and approachable overview (although he ends up with classical liberal, rather than minarchist, conclusions); beginners may wish to start with Peter Leeson and Robert Subrick's synthetic article, "Robust Political Economy," while more advanced readers will enjoy F. A. Hayek's positive case for liberty in *The Constitution of Liberty.* For an overview of the competing strains within the libertarian family, John Tomasi offers a digestible distillate of complex philosophical issues in *Free Market Fairness.* On anarcho-capitalism, Murray Rothbard's *For a New Liberty: The Libertarian Manifesto* is a good place to start; those interested in more rigor and precision (at the expense of simplicity) should turn to the seminal *Anarchy, State, and Utopia,* by Robert Nozick.

CHAPTER THREE

What's Wrong with Conservatism?

A Reply to Schlueter

NIKOLAI G. WENZEL

SCHLUETER MAKES ONE OF THE CLEAREST EXPOSITIONS of conservatism I have seen (for others, see Carey 2004 [1984] or Kirk 1982). But, for all its strengths, natural law liberalism faces the same problems as other brands of conservatism: It is internally inconsistent, it is arbitrary in its preferences, it involves an imposition of private preferences through public means, and it is ultimately inimical to liberty and human flourishing.

In this reply, I will focus on three representative problems: robust political economy, the common good, and a troubling understanding of the American founding. But first, I will discuss the merits of natural law liberalism. Although much in conservatism is problematic, it does contain important lessons for liberty.

Strengths of Natural Law Liberalism

There is much that is good in Schlueter's depiction of natural law liberalism and its position as a bedrock for social organization and human flourishing. Three things, in particular, are pleasing to any friend of liberty. First, the emphasis on an objective moral order is full of promise as a bulwark against the baser instincts of politicians and tyrants. Second, natural law liberalism's emphasis on human flourishing offers a rich overall framework for human life (even if it goes beyond the purview of politics, as I will explain in the following pages). And third, natural law liberalism's emphasis on virtue, character, and the personal foundations of self-governance and a free society contains lessons for libertarians on how to advance the free society.

In many ways, natural law liberalism could serve as a foundation for libertarianism, rather than conservatism! Indeed, Schlueter's articulation of the "equilibrium of liberty" (reason, tradition, and liberty) is superb—but libertarianism repudiates any imposition that would suffocate the very liberty it is supposed to protect. Thus, several difficulties within natural law liberalism contain fatal flaws.

Human Ignorance, Politics, and the Objective Moral Order

The first major difficulty with natural law liberalism comes from the limitations of human knowledge. Natural law liberalism rests on the claim that there exists an objective moral order, that this moral order is discoverable by the human mind, and that it ought then to form the foundation of social, economic, and political organization. In its simplest form, this is a very appealing proposition.

But how are we, fallible human beings with limited cognitive capacities, to discover that objective moral order? What are the criteria for determining what is good and what is evil? How do we account for the changing understanding, over the course of humanity, of what is good and what is evil? And how do we explain the awful things that have been done to promote an alleged good forcefully, from slavery to the execution of those who did not attend weekly church services in colonial times, and from denial of basic rights to women or racial minorities, to arbitrary deprivation of property or life by an absolute monarch? We must remember that all of these things were justified, at some point, by the contemporary understanding of natural law, and all were later rejected by a modified understanding of natural law, after much suffering. For example, Aquinas called for the execution of heretics (Aquinas 1981, Question 11, Article 3) or the physical compulsion (that is, torture) of apostates (Ibid., Question 10, Article 8). Aristotle (in Book I, ii, of the *Politics*, Aristotle 1996) argued that some humans were born for slavery, a point picked up by Aquinas (Ibid., "On Justice") and nineteenth-century American apologists for slavery.

Natural law is certainly tempting. Because it stands as a yardstick outside of politics and human-made "positive law," one can invoke natural law to the torturer, the murderer, and the tax collector. Unfortunately, the limits of reason cast serious doubt on natural law. As legal theorist Alan Dershowitz writes:

If only it were true that a God, in whom everyone believed, had come down from the heavens and given the entire world an unambiguous list of the rights with which He endowed us. How much easier it would be to defend these sacred rights from alienation by mere mortals. Alas, the claim that rights were written down by the hand of divinity is one of those founding myths to which we desperately cling, along with the giving of the Tablets to Moses on Sinai, the dictation of the Koran to Muhammad, and the discovery of the gold plates by Joseph Smith. (Dershowitz 2004, 2)

Wrong interpretations of the natural law

Although natural law has been used in support of such laudable goals as abolition of slavery, habeas corpus, representative government, and rule of law, it has also been used to justify ugly things like slavery, absolute monarchy, or Sharia. In a world without omniscience, imposition of a full system of laws violates the principle that no person has sufficient knowledge to impose ends on others. Appealing as it may be, and as powerful a tool as it may be to justify respect for human dignity and individual rights, natural law can also be a dangerous weapon to impose personal preferences through public means and governmental coercion. Constitutional historian Scott Gordon explains that twentieth-century thinkers like Bertrand de Jouvenel and F. A. Hayek called for a revival of natural law thinking to counter the growth of state power (Hayek, specifically, attempted to reconcile what he called a "nomothetic order" with the knowledge problem; he did so through the idea of emergent, rather than designed, norms; see Hayek 1973, 1976, 1979b). The problem is that

> . . . neither de Jouvenel nor Hayek explains how the doctrine of natural law is to accomplish this task. It seems that natural law (as they conceive it) speaks so plainly on the question of state power that all rational citizens, if they are taught its precepts properly, will oppose any further growth of the state, and indeed demand its reduction. This is doubtful. The specific content of natural law is contained in no document, and those who invoke it are free to proclaim whatever they have in mind. If the history of the doctrine since it was first developed by Thomas Aquinas in the thirteenth century is any indication, the concept of natural law

merely serves to increase the power of any institutions whose members
are bold enough to claim exclusive authority to interpret it. There is more
than one way by which the organized few can dominate the unorganized
many. (Gordon 1999, 13)

Legal philosopher Alf Ross is less tactful in his dismissal:

> Like a harlot, natural law is at the disposal of everyone. The ideology
> does not exist that cannot be defended by an appeal to the law of nature.
> And, indeed, how can it be otherwise, since the ultimate basis for every
> natural right lies in a private direct insight, an evident contemplation,
> an intuition. Cannot my intuition be just as good as yours? Evidence as
> a criterion of truth explains the utterly arbitrary character of the meta-
> physical assertions. It raises them up above any force of inter-subjective
> control and opens the door wide to unrestricted invention and dogmat-
> ics. (Ross 1959, 261)

Finally, Dershowitz points out that

> . . . contemporary apologists for divine law argue that some past claims—
> especially those of which they disapprove—were misreadings or misap-
> plications of God's will. But how can we be sure that today's "correct"
> reading will not be subject to tomorrow's correction? The history of di-
> vine law is a history of repeated corrections of yesterday's lethal misread-
> ings and misapplications. To be an advocate of divine law is constantly
> to have to say you're sorry for the mistakes of your predecessors, and
> your successors will inevitably have to apologize for the mistakes you
> are now making when you claim to know God's true intentions. (Der-
> showitz 2004, 25)

Parenthetically, I am not making a claim for moral relativism—but encouraging caution about claims that there exists a discoverable, universal,
and eternal law. History plainly shows that there is no universal set of ethics.
Maybe every human society has indeed banned murder, but the definition of
murder has been so loosely construed as to make the ban a sham. Burning
heretics at the stake, gassing millions of Jews, and starving millions of dis-
sidents in the Gulag were all apparently ethical according to the norms of the
time. Likewise, almost every human society seems to have frowned on theft

yet allowed it through the coercive apparatus of the state. Frédéric Bastiat gives us a simple test for distinguishing between "theft" and "legal plunder": "How is . . . legal plunder to be identified? Quite simply. See if the law takes from some persons what belongs to them and gives it to other persons to whom it does not belong. See if the law benefits one citizen at the expense of another by doing what the citizen himself cannot do without committing a crime" (Bastiat 2012 [1850]).

As economist Gordon Tullock points out, there have clearly been many different ethics over the years and civilizations; so efforts at claiming knowledge of "the" truth range from the naïve to the dangerously hubristic (Tullock 2005). Likewise, Dershowitz points out that, if natural law were indeed eternal and universal, "then the content of rights would be consistent over time and place. Yet experience shows that nothing could be further from the truth" (Dershowitz 2004, 23). Again, this is not to say, in a relativist bout, that all ethical systems are equal. Rather, it is a reminder that past advocates of natural law thought they held the truth and could coerce others accordingly. Might we not exercise some caution before claiming that, torpedoes and past errors be damned, this time we are right, and we have grasped the truth—especially before we impose our vision on others forcibly? I agree with Schlueter that rejecting natural law in toto because some of its assertions have subsequently been rejected makes no sense—just as it would make no sense to reject science because past scientists have made assertions that were later corrected. However, the issue is not one of rejecting natural law but of rejecting natural law as a justification for coercion.   Isn't any law coercive?

According to natural law liberalism, human reasoning (including the discovery of the objective moral order) takes place within particular traditions. This helps explain why different conservatives attempt to conserve different things. Indeed, conservatism—even Schlueter's natural law liberalism—is a fuzzy and amorphous concept. As one reads through the panoply of schools of thought that call themselves conservative, one is reminded of the proverbial attempt to nail Jell-O to a tree. What, indeed, is a conservative? Conservative theorist Russell Kirk admits openly that "definition of the words 'conservative' and 'conservatism' is not easily accomplished." He continues by explaining that "strictly speaking, conservatism is not a political system, and certainly not an ideology." "Instead," he writes, "conservatism is a way of looking at the civil social order. Although certain general principles held by most conservatives may be described, there exists wide variety in application of these ideas from age to age and country to country." In sum, "conservatism offers no universal pattern of politics for adoption everywhere." Instead, "conservatives reason that social institutions always must differ considerably from nation to nation, since any land's politics must be the product of that country's dominant religion, ancient customs and historic experience" (Kirk 1982, xi, xiv, and xv). I certainly applaud the flexible response to particular circumstances. But where is the underlying principle, beyond prudential adaptation of institutions to circumstances?

Surely there is something to novelist Evelyn Waugh's commentary on Rudyard Kipling's conservatism: "He believed civilization to be something laboriously achieved which was only precariously defended. He wanted to see the defenses fully manned and he hated the liberals because he thought them gullible and feeble, believing in the easy perfectibility of man and ready to abandon the work of centuries for sentimental qualms" (Waugh 1983, 625). But how are we to determine which "old and tried" institutions, which traditions, which products of civilization, are good, and which should be discarded? And according to what underlying principles?

What sense are we to make of such a broad nomenclature, of a family of conservatisms that includes a bit of everything: from an isolationist old right to the interventionism of the neoconservatives, from teetotaling conservative Protestants to conservative Catholics who are quite happy to drink *usque ad hilaritatem*,[1] from free-market conservatives who embrace competition to communitarian conservatives who would thwart the market to protect a community, from profligate conservatives like President George W. Bush to the fiscal conservatives of the Tea Party, from the "bitter gun owners" of the so-called leave me alone coalition[2] to the philosophically sophisticated Burkean conservatives, and from small-government conservatives who fear intrusion into markets and civil society to big-government conservatives who proudly wield the might of the state in the name of national security or national greatness?[3] The list is as long as it is bewildering.

One is left wondering if this contradictory hodgepodge is coincidental. Instead, conservatism—even the limited, principled conservatism espoused by Schlueter—is arbitrary in its claims because it seeks justification for the

public imposition of private preferences. This leads us from the knowledge
problem to public choice theory.   *Geography*

As I have already pointed out, it is dangerous to rely on the political pro- /
cess to determine truth and ethics. As a simple reminder, we must ask what,
indeed, constitutes a "community." If a "community" rejects a new Walmart
in the name of protecting small businesses, what is the "community"? Voters? The consumers that Walmart, in its quest for profit, predicts will choose
to spend money there? Or perhaps a coalition of small businesses seeking to
thwart competition?

Moving from this simple case of market entry to the more complex problem of discovering an objective moral order, we see the danger of using the
coercive power of the state to determine—and impose—one's understanding of truth and virtue. For natural law liberalism, the law is a teacher, and   *God!*
the state can facilitate human flourishing by supporting the pursuit of the
good while "helping" individuals avoid the bad. But, again, who determines   /
the good and the bad, and along what criteria? Who has a privileged access
to the truth, which allows for imposition of that truth on others? If the law
is a teacher, how is the state's interest or a "community's" preference to be
determined? By simple majority? By those who are able to mobilize forces to
impose their preferences on others via the political process? Likewise, if the
government is to be involved in the legislation of morality, who determines
morality? A majority of senators? Or will a supermajority of both houses be
required to define the truth? Conservatism longs for the emergence of law-
makers, of the wise and the good, to guide the ships of state and society
through troubled times, while naively assuming that individuals facing perverse incentives won't use public power for private means.

The very notion that the coercive apparatus of the state can "support" virtue without being coercive is odd and arbitrary, to say the least. Conservatism
would have us believe that a government that can't cover basic functions like
running a trust fund or spending within its means could encourage virtue,
or that a government that can't properly teach children how to read by the
age of eighteen could somehow successfully teach civics. Conservatism would
have us believe that government—by definition an ordering of human affairs
through violence (at best) and the mass murderer of more than 100 million
people in the twentieth century alone (at worst)—could be entrusted with

teaching virtue, or that a government that can't preserve the value of fiat money[4] can somehow guide fallible humans toward an eternal order.

In the words of columnist George F. Will, "Conservatism seems to be saying government can't run Amtrak, but it can run the Middle East." Libertarians and conservatives agree that men are not angels—but libertarians subsequently don't trust anybody with coercive power, whereas conservatives somehow trust the political process and enlightened leaders.

The "Common" Good

Claims of advancing a "common" good are central to natural law liberalism. Schlueter is more cautious in his definition than less careful thinkers who bandy the term about blithely. But he still goes too far. Indeed, to be truly "common," a common good must be, well . . . common! Given the epistemological difficulties of knowing ourselves and knowing what is good for others, we must be very careful in defining *the common good*, lest an allegedly "common" good serve as an excuse, as a friendly sounding veil that enables us to impose private preferences using public means.

Cooperative activities are motivated by the common good of the cooperating parties. That much is not controversial. However, if an activity is not cooperative, if it is not voluntary, then it cannot be motivated by a common good. We thus see the non sequitur of natural law liberalism. A state that does not limit itself to defending individual rights is ipso facto not advancing the common good, as it will impose the preferences of some on others. State regulation of public morality is ipso facto not a common good, as those who violate the public morality (without violating the rights of others) are not included. The drug pusher, the prostitute, and the pornographer, as long as they do not coercively impose their wares on others, are voluntarily providing a service for which there is a willing customer. When the state bans their activities, it is not advancing the common good: The allegedly "common" good of banning the commerce clearly does not include the interests, desires, and preferences—and thus the good—of the suppliers and consumers who are thwarted. Because some parties are excluded as a result of prohibition, the alleged good cannot, by definition, be "common." If an activity is cooperative but others don't approve of it, that activity is still a good common to those

"Radical" Individualism throughout...

who participate in it. Just as voluntary polygamy is a common good for the parties involved, involuntary monogamy is not.

Likewise, the scale of the political association makes it difficult for its activities really to be common, if the state does more than protect individual rights. An individual can understand a marriage, an orchestra, a friendship, a commercial transaction—and, to a large extent, a business firm. But at vast scales, it is hard to speak of a truly common good. An army, for example, may very well be dedicated to a common good of national defense. But it is frequently dedicated to conflicting goods of national expansion, advancement of generals or politicians at the expense of troops, and the like. Likewise, although one would hope that military procurement actually serves military purposes, it can easily fall prey to rent seeking, as defense contractors capture the political process. At the broadest level, the pork-barrel morass of $4 trillion in annual federal spending, or the 80,000 pages of new federal regulations that come out each year as part of the U.S. government's efforts at redistribution and rent seeking, are hardly representative of a "common" good. So many interests are represented, so many compromises made, so many logs rolled, so many dollars taken and redistributed, that we cannot coherently speak of a good that is truly "common."

All of this should not be taken as a blanket rejection of the common good. Surely there is something to a broad institutional blanket, a framework within which individuals can peacefully cooperate. Rule of law, free markets, and the opportunity to pursue happiness are all part of a common good. But anything beyond this, any imposed detail, will not be truly common. For a superb definition of the common good, see philosopher Jason Brennan, who defines it with delicious narrowness, as a combination of institutions—such as social order, shared ethical/social norms, rule of law, and markets—that are indeed to *everyone's* advantage (Brennan 2012a). We return to Buchanan's reminder that it "is impossible for an external observer to lay down criteria for 'goodness' independent of the process through which results or outcomes are attained" (2000a [1975], 19). The common good, properly understood, must be means oriented: that is, it provides the framework within which individuals can determine and pursue their own ends. It cannot be ends oriented, as nobody has the knowledge to determine ends for others.[5] In the words of the Declaration of Independence, one of the purposes of legitimate government is to secure each individual's right to the "pursuit of happiness." The Declaration does not grant to the state the power to define that happiness and then impose it.

We know what happiness is !!!

Tensions within the American Founding

Although I largely embrace the philosophy and institutions of the American founding, they are not central to my argument. First, the American founding is but one of many (and incomplete) historical attempts to establish a constitution of liberty—along with ancient Greece, ancient Rome, the Venetian Republic of the thirteenth century, the Dutch Republics of the sixteenth century, and seventeenth-century Britain (Gordon 1999). I thus prefer to rely on underlying principles, rather than one historical moment. And, second, there is no single philosophy of the American founding, and the prevalent philosophy is mixed on the subject of liberty.

In many ways, the U.S. Constitution, American political life, and American political culture are all very libertarian. In many other ways, American politics from the founding to the present has been one great story of assaults on liberty, as various interests have used public power to advance their private preferences.

The U.S. Constitution was largely a libertarian document, as it checked the illiberal activities of the states while rejecting many centralizing impulses. However, in many ways, the Constitution betrayed the Revolution: The Declaration represented the more libertarian element in American politics, but centralizing forces rallied in 1787 to impose a strong central government.

Perhaps the easiest way to address libertarianism in the American founding is to ask the simple question, "Is a return to the Constitution a return to libertarianism?"[6] To that question, I offer an unequivocal answer: "YES! . . . mostly."

We can think of the Declaration of Independence as a philosophical statement, followed a decade later by the U.S. Constitution as the institutional implementation of the Declaration's principles. What, then, is the philosophy of the Declaration? "We hold these truths to be self-evident, that all men are created equal, that they are endowed by their Creator with certain unalienable Rights, that among these are Life, Liberty and the pursuit of Happiness." There, simple and straightforward, a minimalist philosophy with which any libertarian would agree. The next step moves from metaphysics and ethics to politics, with a statement on the purpose of government: "To secure these rights, Governments are instituted among Men." And, "whenever any Form of Government becomes destructive of these ends, it is the Right of the People to alter or to abolish it, and to institute new Government, laying its foundation on such principles and organizing its powers in such form, as to them shall seem most likely to effect their Safety and Happiness."

There, then, is the political philosophy of the Declaration: The purpose of government is to protect rights. Period.[7]

The next question, of course, is one of implementation. If the purpose of government is to secure rights, how should government go about doing so? We now move from philosophy to institutions, and to the Constitution as implementation of the Declaration. By and large, the enumerated powers granted to the federal government under Article I, section 8, are in line with libertarian philosophy, the defense of liberty, and the spirit of 1776. The Constitution grants protective powers, lapses into gray areas with productive powers, and eschews outright redistributive powers or the legislation of morality. Ultimately, I must agree with Calvin Coolidge, who is said to have proclaimed in a speech that "to live under the American Constitution is the greatest political privilege that was ever accorded to the human race." Coolidge's assessment notwithstanding, there were big problems with the founding, from the beginning.

The first—glaring—problem with the U.S. Constitution is the question of slavery. Not only is slavery tolerated, in clear violation of the principles of the Declaration, but the Constitution does not even face it squarely. Indeed, the Constitution limits itself to milquetoast and obfuscatory language about the three-fifths compromise for congressional representation (Article I, section 2), a moratorium on the "Importation of such Persons as any of the States now existing shall think proper to admit" after 1808 (Article I, section 9), and an obliquely worded fugitive slave clause (Article IV, section 2). To be sure, the founders had to compromise on slavery, lest the entire constitutional project founder. However, many of the founders believed in slavery, so it is hard to disentangle the problem from the Constitution.

Second, the Constitution contains rather illiberal language on the matter of regime preservation, which corroborates the old saw that today's revolutionary is tomorrow's reactionary. A libertarian argument can be made for preserving a regime that preserves liberty, so long as liberty is the ultimate goal. But regime preservation is usually more concerned with preservation of the regime tout court. One wonders about the use of the militia to suppress insurrections (Article I, section 8), the suspension of habeas corpus in case of rebellion or when the public safety requires it (Article I, section 9),[8] or the definition of treason against the United States as levying war against them (Article III, section 3). What happened to the American tradition of direct resistance to government power, or the revolutionary spirit of 1776? American history contains a long tradition of illiberal raison d'état as justification for curbing liberty and individual rights, in the name of regime preservation.

Third, the Constitution is problematic on the question of respect for individual rights by the states. Was the Constitution applicable solely to the new federal government, leaving the states great leeway to do anything within their borders? Or did the Constitution establish parameters that the states were bound to follow—but within whose confines they could act as they saw fit, as proverbial laboratories of democracy? History, indeed, points to glaring state abuses, from slavery and self-incrimination in criminal cases to established religions that lasted well into the nineteenth century, police powers that would make any friend of liberty blanch, and healthy doses of economic dirigisme and support of state-sponsored monopolies. Alas, the Constitution is vague on this matter. Article IV, section 2, guarantees that "the Citizens of each State shall be entitled to all Privileges and Immunities of Citizens in the several States." But even this was not clear—and it took half a million dead and the fourteenth amendment to clarify this article's meaning as well as the applicability of the Bill of Rights to the states (see Neily and McNamara 2010). Article IV, section 4, states that "The United States shall guarantee to every State in this Union a Republican Form of Government." But that's it. It was not until the Reconstruction era that the limits to the powers of the states were explicitly defined. Legal scholars Neily and McNamara explain that "the Privileges or Immunities Clause [of the Fourteenth Amendment] was very carefully, very deliberately crafted to make clear that citizens hold basic civil rights—some specifically enumerated in the Constitution and some not—that state and local governments must respect." Indeed, as late as the mid-nineteenth century, the U.S. Supreme Court had ruled that the Bill of Rights did not apply to the states. The Fourteenth Amendment's explicit language was meant to clarify things, but the amendment was eviscerated by the Supreme Court within a decade of its ratification (again, see Neily and McNamara 2010). The controversy lingers today, as states routinely violate the Bill of Rights and frequently get away with it. In point of practice, the U.S. Constitution has allowed the states to thwart individual liberties.

Fourth, the Constitution paves the road for redistribution, social engineering, and the rent-seeking gravy train. Clauses such as "the general welfare" and "necessary and proper" have been routinely abused as an excuse for redistribution and intervention, even if the language is rather evident. Alas, the Constitution also sowed the pernicious tare of economic powers, from postal roads to coining of money and the national debt. Although such powers may have seemed necessary for establishing a union sufficiently strong to protect liberty, they contain the roots of ugliness and have indeed given us an inefficient postal monopoly, a national debt that exceeds 100 percent of America's annual production, a federal government that spends more than a third of national production (60 percent or more of which is not explicitly authorized by the Constitution and thus unconstitutional), and an unelected committee in Washington, DC, that artificially sets the price of money, giving us an ugly cycle of inflation and recession.[9] Regardless of original intent versus later interpretation, the Constitution plainly hands a portion of the economy's commanding heights to the federal government.

Beyond these specific problems, we must remember that there is no such thing as "the" American founding (generally see McDonald 1985, Beard 2004 [1913], Hardin 1999, Wood 1969, or Hummel and Marina 1981). There were multiple competing factions, ideologies, and interests, ranging from the agricultural to the mercantile, from the radicals to the nationalists, from advocates of states' rights to proponents of a strong central government, from republicans to monarchists, and from democrats to aristocrats (see Hardin 1999). Likewise, there were multiple understandings of liberty at the founding, from the "liberty to act virtuously" of the Puritans and the socially stratified liberty of the Virginia Cavaliers, to the social pluralism and egalitarianism of the Quakers and the "libertarian" individualism of the back-country settlers (see Fischer 1989). The Constitution of 1787 was, itself, the result of political compromise on matters ranging from slavery to representation in the Senate, and from state versus popular sovereignty to the inclusion of a Bill of Rights. The Federalists won, but it would be incorrect to refer to the Federalist vision, as outlined in *The Federalist Papers*, as "the" American founding's philosophy (see also Wood 1969, 483).

Indeed, there exist competing interpretations of the founding, contrary to the monolithic view that often prevails. As a telling example, one panelist at the 2011 American Political Science Association panel that prompted this commentary stopped the discussion at one point. His voice dripping with exasperation, he said something to the effect of: "Listen. The American constitutional convention was not a public choice story. The founders wanted ordered liberty, and they were going to implement it through the Constitution." On the other hand, we have a much more tempered view: 1787 as "repudiation of 1776," or "the Constitution as betrayal of the revolution" (Wood 1969, 519).[10]

In sum, there are four big problems in the orthodox view, espoused by Schlueter, of the "founding as liberty."

First, the victorious Federalists did not spring forth ex nihilo. Economic historian Jeffrey Hummel notes that they emerged from an older American "nationalist" tradition that wanted a strong central government with the hierarchical features of eighteenth-century England (see also Wood 1969, 492). While the nationalists were largely absent from the 1776 drafting of the Declaration of Independence, they dominated the 1787 convention—which, we must remember, was an unconstitutional circumvention of the states' powers under the amendment procedures set forth in the Articles of Confederation.

Second, dissenting voices argue that "the prevailing rule prior to the Constitution was complete free trade among the states" with a few minor exceptions (Hummel and Marina 1981). The whole commercial justification for the Constitution thus appears to be a sham. What is more, "if a general reduction in trade restrictions was what the Nationalists were really after, this would hardly have justified a central government with the power to tax" (Ibid.).

Third, the Constitution of 1787 reads like a postrevolutionary entrenchment of power by yesterday's revolutionaries, who have become today's reactionaries. We see this in the Constitution's emphasis on order, as well as its underlying preoccupation with anarchy over leviathan, as evinced by such provisions as suspension of habeas corpus in times of rebellion and calling forth the militia to preserve the status quo and quash insurrections (Wood 1969, 432–433). Hummel worries about this end to the American tradition of direct action; Wood similarly refers to "the people out of doors" as a powerful check on tyranny that lasted only until 1787 (generally, see Hummel and Marina 1981 and Wood 1969, 319–321).

Fourth, the commercial powers granted to the central government in the 1787 Constitution—especially in light of the argument that interstate trade was alive and well under the Articles—smack of an excuse for a nationalist takeover. The federalists imposed a number of internal taxes and regulations, which were later repealed by Presidents Jefferson and Madison. These internal taxes were not reinstated until the next big grab for central power, under Lincoln's final destruction of federalism (see Hummel 1996). All of this amounts to a nationalist excuse for imposing a strong central government (Wood 1969, 504 and 525). Alleged state abuses and commercial shenanigans were merely a convenient excuse for setting up a vastly more powerful central apparatus than was needed to remedy the alleged shortcomings of the Articles.

The Constitution of 1787 can thus be seen as a thoroughly aristocratic document that entrenched many existing power structures at the expense of liberty; in the words of President John Quincy Adams, the Constitution was designed "to increase the influence, power and wealth of those who have it already" (Ibid., 513–514). This elite takeover can be seen as the culmination of the nationalist project and definitely not the culmination of 1776 (Ibid., 499). In many ways, the Constitution was a "repudiation of 1776" and betrayed the Revolution (Ibid., 519 and 563; generally, see also Hummel and Marina 1981).

It is plain that competing strains linger in American political life. Although there has been a libertarian streak since the founding, there has also been an interventionist one (again, see Fischer 1989 for details on competing visions of liberty in American colonial and revolutionary times). It is thus curious to appeal to "the" American founding as an era, or a discrete and homogeneous intellectual movement, rather than appealing to ahistorical and universal principles as a foundation for social organization.

Conclusion

Although natural law liberalism, as presented by Schlueter, contains much that is appealing, it also contains many difficulties and internal tensions. Fundamentally, natural law liberalism rests on assertion rather than argument, on circumstance rather than principle, and (ironically) on subjective preferences rather than objective norms. It is no wonder that there are so many different and conflicting forms of conservatism because none is based on principle or coherence but rather on an arbitrary set of personal preferences that is imposed as *the* truth on everybody, through the political process.

For Further Reading

The clearest case against conservatism comes from F. A. Hayek's pen, in his essay "Why I Am Not a Conservative" (in Hayek 1960); although Hayek is writing against European conservatism, his critique applies to contemporary American conservatism, including natural law liberalism. Alan Dershowitz raises fundamental questions about natural law in *Rights from Wrongs* (while his analysis is damning, his conclusion is somewhat disappointing and thin gruel against those who would violate rights). Readers may wish to revisit Mark Pennington's *Robust Political Economy* for the basic economic case against conservative interventionism. The simplest, most straightforward questioning of American founding homogeneity can be found in the debate between Jeffrey Hummel and William Marina, "Did the Constitution Betray the Revolution?"; a more thorough case can be found in Gordon Wood's *The Creation of the American Republic: 1776–1787*.

CHAPTER FOUR

What's Wrong with Libertarianism?

A Reply to Wenzel

NATHAN W. SCHLUETER

THERE IS MUCH IN DR. WENZEL'S ABLE DEFENSE of libertarianism with which conservatives can wholeheartedly agree. Like libertarians, conservatives believe that political institutions should "minimize harm and maximize the opportunities for human flourishing." Conservatives also agree with libertarians that human beings are neither omniscient nor reliably benevolent and that human beings do not necessarily act "selfishly in markets and selflessly in government." Conservatives wholeheartedly share the libertarian call for "limited government, to minimize opportunities for government capture, redistribution, and advancement of private preferences through public means." Likewise, conservatives share with libertarians a "prudent and principled rejection of social engineering," and conservatives deny that government, or any individual, should "determine ends for others." Finally, conservatives celebrate the singular ability of free associations, including the free market, to coordinate human actions, provide for human needs, and promote human flourishing. (It is true that traditionalist conservatives sometimes speak as though they are suspicious of the free market, but what concerns traditionalist conservatives is really corporate capitalism.[1])

In the most fundamental sense, the difference between conservatism and libertarianism turns on the degree to which politics can be understood in terms of economics. As Wenzel's term *robust political economy* suggests, libertarians tend to view politics through the lens of economic assumptions about human action. This lends an attractive clarity and neatness to the libertarian account of politics. But, as I hope to show, that clarity and neatness are achieved only by ignoring or downplaying certain aspects of human nature that make politics, messy and imperfect as it is, a permanent feature of human existence.

Conservatives, while acknowledging the importance of economic analysis for public policy, deny that political life can be correctly understood in economic terms. To see why, I will treat three significant difficulties in Wenzel's arguments that stem directly from the economic assumptions he brings to those arguments. Each of these difficulties is related to a different thinker and associated with a different approach to libertarianism. First, in the next section I will treat James Buchanan and public choice theory. In the following section, I will treat F. A. Hayek and the knowledge problem. Finally, I will treat Robert Nozick and the principle of self-ownership. Along the way I will continue to build my case for conservatism, especially by addressing the challenge of pluralism in the penultimate section.

Interestingly, although Wenzel relies on the arguments of Buchanan and Hayek in his defense of libertarianism, neither Buchanan nor Hayek is a libertarian in Wenzel's sense of the term. And although Nozick *is* a libertarian in Wenzel's sense of the term, Nozick's arguments in defense of libertarianism actually undermine Wenzel's position.

James Buchanan and Public Choice Theory

Wenzel begins his argument with public choice theory. Launched by Nobel laureate James Buchanan, Gordon Tullock, and others in the 1960s, public choice theory challenges the common assumption that human beings pursue private interests in the market and public interests in government. Because "the *same* individual participates in both processes," public choice theorists emphasize (Buchanan and Tullock 1999, 19), this assumption is unwarranted and leads to an unreasonable preference for government over the market in providing goods and solving coordination problems. Any theory of market failure must also be balanced by an acknowledgment of government failure.

Instead of assuming that human beings in politics seek "the public interest" or "the public good" (Buchanan and Tulloch 1999, 19), public choice theorists assume that "man . . . is a utility-maximizer in both his market and his political activity" (23), and they regard "political activity as a particular form of *exchange*" (23). Buchanan and Tulloch insist that the economic or libertarian assumption does not necessarily mean that human beings are egoistic or materialistic, as conservatives sometimes allege.[2] As Buchanan and

Tullock point out, "the purely economic man" who "is motivated solely by individual self-interest in all aspects of his behavior, has always represented a caricature designed by those who have sought to criticize rather than appreciate the genuine contributions that economic analysis can make" (Buchanan and Tullock 1999, 16). Economic analysis only requires Philip Wicksteed's principle of "non-Tuism," which requires that "the interest of [the] opposite number in [an economic] exchange be excluded from consideration" (17).

Nevertheless, although Buchanan and Tullock repudiate the egoistic interpretation of economic behavior, their description of utility-maximizing behavior does favor a more narrowly self-interested view of human action. They appear to be neutral with respect to the "utility-function" economic actors might have: "[St.] Paul may be acting out of love of God, the provincial church, friends, or self without affecting the operational validity of theory of markets" (1999, 17). But they also assert that "self-interest, broadly conceived, is recognized to be a strong motivating force in all human activity." And because the ethical and moral principles required to restrain self-interest are "scarce," the models of economic analysis should "assume the pursuit of private interest" (27).

Public choice theorists also embrace a contract theory of government. That is, they conceive of individuals as prior to and independent of the state, which they regard simply as a means for better achieving their private ends. In the words of James Buchanan, "Collective action is viewed as the action of individuals when they accomplish purposes collectively rather than individually, and the government is seen as nothing more than the set of processes, the machine, which allows such collective action to take place" (Buchanan and Tullock 1999, 13).

As we shall see, these economic assumptions, however appropriate in the market, not only fail to account for political behavior but also even endanger it. Public choice theory is subject to a fatal objection, which might be called the dilemma of public choice theory: Either public choice theory is *descriptive*, or it is *prescriptive*. If it is intended to be descriptive, it is undermined by empirical evidence. If it is intended to be prescriptive, it in fact undermines political life altogether. I shall consider each of these possibilities in turn.

Public choice theorists do not claim that their *"economic-individualist* model of political activity" (Buchanan and Tullock 1999, 30) is a complete or even accurate description of how human beings always behave. Their individualism is only a "methodological individualism" (30), they insist, designed to help explain "*one* aspect of human behavior" (20), and the validity of that model must be empirically tested against the real world. How does the test hold up?

The first and most important thing to notice is the degree to which public choice assumptions contradict the ordinary understanding and experience of political life. According to that ordinary understanding, members of the political association are not utility maximizers but *citizens*. Citizens recognize the political association as partially constitutive of their personal identity ("I *am* an American") and not merely as an "impersonal machine" for realizing their private ends. To be a citizen is to recognize the good of the political association—common legal institutions, common history, common national heroes, common symbols like flags and monuments, and common traditions of language, custom, celebration and practice—*as one's own good.* For the citizen, political life is animated by a shared conception of the common good, whose contours are worked out, developed, and revised through experience and rational deliberation. Thus, the citizen perspective fundamentally contradicts the public choice assumptions of non-Tuism and politics as exchange. Politics is fundamentally cooperative, not competitive, and the public choice model of "politics as exchange" rests on a corrupt idea of the political process, not its proper form.

Buchanan, Wenzel, and other libertarians strongly object to this ordinary understanding of politics. Instead they promote what Buchanan calls "politics without romance." "Public choice is like the small boy who said that the king really has no clothes," Buchanan writes. "Once he said this, everyone recognized that the king's nakedness had been recognized, but that no-one had really called attention to this fact" (Buchanan 2003, 7). Using the same metaphor, Murray Rothbard describes the libertarian "as the child in the fable, pointing out insistently that the emperor has no clothes." It is one of the prime tasks of the libertarian, he writes, "to spread the demystification and de-sanctification of the State among its hapless subjects. His task is to demonstrate repeatedly and in depth that not only the emperor, but even the democratic State has no clothes; that all governments subsist by exploitive rule over the public" (Rothbard 2006, 29–30).

Unfortunately for the public choice model, a substantial number of people seem to prefer their clothing, thinking and acting like citizens rather than utility-maximizing individuals: They honor the important political figures and events of their history; they respect their flag; they learn their national anthem; they take time to vote, even when they know their individual vote has only an infinitesimal chance of affecting the outcome of the election, and often against what libertarians regard as their own individual interests; and, in exceptional cases, they are willing to expend their "last full measure of devotion" in service to their country.[3] Could all of this really be the behavior of alienated suckers brainwashed into false consciousness by exploitative elites?

Public choice theorists are fond of pointing out it is the *same* human beings who participate in the market and in politics, that human nature does not change when human beings move from one institutional setting to another. But they draw the false conclusion from this premise that human beings *behave* the same way in all institutional settings. But Wenzel himself points out "the disastrous consequences of mixing the worlds of markets and civil society." "Surely we would not want to apply market rules to the family," he writes. And in fact, ordinarily human beings *do behave* very differently according to the different institutional contexts of the market and the family.

It is telling that public choice theorists, who profess a sensitivity to the role of incentives in human behavior, miss the ways in which different social and institutional contexts can and do elicit very different kinds of attitudes and behavior. There is a substantial body of literature that demonstrates that market norms, when applied to nonmarket institutions and practices, can sometimes crowd out valuable nonmarket norms and undermine social capital. One of the more famous studies supporting this claim is Richard Titmuss's study on blood supply (Titmuss 1971). Titmuss compared the blood collection system in the United States, where some of the blood is purchased by commercial blood banks, and the United Kingdom, where the entire blood supply is donated. Michael Sandel summarizes the result:

> Titmuss presented a wealth of data showing that, in economic and practical terms alone, the British blood collection system works better than the American one. Despite the supposed efficiency of markets, he argued, the American system leads to chronic shortages, wasted blood, higher costs, and a greater risk of contaminated blood. (Sandel 2012, 123)

Although some aspects of Titmuss's study have been challenged (see Leonard 2004), the substance of his theory has been empirically confirmed in subsequent studies (see Frey and Jegen 2001 and Janssen and Mendys-Kamphorst 2004).

Politics clearly involves some of the competitive behavior and bargaining between private interests that one finds in the market. The American founders were well aware of this and sought to provide for it (see especially the analysis of faction in *Federalist 10*). But politics also vitally depends on non-economic social capital. The institutional context for the political association, what gives politics its meaning and purpose, is not utility maximization but normative considerations of justice and the common good. It is true that the public profession of these ends is often merely a pretext for private ends, but, in the words of La Rochefoucauld (Maxim 218), "Hypocrisy is a tribute vice pays to virtue" (LaRochefoucauld 1959, 65).[4]

Here we come to the second aspect of the public choice dilemma: As a prescription, public choice theory would destroy political life altogether. To see this better, we might ask: What if people actually *did* think and behave the way public choice theory suggests and no longer used "public service" and "the common good" as a pretext for their utility-maximizing political behavior? What if, instead, elected officials frankly declared their votes for sale to the highest bidder, and voters sold their votes to office seekers?

This would in fact be the end of politics, where rule must always respond (even if sometimes hypocritically) to the demands of deliberation and justice, and would leave in its place only naked domination by force of the greatest number. One is reminded here of Edmund Burke's prophetic warning against the coming age of "sophisters, economists, and calculators":

> All of the superadded ideas, furnished from the wardrobe of the moral imagination, which the heart owns and the understanding ratifies as necessary to cover the defects of our naked, shivering nature, and to raise it to dignity in our own estimation, are to be exploded as a ridiculous, absurd, and antiquated fashion. (Burke 1987, 67)

It is fascinating to see James Buchanan acknowledging this weakness in public choice theory twenty-five years after publishing his path-breaking book in public choice economics, *The Calculus of Consent*. In an uncommonly insightful essay "Is Public Choice Immoral? The Case for the Noble Lie," cowritten with Geoffrey Brennan (1988), Buchanan fretted that the individualist model of human behavior used by public choice theorists to *explain* human behavior might actually erode the standards for behavior in public life, resulting in *worse* consequences.

As Buchanan and Brennan put it, "The maintenance of the standards of public life, it could be argued, may require a heroic vision of the 'statesman' or 'public servant,' because only by holding such a vision can the possibility of public-interested behavior on the part of political agents be increased" (Brennan and Buchanan 1988, 184). In practice, therefore, "politics without romance" could be a prescription for disaster. Notably, Buchanan and Brennan deploy Rothbard's clothing image once again, only this time with a sympathetic nod to Burke:

> We may agree that public choice analysis allows us to see politics without blinders. In that sense, we play the role of the boy who called attention to the emperor's nakedness. But the familiar story might be given quite a different twist if it went on to relate that the emperor fell into disgrace, that the nobles fought among themselves, that the previously stable political order crumbled into chaos, and that the kingdom was destroyed. The moral might then have been *not* that one should call a spade a spade, whatever the possible consequences, but rather that a sensitivity to consequences might require one to be judicious in exposing functionally useful myths. (Brennan and Buchanan 1988, 185)

To see such a sober acknowledgment of the limits of libertarianism by these two libertarian thinkers is commendable. But we should be troubled by their conclusion that politics requires "functionally useful myths" to support "public interested behavior." This claim, which is reminiscent of Plato's "noble lie" and the "civil religion" of Jean Jacques Rousseau, reflects the persistent libertarian denial that there is a *real* political good, different from individual preferences and identifiable by reason, that can actually guide moral and political judgments. But this denial profoundly undermines the coherence of public choice theory, which simultaneously repudiates and requires "romanticism" in politics. Indeed, Buchannan and Brennan concede in the preceding passage that the "realistic" model of human behavior that underlies public choice theory, if actually embraced by the people they claim to describe, might actually make political life impossible. And Brennan (with Alan Hamlin) has since significantly revised the assumptions of public choice theory to better account for actual political behavior like voting by including moral motivations into the behavioral assumptions (see Brennan and Hamlin 2000 and 2008). Skeptics may doubt, however, whether public choice theory can admit this assumption without a more radical revision of the whole theory. (I will have more to say about this in the next two sections.)

None of this is to deny the value of public choice theory at the level of public policy. By highlighting the nature and causes of government failure, public choice theorists help counteract a pervasive proclivity among politicians and ordinary citizens to seek government solutions to every social and economic problem. As the public choice theorists point out, many social and economic problems can be resolved more easily and efficiently by voluntary cooperation. This is especially true when one considers that government action often imposes heavy costs, not only costs of decision making but also the costs of decision themselves, which can be adverse to members of the political association (see Buchanan and Tullock 1990, especially chapter 5).

Granting this, it is important to see that the leading public choice theorists do not support Wenzel's libertarianism. Unlike Wenzel, public choice theorists acknowledge that "utility-maximizing" individuals will sometimes have good reasons to support government action, beyond the mere protection of individual rights and private property. This is true (they argue) whenever the expected costs of government action to achieve some preference are less than the expected transaction costs of voluntary organization (see Buchanan and Tullock 1990, 62):

> The fact that individuals, if left full freedom of private choice, may not educate their own children sufficiently, may not keep their residences free of fire hazards, may not free their premises of mosquito-breeding places, may not combine in sufficiently large units to purchase police protection most efficiently, etc.: all these suggest that such activities may rationally be thrown into the public sector. (Buchanan and Tullock 1990, 75)

Where there is a clear case for government action, public choice theorists remind us how important it is to choose decision-making rules that are most likely to identify the *genuine* places for government action (in part by weighing the costs of government action against the benefit of voluntary solutions), and, when government action is chosen, to effect that action most efficiently. And here it is evident that the current rules for government action are *not* well designed. How exactly those rules might be improved (for example, by requiring supermajorities for regulations, mandating a long waiting period before a final vote, attaching automatic sunset provisions to all regulatory legislation, recognizing regulations as "takings" under the Fifth Amendment, allowing legislative vetoes of administrative actions, and so on) is beyond the scope of this book, but conservatives welcome the conversation.

Despite its salutary warnings, public choice theory simply cannot account for political life in the most fundamental sense. *Within* politics, properly understood, public choice theory can be a valuable tool for citizens and political leaders. *Without* politics, as an ultimate account of political life, it can profoundly undermine the conditions for free government.

F. A. Hayek and the Knowledge Problem

Wenzel's second argument in defense of libertarianism also relies on a misapplication of economic assumptions, in this case F. A. Hayek's "knowledge problem."

For Hayek, the knowledge problem argument is primarily directed against central economic planning. Hayek observed that the data on which central planning depends "are never for the whole society 'given' to a single mind which could work out the implications, and never can be so given." These data only exist "as the dispersed bits of incomplete and frequently contradictory knowledge which all the separate individuals possess" (Hayek 1945, 519). The knowledge problem is "how to secure the best use of resources known to any of the members of society, for ends whose relative importance only those individuals know" (Hayek 1945, 520).

The principal solution to the knowledge problem is the price system, which grows spontaneously from the particular actions of individuals responding and adapting to particular circumstances of time and place that only those individuals know and that provide those individuals with information for making the best use of resources. The price system is best understood as a complex, self-regulating "system for communicating information"

(Hayek 1945, 526), allowing human beings to benefit greatly from the knowledge of others.

Wenzel refers to Leonard Read's clever fable *I, Pencil* to illustrate the point. When one turns from something as seemingly simple as the production of a pencil to the extraordinarily complex achievements of science and culture, the value of spontaneous orders for generating knowledge for the benefit of others becomes clear. As Wenzel nicely puts it, "Based on the critical fact of limited human knowledge, Hayek emphasizes the importance of [free] institutions in creating and communicating knowledge—over time of accumulated stocks (via traditions, cultural heritage, or teaching), but also among contemporaries. This includes the communication of economic knowledge through prices, and social knowledge through approbation and custom."

Thus Hayek takes as his primary task the promotion of the "Great Society" (not to be confused with Lyndon B. Johnson's Great Society!), an overall, open-ended spontaneous social order, governed by impersonal and general rules, which emerges from the free interactions of individuals and groups pursuing their own relative ends (see Hayek 1976, 4, 12). Hayek understood that the Great Society requires the assistance of orders that are not spontaneous: "In any group of men more than the smallest size, collaboration will always rest both on spontaneous order as well as on deliberate organization" (Hayek 1973, 46). This especially includes the organization of government (Hayek 1973, 47). But government must always be at the service of the Great Society, not a substitute for it.

As Wenzel acknowledges, Hayek does not draw from his premises libertarian conclusions, which he associates with the French rationalist tradition. His remarks, in which he appeals directly to Edmund Burke in support of his argument, are worth quoting at length:

> Nor Locke, nor Hume, nor Smith, nor Burke, could have ever argued, as Bentham did, that "every law is an evil for every law is an infraction of liberty." Their argument was never a complete laissez-faire argument, which, as the very words show, is also part of the French rationalist tradition and in its literal sense was never defended by any of the English classical economists. They knew better than most of their later critics that it was not some sort of magic but the evolution of "well-constructed

institutions," where the "rules and principles of contending interests and compromised advantages" would be reconciled, that had successfully channeled individual efforts to socially beneficial aims. In fact, their argument was never antistate as such, or anarchistic, which is the logical outcome of the rationalist laissez faire doctrine; it was an argument that accounted both for the proper functions of the state and for the limits of state action. (Hayek 2011 [1960], 119–120)

In the same book that Wenzel appeals to in his defense of libertarianism (*The Constitution of Liberty*), Hayek states that "although a few theorists have demanded that the activities of government should be limited to the maintenance of law and order, such a stand cannot be justified by the principle of liberty." Rather, Hayek maintains "that there is undeniably a wide field for non-coercive activities of government and . . . there is a clear need for financing them by taxation" (Hayek 2011 [1960], 374).

What kind of activities does Hayek have in mind? Here are just a few of the things he mentions in the *Constitution of Liberty* (2011 [1960]): sanitation and roads (209); compulsory military service (210); "a reliable and efficient monetary system . . . the setting of standards of weights and measures; the providing of information gathered from surveying, land registration, statistics, etc.; and the support, if not also the organization, of some kind of education" (332); "provision for the indigent, unfortunate and disabled"; "social insurance"; subsidizing "certain experimental developments" (374); "parks and museums, theaters and facilities for sports . . . security against severe physical privation, the assurance of a given minimum of sustenance for all" (375–376); licensing requirements for the sale of poisons and firearms (336). Hayek also held that "contracts for criminal or immoral purposes, gambling contracts, contracts in restraint of trade, contracts permanently binding the services of a person, or even some contracts for specific performances [should not be] enforced" (339).

How does Hayek reconcile his opposition to central economic planning with support for this robust array of government action? In the first place, Hayek observes that there are collective goods that cannot be provided (or not very well) without the assistance of government. He quotes Adam Smith, who approved of "those public works, which, though they may be in the highest degree advantageous to a great society, are, however, of such a nature, that the profit could never repay the expense to any individual or small number of individuals."[5] Roads, for example, are often useful to large numbers of people but require considerable expense to build and maintain. Because in most cases it is very difficult to capture those costs by charging individual users of the road and preventing free riders, there is little economic incentive to build roads. These difficulties can be overcome by some of kind of tax (say, on gasoline), which both raises revenue for building and maintaining the road and prevents free riding.

Still, Hayek argues, the need for government action should never be presumed and should always be subject to a careful cost–benefit analysis (2011 [1960], 332–333). (And here again, economists and public choice theorists can play a very important role in shaping the decision-making process). Hayek also maintains that, in those cases where government action is justified, it should be provided according to general rules rather than "specific orders and prohibitions" (332) and should be provided in a way that relies as much as possible on the initiative and activity of nongovernmental agencies, rather than government agents (339). Finally, Hayek maintains that government may not reserve "for itself the exclusive right to provide particular services" (332).

Subject to these conditions, such government activity does not involve coercion, Hayek argues, nor does it unduly disrupt the spontaneous order of the Great Society, because it is not concerned with dictating specific ends of action but only with supplying "means which individuals can use for their own purposes" (2011 [1960], 332). So although Wenzel agrees with Hayek on the knowledge problem, Wenzel departs from Hayek's conclusions about what the knowledge problem means for the scope and limits of political authority. But Wenzel and Hayek agree at a deeper level.

Because for Hayek both the means and ends of human action evolve through the operation of spontaneous forces, Hayek shares with both libertarians and progressives the belief that government should be neutral with respect to the means and ends of individual choices. "Moral beliefs concerning matters of conduct which do not directly interfere with the protected sphere of other persons," Hayek writes, "do not justify coercion" (2011 [1960], 524).[6] In the language of contemporary political theory, Hayek seems to be an "antiperfectionist," in contrast to "soft perfectionists" who believe that government, in protecting the conditions for human flourishing, must favor some conceptions of the good and discourage others. But Hayek's blanket promotion of an abstract antiperfectionism principle against the reason of tradition and experience suggests a Cartesian rationalism lurking within his otherwise Humean sensibility.

On the Humean side, Hayek's antiperfectionism rests on an "empiricist evolutionary" account of moral reason that is skeptical, historicist, and emotivist.[7] That is, for Hayek all moral knowledge grows out of tradition, but "tradition is not something constant but the product of a process of selection guided not by reason but by success." "Progress," Hayek claims, is "a process of adaptation and learning in which not only the possibilities known to us but also our values and desires continually change" (Hayek 2011 [1960], 94). But how can this account of reason support Hayek's claim that a free society depends on a firm belief in "fundamental values" (Hayek 2011 [1960], 49), "ultimate ideals" (131), and "supreme principles" (131)?[8] How can principles that are derived from the evolutionary process guide the evolutionary process? Indeed, what does "improvement" in terms of evolution even mean? (Hayek's reference to "success" is telling).

When Hayek turns to the common law, he abandons emergent institutional knowledge in favor of an abstract principle. For Hayek, the common law exemplifies how a decentralized and spontaneous legal order can emerge, but he incorrectly interprets the common law in an antiperfectionist way (see especially Hayek 1973, 72–123). Although it is true that the common law emerged through the decentralized discovery and development of abstract rules by judges in response to particular cases, the common law recognized moral harm as a form of injustice. As Sir William Blackstone, in his magisterial and highly influential summary of the common law points out, the common law distinguishes "private nuisances," which involve harms to specific people, from what he called "common nuisances" (later called "public nuisance"), or actions that harm the whole community in general and not merely some particular person (see II.13 of Blackstone's *Commentaries on the Laws of England*). According to the common law, a person is guilty of a public nuisance "if the effect of the act or omission [of that person] is to endanger the life, health, property, morals, or comfort, of the public."[9] This view of the common law not repudiated by any classical liberal (Adam Smith, David

Hume, Adam Ferguson, Edmund Burke, and the like), was adopted by virtually all of the earliest state constitutions without protest, and continues to exist in some form today in the laws of every state.

The suspicion of a Cartesian Hayek is strengthened by his hope that by "extending the rules of just conduct to the relations with all other men," we might one day "approach a universal order of peace" and "integrate all mankind into a single society" (1976, 144; see also 58). The realization of this hope is predicated on the complete privatization of competing conceptions of the good, which Hayek reduces to subjective personal preferences. Thus, for Hayek, the only obstacles to this universal "Open Society" (112), bound by impersonal, economic ties (112), are atavistic tribal instincts for a Closed Society, rooted in "feelings of personal loyalty" (143), "a common scale of concrete ends" (114), and the desire for "friend–enemy relations" (149).

But conservatives are very doubtful that the elimination of political boundaries is either possible *or* desirable, and this doubt is amply justified by history and experience. And although the deepest reasons for this doubt are very difficult to identify and articulate, they are related to the fact that human beings are strong evaluators and not merely preference calculators and that evaluative judgments demand expression, education, and moderation within at least a soft perfectionist political order.[10] (I shall say more about this in the following pages). But Hayek excludes this possibility by only considering two political alternatives: a global Open Society, bound by impersonal, economic ties, which excludes from law any conception of the good, or a parochial Tribalism, bound by personal ties of kinship, which seeks to impose on society an arbitrary hierarchy of goods. But unable to surrender their strong evaluative convictions about goodness for the sake of the universal antiperfectionist state, yet educated to believe those judgments are nothing more than passionate intensity, Hayek's human beings are deprived of the only kind of regime that has actually proven itself capable of supporting a decent, stable, and prosperous way of life, a regime that is neither dedicated to a fixed hierarchy of ends nor indifferent to the good.

In short, the antiperfectionism of modern liberals and libertarians reflects a Cartesian rationalism that flies in the face of human history and experience. But can the soft perfectionism of conservatism be defended? This question is especially pressing in light of the fact of moral pluralism within free societies.

The Challenge of Pluralism: Private Preferences, Public Reason, and the Common Good

It is important to notice how Hayek and Wenzel couch their principle of government neutrality. First Hayek: "Where private practices cannot affect anybody but the voluntary adult actors, the mere dislike of what is being done by others, or even the knowledge that others harm themselves by what they do, provides no legitimate ground for coercion" (Hayek 2011 [1960], 212). For his part, Wenzel repeatedly declares that libertarianism prohibits "the imposition of private preferences through public means."

To all of this the conservative wholeheartedly agrees. Government should never be used to prohibit what some persons merely "dislike" or to promote "private preferences." But conservatives insist that moral principles are not based on what people "dislike," nor are they equivalent to "private preferences." The libertarian penchant for describing the conservative concern for public morality as a matter of taste or private preference reflects the same economic bias that infects other parts of libertarianism. To see why this description fails, consider a much-celebrated (but probably apocryphal) conversation between Winston Churchill and a socialite:

> Churchill to socialite: "Madam, would you sleep with me for five million pounds?"
> Socialite: "My goodness, Mr. Churchill . . . Well, I suppose . . . we would have to discuss terms, of course . . .
> Churchill: "Would you sleep with me for five pounds?"
> Socialite: "Mr. Churchill, what kind of woman do you think I am?!"
> Churchill: "Madam, we've already established that. Now we are haggling about the price."

The humor in the punch line of this story depends on recognizing the difference in natural language between the logic of moral judgments and the logic of preferences. Preferences refer back to the subject and are therefore expressed in the first person ("I don't like bananas"). Moral judgments, on the other hand, purport to make true statements about the structure of reality and are therefore expressed in the third person ("rape is wrong").

It follows that whereas the objects of preferences are saleable, the objects of moral judgments are not. As the Churchill story illustrates, anyone who would put a price on her or his moral judgment has in fact transformed that judgment into a preference. Thus, there can be no market for moral judgments, without destroying what moral judgments are. The libertarian reduction of the logic of morals to the logic of preferences also has absurd results. It makes moral statements like "rape is wrong" into preference statements like "I don't like rape (but others might)." It therefore equates the statement "rape is wrong and therefore should be prohibited" with the statement "I don't like eating bananas; therefore eating bananas should be prohibited."

The fact that moral judgments and private preferences are different, however, does not by itself justify different principles with respect to government action. Further conditions are required.

Recall what I said about government and the common good in my chapter on conservatism. Human beings can only fully flourish through their own self-constituting choices, alone and in association with others and there are as many ways to flourish as there are human beings. The object of political authority, therefore, is not to direct human beings to particular ends of human flourishing but to protect and promote the *conditions* for human flourishing. That those conditions include freedom from physical harm every libertarian will concede, but there are also nonphysical harms that are proper objects of government action. These include harms to reputation (for example, defamatory speech, libel, and slander), harms to social order (such as open borders), and harms to moral culture (including pimps, prostitutes, drug pushers, panders). Either such nonphysical harms exist, or they do not. If they do exist, they are a proper object of political authority. If they do not exist, they are not. Do they exist?

That reputation is a good that can be harmed by the false speech of others is too obvious to be argued for. The question of social order and open borders I shall treat in my case studies, though what I say here about moral ecology will relate to that subject as well.

If there is one universal and consistent theme among the American founders it is this: Without virtue a free society is impossible. As George Washington put it in his second Inaugural Address: "Of all the dispositions and habits which lead to political prosperity, religion and morality are indispensable supports." With this claim Wenzel seems to agree. (I say "seems" because Wenzel also seems to endorse the Smithian suggestion that "individual self-interest" rightly channeled is sufficient for free government). But the founders also agreed that political authority has a legitimate, if secondary, role to play in preventing moral harm and promoting good character. The following statement, affixed to the Declaration of Rights of the first Virginia Constitution, was typical and uncontroversial:

> SEC. 15. That no free government, or the blessings of liberty, can be preserved to any people, but by a firm adherence to justice, moderation, temperance, frugality, and virtue, and by frequent recurrence to fundamental principles.

Lest one think such language was merely expressive, consider this passage from the first Pennsylvania constitution:

> SECT. 45. Laws for the encouragement of virtue, and prevention of vice and immorality, shall be made and constantly kept in force, and provision shall be made for their due execution.

Legal provision for public morality was not limited to the state constitutions. One of the first laws passed by Congress under the Constitution of 1787, the Northwest Ordinance, stated: "Religion, morality, and knowledge, being necessary to good government and the happiness of mankind, schools and the means of education shall forever be encouraged" (Article 3).

In their political concern for public morality, the American founders were simply reflecting the consensus of the Western legal tradition, which rests on three salient claims. First, there is a class of actions involving moral harm to oneself. That is, some actions are wrong and harmful to individuals even when those individuals engage in those actions voluntarily. Second, such actions, when engaged in by consenting individuals, can also harm nonconsenting, third-party individuals. Third, laws that prohibit such actions not only prevent particular moral harms to individual parties; they also reinforce and promote general norms of behavior. In other words, law is not merely coercive; it is also expressive. The law *educates.*   Mosaic Covenant

On the first point: Libertarians often seek to avoid the question of whether there are any wrongful actions other than coercion. Wenzel, for

Here's the rub

example, claims that the libertarianism he is defending is only a "*political philosophy*; it does not make claims beyond politics." But it is very doubtful whether such a neat line of demarcation between politics and ethics can be drawn. For if there are wrongful actions that do not involve coercion and *if* those actions can cause harm other than coercion to others, then to permit such actions without good reason is unjust. (For a richer elaboration of these and the following arguments, see George 1995, 1999, and Finnis 2011). Conservatives believe that there is such a class of wrongful, noncoercive actions, including assisted suicide, prostitution, pornography, and the sale and consumption of addictive mind-altering drugs. Such actions, they argue, directly harm basic goods that constitute human flourishing, such as life, conjugal union, and personal integrity. They also harm the moral character of the persons who engage in them, making it more difficult for them to recognize and embrace those basic goods.

If these actions are themselves wrong, then it is unjust to offer them to others. Libertarians antecedently deny that a voluntary transaction can ever be unjust, but this denial flies in the face of human experience. Human action is not simply motivated by a subjective scale of preferences that can be priced; it is motivated by an orientation toward real, intelligible goods that give reasons for action. Often human beings experience strong attractions to objects that conflict with this deeper orientation and desire toward basic goods. To elicit and feed such attractions in others is to cause them unjust harm, which the law might reasonably prevent.

But the law does not merely prevent wrongful acts; it also shapes attitudes, understandings, and character. Those who doubt this point should examine the difference in attitudes toward racial discrimination in America before and after the Civil Rights Act of 1964 or the availability of pornographic materials before and after *Roth v. United States* (1957), or the stability of marriage before and after the introduction of no-fault divorce laws in the 1970s. The law, both by prohibition and by silence, is a powerful signal of acceptable behavior and thus a powerful influence on character. When the behavior in question involves moral norms that are consequential for the rest of society, it is a proper object of law.

The Law educates...

If these conservative claims are true, then the pretended libertarian separation of politics and morality is a fraud. If the activities of pornographers, prostitutes, pimps, and drug pushers cause real harm to third parties and to the moral ecology of the social order, if the proliferation of sexually explicit advertising and hard drugs makes it more difficult for individuals to pursue the basic goods that constitute human flourishing and more difficult for parents to raise their children with personal integrity and good character, then to protect the "right" to these activities is to violate the rights of others.

The upshot of the foregoing arguments is that libertarianism is not neutral between competing conceptions of morality. Libertarianism essentially denies that both self-regarding harms and moral harms exist and maintains that the only real injustice is coercion. Accordingly, it promotes a legal regime in which some individuals are legally entitled to harm others in noncoercive ways. What arguments do libertarians offer for this moral theory? Typically they are arguments of moral skepticism: "How are we, fallible human beings with limited cognitive capacities, to discover the objective moral order?" Wenzel asks. "What are the criteria for determining what is good and what is evil?"

Unfortunately skepticism about moral knowledge will not support the libertarian position any more than the conservative one. (Indeed, it very well might undermine both!) This is especially true if libertarianism rests on a positive moral philosophy, as I have claimed it does. The difference between conservatism and libertarianism is not between moral dogmatism and moral skepticism but between two competing claims to moral knowledge. But, in this case, the proper default position is not libertarianism, as Wenzel suggests, but conservatism. Why?

Put most simply, if a legal regime of moral neutrality is *in principle* impossible (as I think it is), then the next fairest and most stable alternative in a pluralist society is to have a well-designed deliberative decision mechanism in which citizens are obligated to ask for and offer *public reasons* (that is, reasons that others can recognize in principle and not special divine revelation, expressed preferences, or private interests) for the policies they oppose or support. That mechanism should be part of a constitutional design in which so far as possible, not "the *passions* . . . but the *reason*, of the public . . . sit[s] in judgment" (to use the words of James Madison in *Federalist 49*). This was the deliberate purpose behind the various devices in the American Constitution (for example, a written constitution of enumerated powers; the separation of

I don't think pluralism leads to flourishing.

powers; staggered elections and election requirements; bicameralism; federalism; and so on), a constitution that was itself the product of deliberation
within a pluralist social order. As Charles Kessler puts it, "Without denying
the plan's [that is, the plan of the Constitution] origin in political give and
take, *The Federalist* thus interpreted the Federal Convention as having been
a forum not for (at least not mostly for) self-interested bargaining, but for
public-spirited deliberation" (Kessler 1999, viii).

It is important to emphasize what the preceding conservative argument is
and is not saying. It is *not* saying that the law can "make men moral." Only
human beings can make themselves moral through their own self-constituting
choices. It *is* saying that the law can assist people in making themselves moral
by protecting the cultural conditions for authentic freedom. It is *not* saying
that morality consists in conforming to a single idea of human flourishing,
such as participation in politics or contemplation. There is a diversity of goods
through which human beings flourish, and an infinite number of ways in
which those goods may be participated. It *is* saying that there are some actions
that are never good because they directly frustrate or undermine the achievement of the basic goods that are the fundamental reasons for human action. It
is *not* saying that the U.S. Constitution gives the national government power
over morals legislation. It does not. In our system of government, these decisions are reserved to the state and local governments. Finally, it is *not* saying that every moral wrong must be legally prohibited. There are often good
and even conclusive reasons to refrain from prohibiting behavior that violates
moral norms that are consequential for the rest of society. These include the
strong opposition of public opinion, the public expense of enforcement that
could better be spent elsewhere, the danger of abuse of public authority, the
incitement to crime, and a host of other prudential considerations. It *is* saying
that it is not wrong in principle, and indeed it is sometimes a requirement of
justice, to prohibit immoral actions by law.

Robert Nozick and Self-Ownership

There is one further argument for libertarianism that Wenzel does not directly make but that moves with logical consistency from premises that Wenzel seems to share to conclusions that Wenzel seems unwilling to make. This
is the argument from self-ownership. According to this argument, every hu-

man person owns him- or herself. The only alternative, it is claimed, is that some persons own other persons. This is called slavery, and it is wrong precisely because it violates the principle of self-ownership. (Or why else is slavery wrong?) But slavery was not abolished with the Thirteenth Amendment. It exists every time persons are coerced who have not themselves threatened or violated the self-ownership principles of another.

Against this background, libertarian Robert Nozick in his classic work *Anarchy, State, and Utopia* baldly declares that "taxation of earnings from labor is on a par with forced labor" (Nozick 1974, 169). The argument is simple: Taking someone's earnings from hours of labor (by taxation) = taking someone's hours of labor = making someone work for someone else. It does not matter that persons could avoid the tax by refusing to work because the tax still coercively limits the alternatives persons may choose. As Murray Rothbard puts the challenge, "*How* can you define taxation in a way which makes it different from robbery?" (Rothbard 2006, 63).

The protection of property rights (first in oneself and then by extension to the things one has justly acquired), therefore, exhausts the scope of legitimate coercion, and every self-owning human being has the right to protect his or her property. Starting from these premises, the pressing questions become: How does the state gain a legitimate monopoly on the legitimate use of coercion? How can the state tell those who refuse to join it that they may not judge for themselves whether their rights have been violated and enforce their judgments by punishing those who infringed them (see Nozick 1974, 24)? And how can the state legitimately tax people to support that monopoly?

What is Wenzel's response to this challenge? Wenzel argues that government is a "necessary evil." But what can that phrase possibly mean, and what could it not justify? What Wenzel seems to mean is that it is sometimes legitimate to violate the rights of others to prevent greater evils, such as the violent state of civil war that might ensue without the state. But isn't this precisely the kind of redistributive behavior Wenzel condemns throughout his defense of libertarianism? And isn't it based on the kind of utilitarian reasoning that Wenzel claims to repudiate? And on what principle can an exception to redistribution be made here that cannot be made elsewhere? And by whom?

For good reasons Nozick repudiates utilitarian justifications of the state. If people have rights, there is no sense in saying that it is right (even by necessity) to violate them, period. If the state can be justified at all, it must be in a way that does not violate anyone's self-ownership rights. Nozick attempts to show how a legitimate state *might* arise "spontaneously," first from the voluntary creation of private protection agencies and then from the free interactions of private protection agencies within a prestate situation. In this account, the "state" is nothing more than the dominant protective agency (DPA) in a given geographical area, paid for by the members of that association. Nonmembers of the DPA within a given region are not taxed (and so that right is not violated), and, although they are prohibited by the DPA from enforcing their own rights, they are also compensated for the prohibition.

Nozick's argument is too subtle and complex for a thorough treatment here. Needless to say, it has been sharply criticized by more extreme libertarians like Murray Rothbard (Rothbard 1977). I shall leave those arguments for the libertarians and focus on the same conservative objections I made to social contract theory in my first chapter and to public choice theory in the preceding pages: Not only has no state ever arisen in the way Nozick describes it (making all existing states illegitimate), but the political association simply cannot be understood or accounted for as a contract between prepolitical, self-owning persons.

Nozick's mistake is rooted in the principle of self-ownership. There is something powerfully intuitive in this principle, something that captures our moral judgment that human persons have an intrinsic dignity and therefore must never to be used by anyone simply as a means. But on closer examination the defects in this principle become clear.

The language that I have just used comes from Immanuel Kant, and indeed it is to Kant that Robert Nozick appeals in making his case for the principle (Nozick 1974, 30–33). Nevertheless, Kant himself explicitly repudiated this principle. In the first place, Kant regarded the notion of self-ownership as self-contradictory: Persons are *subjects* of ownership, whereas ownership is of things. Were persons to own themselves, they would be simultaneously persons and things, which is impossible (Kant 1997, 157–158).

The only way to avoid this self-contradiction, Kant suggested, is to divide the self partly into a person (such as the conscious, thinking part of the self) and partly into a thing (such as the body part). This entails an untenable body–self dualism. As Robert George has written, "The dualistic view of the human person makes nonsense of the experience all of us have in our activities of being dynamically unified actors—of being, that is, embodied persons, and not persons who merely 'inhabit' our bodies and direct them as extrinsic instruments under our control, like automobiles" (George 2002, 9).

Another difficulty with the principle of self-ownership is that it makes all forms of rule without consent equivalent to slavery. But surely there is a difference between the rule of parents over their children (though the children do not consent to it) and the rule of the master over the slave? At least Rothbard is consistent when he declares that parents may not physically restrain their small children from running away. For his part, Nozick, in over 300 pages of densely elaborated arguments on the principle of self-ownership, dedicates barely two pages to this problem and only then to show why John Locke's argument against the ownership of children is problematic (Nozick 1974, 287–289).

Just as the principle of self-ownership makes it difficult to justify parental authority, so it also in fact makes it difficult to justify state authority. On what grounds can the state claim exclusive authority over the authorized use of force over those who have never consented to it? And how will the state finance this authority without taxation? And if (as libertarians believe) the state can exercise legitimate authority over nonconsenting individuals to prevent coercion and can tax those individuals to pay for its activity, then why can't it use this same authority for other reasons? Libertarians rarely face up to this question squarely.

In short, the principle of self-ownership cannot do the work libertarians want it to do. But rejecting the principle of self-ownership does not require one to reject the principle of intrinsic human dignity altogether. Thinkers as diverse as Augustine, Thomas Aquinas, and Thomas Jefferson all affirmed basic human equality and dignity without reaching libertarian conclusions, by offering an account of human dignity that corresponds better to the conditions and requirements for human flourishing.

Conclusion

Conservatives agree with libertarians that politics in America (and, indeed, in the world) is in very bad shape. With libertarians, they strongly oppose the administrative state, which is corrupt, inefficient, unjust, and unconstitutional. Conservatives also favor limited government and a strong civil society in which human beings pursue their own flourishing, alone and in association with others. These associations include the free market (which should not be confused with the crony capitalism that today passes for the "free market"), as well as familial, religious, fraternal, and other social institutions.

But to conservatives, libertarianism looks like an understandable but utterly implausible reaction to the current state of affairs. It offers no real alternative to those affairs. Instead, it eviscerates the real ground on which progress can be made against the modern state. That state did not arise from American conservatism but in explicit opposition to the principles of the American founding (see Pestritto and West 2005). Modern liberals succeeded, in part, by appealing to notions of citizenship, justice, and the common good in ways that ordinary Americans recognize and approve of. Libertarians, on the other hand, regard government as a "necessary evil." They do not understand the nature of the political association; insofar as they undermine the self-understanding and norms that underlie citizenship, libertarians inadvertently assist in the growth of the managerial administrative state. If there is hope for the restoration of a decent political order, it rests in those who understand the nature of politics, the specific *good* of politics and the *limits* of politics, better than modern liberals or libertarians. That hope rests in conservatism.

For Further Reading

In *What Money Can't Buy: The Moral Limits of Markets*, Michael Sandel offers an entertaining and insightful account of the limits, and dangers, of relying exclusively on economic analysis for making sense of moral and political life. John Tomasi, in *Free Market Fairness*, defends classical liberalism against both libertarianism and progressivism, offering along the way a friendly critique of Hayek. For a richer account of public choice theory that incorporates moral motivations into the analysis, see Geoffrey Brennan and Alan Hamlin, *Democratic Devices and Desires*. Notably, Brennan and Hamlin begin each chapter of this book with a quote from *The Federalist Papers*. For a defense of the classical understanding of politics and morality, see Robert P. George, *Making Men Moral*.

CHAPTER FIVE

Libertarian Case Studies

NIKOLAI G. WENZEL

THE DEBATE BETWEEN LIBERTARIANS AND CONSERVATIVES is not merely theoretical. Ideas have consequences that bear directly on the quality of our lives and broader human flourishing. Those consequences in turn provide a test for the adequacy of the ideas behind them.

The debate is played out in a number of contemporary political issues. The next two chapters will focus on three of those issues: immigration, education, and marriage. Each of these issues is consequential and goes to the heart of the disagreement between libertarians and conservatives. In this chapter, I will examine each of them from a libertarian perspective, arguing that the interventionism of conservatism is inherently self-defeating, in terms of lost liberty and unintended consequences. In the next chapter, Schlueter will argue that the libertarian position is flawed.

Immigration

Immigration provides a rich and indicative case study for the conservative–libertarian debate. Indeed, it cuts to the heart of individual rights versus the public imposition of private preferences; it also raises questions of economics, culture, central planning versus spontaneous order, provision of government services, national security, and, fundamentally, the role of force in organizing human interactions.

THE CLASSICAL LIBERAL AND ANARCHO-CAPITALIST APPROACHES

The classical liberal case for immigration gives prima facie deference to the right of individuals to cross borders freely and the rights of employers and employees to engage in contracts without outside interference. However, a classical liberal would also give consideration to other goals, such as security, government services, or access to welfare. Hayek, for example, argued that "while I look forward, as an ultimate ideal, to a state of affairs in which national boundaries have ceased to be obstacles to the free movement of men," he also expressed a worry that led him to favor some immigration restrictions, based on prudential considerations: "I believe that within any period with which we can now be concerned, any attempt to realize it would lead to a revival of strong nationalist sentiments."[1] Similarly, Milton Friedman epitomizes the classical liberal vision:

> Immigration is a particularly difficult subject. There is no doubt that free and open immigration is the right policy in a libertarian state, but in a welfare state it is a different story: the supply of immigrants will become infinite. Your proposal that someone only be able to come for employment is a good one but it would not solve the problem completely. The real hitch is in denying social benefits to the immigrants who are here. That is very hard to do, much harder than you would think as we have found out in California. But nonetheless, we clearly want to move in the direction that you are talking about so this is a question of nitpicking, not of serious objection.[2]

Philosopher Nicolas Maloberti (2011), likewise, examines immigration from a classical liberal perspective and arrives at a different conclusion. In line with traditional classical liberal thinking, he concedes that "in certain extraordinary circumstances, individuals' rights might be permissibly infringed if such infringement were necessary to procure the sort of environment in which the benefits that those rights provide can be enjoyed securely." However, he concludes that "immigration barriers are not merely unnecessary to that effect; they are detrimental because they raise individuals' mobility costs and thereby lower the competitive pressures on governments."

In sum, classical liberalism could in theory call for restrictions on immigration, in the name of market preservation or other public purposes. However, Maloberti continues:

> Considered under ideal conditions, immigration barriers constitute an unjustified infringement on individuals' ownership rights because it is

difficult to identify a purpose that such an infringement might serve that would outweigh the disadvantages created by eliminating important competitive pressures on governments. Considered under nonideal conditions, the problem is, roughly, that immigration barriers cannot be seen as the choice of a lesser evil in the face of either an expected extension of the redistributive state or an expected threat to liberal institutions. On the contrary, because immigration barriers relax the constraints governments face, they should be seen as a major contributor in creating the conditions for the perpetuation of the sort of political arrangements that classical liberals oppose. If individual sovereignty is to be protected, the state's sovereignty over a particular territory should not include a prerogative to determine who is to inhabit it. I do not claim that there should be no borders or that anyone willing to enter a country should be allowed to do so. I claim, rather, that from a classical-liberal perspective there are no good reasons for preventing the entry of those who merely intend to advance their own well-being within the constraints imposed by respect for other people's rights.

Under classical liberalism, the debate remains open. Although a classical liberal might place minimal limits on immigration, for considerations such as burdens on the public infrastructure, passport controls against terrorism or crime, or access to welfare, we have the other extreme of anarcho-capitalism. Recall that, under anarcho-capitalism, there is no state; rights are protected and collective action problems are solved through the voluntary forces of market and civil society. With no state, there will be no immigration policy. But lack of government does not imply lack of governance. There is no government welfare and thus no problem of access to welfare. Immigrants would be free to travel, so long as they could find somebody willing to employ them, to rent or sell housing to them, and so on. The labor market would solve most problems, as an excess supply of immigrants would drive down wages and thus decrease the incentive for immigration. Other markets would solve other problems; for example, prices would rise in electricity or educational markets if the demand increased from immigration, thus attracting new suppliers into the market. On a voluntary basis, clubs and other associations could voluntarily subsidize immigration or create voluntary arrangements that ban newcomers (such as Homeowners' Associations).

A RIGHTS-BASED ARGUMENT FOR OPEN BORDERS

Having outlined the classical liberal and anarcho-capitalist approaches to immigration, I now turn to minarchy, starting with a foundation in individual rights. I will then turn to robust political economy. Libertarian commentator Jacob Hornberger reminds us that, in times of crisis, it is good to return to first principles (Hornberger 2004, 161). This is particularly helpful in the case of immigration because there is so much emotion, and so much economic fallacy, lumped into the arguments.

Instead of starting with the construct of the nation-state and national/political borders, I begin with the individual. An individual wishes to move from point A to point B for peaceful purposes. From a libertarian perspective, it would be a violation of our individual's rights if somebody else were to prevent that person from doing so (unless, of course, he or she violates somebody else's rights along the way). The same goes for an individual contracting employment: Smith agrees to provide his labor to Jones at a certain wage, and Jones agrees to pay Smith that wage. It would be a violation of the rights of both Smith and Jones if a third party were to come along and interfere with the contract.

Moving from individuals to countries, the same principle applies. If an individual seeks to move from country A to country B without violating the rights of others, then any attempt to prevent him or her from doing so would be an unacceptable violation of rights against that person. Likewise, if Smith from country A is willing to sell her services to Jones from country B at a wage that is mutually acceptable, it would be a violation of both their rights for a third party to prevent them from doing so.

MINARCHY AND ROBUST POLITICAL ECONOMY

Returning to the language of robust political economy, restrictions on the free movement of individuals across borders thus amount to one of three things: (1) violating the rights of others; (2) attempting to impose knowledge on others; and (3) advancing private preferences coercively through public means. Naturally, libertarianism rejects all three.

Economist Bryan Caplan writes of a number of biases from which people tend to suffer, biases that are not grounded in fact or logic (Caplan 2008). One of these biases is an antiforeign bias, according to which people tend to be suspicious of foreigners, instinctively and prior to any argument in fact or logic. Even though there may be no direct personal, affective, or intellectual ties, people tend to value arbitrarily their compatriots over foreigners. Although antiforeign bias is certainly one reason for restricting the free movement of individuals, there are others that are more sophisticated. I will now address three arguments for immigration restriction, through which I will make the minarchist case for open orders, based on robust political economy.

Cultural Homogeneity and the Foundations of a Free Society
Cultural arguments against the free movement of peaceful individuals take two forms, cultural homogeneity and the cultural foundations of a free society.

According to cultural homogeneity arguments, there exists a domestic culture that is worth preserving, and this culture is threatened by the influx of foreigners from different cultures. This attitude is exemplified by a 1964 position paper by the Daughters of the American Revolution, arguing that national origin quotas should be retained (Duncan 1964, 61). The position is based on the argument that there was a specific cultural identity, carried by a historically Anglo-Saxon population base in the United States, that produced the American heritage. That heritage is worth preserving by favoring immigration from Anglo-Saxon countries while severely restricting immigration from other sources. The position paper continues by arguing that immigration is a privilege rather than a right, and immigration policy should address the problems of newcomers assimilating into the existing culture. Such arguments are reflected in more recent claims that immigration harms American culture. English is the national language; current U.S. culture is more worthy of preservation than multiculturalism; the nation is responsible for the defense and preservation of a particular society; immigrants don't come as individuals but as bearers of their cultures; and immigration policy should favor assimilation and "suitability for membership" in U.S. society (Auster 2002).

A similar line of reasoning worries about the cultural foundations of a free society. The institutions of liberty do not spring forth randomly; rather, they are the necessary consequence of an underlying political and constitutional culture that supports liberty. The people of a free society must be self-governing, must have civic virtue, and must support rule of law and limited government. Immigrants, who are typically fleeing the consequences of illiberal government, are typically not steeped in a culture that supports liberty. Allowing too many immigrants into the country will stymie assimilation, with negative consequences for liberty. Immigration policy should thus restrict overall numbers and exclude immigrants with ideologies at variance with the U.S. republican form of government (Duncan 1964).

These arguments have superficial appeal. In fact, most libertarians would agree with the challenges identified—if not with the proposed coercive solution. It is quite probable (given historical experience) that immigration will change the host country's culture. It is also clear that the institutions of liberty rely on specific cultural and philosophical foundations.[3] However, the knowledge problem plainly indicates that we do not know the costs and benefits of preserving a particular cultural snapshot. Indeed, who really knows the ideal number of immigrants to the United States and the ideal breakdown by country of origin? For all the "seen" benefits (if indeed they are benefits) of blocking individual immigrants, what are the "unseen" costs—in lost creativity, or economic growth, or who knows what else? Backing up for a moment, which American culture are we preserving in this heterogeneous country of multiple origins? (See Hornberger 2004.) Newcomers are typically viewed with suspicion (see Wattenberg 2002). But one wonders what the country would look like if earlier attempts at preserving American culture through immigration policy had been successful—starting with Catholics, the Irish, Eastern Europeans, or Chinese immigrants.

We also see a clear public choice problem: Many opponents of the free movement of peaceful individuals are hiding behind cultural homogeneity arguments to protect their own interests and advance their own preferences through the political process. Public choice economists refer to strange political bedfellows as a "Baptists and bootleggers" story (see Smith and Yandle 2014). In what appears to be a contradiction, Baptists and bootleggers are allied in their desire to ban alcohol sales, if for completely different reasons. The Baptists want the sinful temptation banned, whereas the bootleggers are pleased to reap the higher profits from engaging in a banned activity. But the story doesn't end there, as both parties advance each other's interests. The bootleggers can hide behind a veneer of Baptist respectability, while the

Baptists will benefit from the financial support and rent seeking of the boot-leggers. Thus do we see cultural or nationalist arguments as a front for naked job protectionism.

Many others, who would block immigration for sociotropic rather than selfish reasons, honestly believe they have the requisite knowledge to impose ends on others. Either way, we have imposition of private preferences through public means. What is more, the reductio ad absurdum of cultural preservation would lead to exclusion of some Americans within the United States of America. Indeed, once we have defined Americanness and the power of the state to exclude those who do not fit specific criteria, why not deport those who do not fit those criteria? Surely the substance of belief and culture is more important than the accident of birth. Why not throw out Democrats? Or Republicans? Or climate change "deniers"? Or opponents of national-ized health care? Or atheists? Or Catholics? By this logic, states with high economic freedom (like Virginia or Texas) could exclude people from states with low economic freedom (like California, Illinois, or New York), on the grounds that those workers are fleeing the consequences of interventionism to seek opportunity—but that they also carry with them the cultural seeds of interventionism.

Finally, immigrants typically leave their home country to seek opportu-nity (controlling for government services and "welfare shopping," a problem I address in the following pages). We can thus reasonably assume that they will be hard workers and risk takers. In fact, recent research finds a small but positive increase in a country's institutional quality as a result of immigration (Clark et al. 2014).

Economics

A second argument against the free movement of peaceful individuals across borders is economic. On the microeconomic level, native workers (or the trade unions that represent them) fear that immigrants will take "their" jobs. On the macroeconomic level, there is some concern that immigration hurts the host economy because many immigrants are low skilled.

In strict economic terms, the bottom line is not clear, as there are some conflicts in the literature (likely from philosophical bias on both sides). But it appears that the net economic benefit of immigration is small, but positive. What is more, this gain from immigration has hitherto been underestimated, as it has not taken into account the economic loss from rent seeking by various interest groups seeking to benefit themselves through immigration restrictions (Powell 2012; see also Borjas 2008). Although the overall benefit is positive, immigration does indeed involve some redistribution of wealth. Native consumers benefit from lower prices, native capital owners benefit from lower wages, and some native workers are hurt by the competition. Setting aside the rights of peaceful individuals to move freely across borders and the rights of workers and employers to contract freely, we must ask why one group should benefit at the expense of another through force. Why should native consumers and native capital owners be taxed to protect the native workers who cannot offer labor services as efficiently as their foreign competition? If we were to expand this logic, we could justify protection of inefficient domestic industries from more efficient foreign competition (effectively taxing domestic consumers and domestic users of the foreign inputs), or we could ban farm machinery to protect inefficient agricultural workers from modern technology, at the expense of consumers who would see a massive increase in the price of food.

Government Services

A third argument against allowing peaceful individuals to move freely across borders involves the provision of government services. First, unrestricted immigration means an increase in population and thus a strain on government services.[4] Second, if the host country offers welfare services, immigrants may engage in forum shopping, that is, immigrating for public benefits rather than to seek jobs (see, for example, Eldredge 2004). However, both of these arguments are missing the fundamental problem. Indeed, these are not problems of immigration but problems with interventionism—an approach that libertarianism rejects in the first place.

With immigration and the strain on government services, the fundamental problem is not one of immigration but of state-based provision of services. In slightly technical economic terms, the tension is not driven by an increasing demand but by a fixed supply that is unresponsive to market forces. In a market system, increased demand would lead to a higher price and quantity supplied in the short run; then the higher price would attract entrepreneurs into the market, thus increasing supply. In the current interventionist system, supply is determined through the political process, and prices are rigid. Any increased demand will cause a shortage, with allocation through waiting, corruption, strained capacity, or government fiat, rather than through market efficiency. A typical example of this is a traffic jam during rush hour on zero-price roads or a lottery for entry into the best government schools.

In sum, the fear about immigrants putting a strain on government services—services that are not legitimate functions of government, according to minarchist libertarianism—is a consequence of government overstepping its bounds in the first place. Under libertarianism, the state will not provide education or health care, so immigrants will be served by the market and civil society. Likewise, in a free society, there is no coerced charity, so there is no incentive for immigrants to seek handouts. It is thus inappropriate to blame immigration for what are really the shortcomings of a coercive, redistributive state.

CONCLUSION: NATIONAL SECURITY AND OPEN BORDERS

A free society allows free movement of peaceful individuals across borders. In a free society, the market will regulate movements; a sudden influx of workers would cause a drop in wages (for a particular segment of the labor force), thus reducing the desirability of crossing a border for a job. Likewise, the market would efficiently regulate access to private services through the price mechanism and the ensuing incentives to entrepreneurs.

What about the final element of concern about immigration, national security, especially in a post-9/11 world? Returning to first principles, libertarianism argues that the only legitimate function of the state is the defense of individual rights. Thus, national security falls under the proper purview of the state. The state may use coercive power to prevent the violation of rights, but a border crossing would be akin to crossing a state line, where individuals are not thwarted in their movement or considered guilty until proven innocent. Besides, a libertarian state would not meddle in the affairs of other countries, thus almost completely eliminating the prospect of terrorism or aggression by another state.

Lunacy...

Education

Education is important—nay, crucial—for self-governing citizenship and the ability to participate in markets, civil society, and limited government. But how will it be provided? Libertarianism turns to markets and liberty, rather than state interventionism.

In this section, I will discuss (1) the purpose of education; (2) the classical liberal response; (3) the rights-based case against state provision (in the anarcho-capitalist and minarchist traditions); (4) robust political economy and the case against state provision (again, for both anarcho-capitalism and minarchy); and (5) liberty as an alternative to state involvement.

THE PURPOSE OF EDUCATION

The arguments typically marshaled in favor of state support of education are three. First, an educated citizenry is required for self-governance and the informed choices of democracy. Therefore, to protect the free society, the state must ensure a basic level of education within the population. Second, participation in the free market is impossible without a basic set of skills that would-be consumers and employees must possess. Without these skills, economic activity is impossible, even if markets are de jure open (think, perhaps, of reading, basic arithmetic, writing, and basic logic to understand contracts or have the wherewithal to seek legal counsel). Therefore, to allow the free market to function, the state must ensure a basic level of education within the population. Third, beyond basic skills, citizens must develop an attachment to the regime, so that they will defend it in case of external attack and respect it internally, thus minimizing the cost of constitutional enforcement (see Hobbes 2002; see also Hayek 2011 [1960], 62) on the inverse relationship between morality and the need for coercion). Whereas the first two arguments are cognitive, this third one is affective. The state must ensure the education of citizens, including civics and teaching of virtue through the law.

I will argue, from a libertarian perspective, that all three of these claims jump from an important goal to state provision in a glaring non sequitur. In fact, state intervention in education is not only self-defeating; it also brings about unintended consequences.

Before looking at the means of delivering education, it behooves us to ask a more fundamental question: What, really, is the purpose of education?

Because of knowledge considerations, this question can be answered only by each individual making the choice of pursuing an education.[5] Some will seek basic skills, and others advanced skills; some will seek technical training, and others will seek the general inquiry of the liberal arts. The homogeneity imposed by the state, especially at the K–12 level, is an affront to individual liberty and efficient allocation of resources. Note that this is not an argument for moral relativism. As a college professor and as an economist, I have strong views about the liberal arts and the overly technical turn of both the economics profession and undergraduate education generally. Although I will strongly encourage liberal learning for those students who seek it, I would never impose it by the sword for everybody.

CLASSICAL LIBERALISM AND STATE SUPPORT OF EDUCATION

Classical liberalism places a prima facie priority on individual rights and a prima facie deference to markets and civil society over state provision of goods. Only in cases of market failure is government involvement acceptable and then only to the limited extent required to fix the market failure. The classical liberal approach precludes outright, wholesale, and monopolistic provision of education. But classical liberalism does not completely reject state involvement (as do anarcho-capitalism and minarchy). Instead, classical liberalism calls for government to play a supporting role, and even that only in cases of market failure. Thus would tax-exempt status for schools be acceptable, as would scholarships or other forms of tailored public assistance for the poorest students, to guarantee a basic education for all.

The classical liberal approach to education is exemplified by Milton Friedman's (1962) argument. Because it also illustrates the prudential and limited approach of classical liberalism in general, this argument is worth quoting here at length:

> A stable and democratic society is impossible without a minimum degree of literacy and knowledge on the part of most citizens and without widespread acceptance of some common set of values. Education can contribute to both. In consequence, the gain from the education of a child accrues not only to the child or to his parents but also to other members of the society. The education of my child contributes to your welfare by promoting a stable and democratic society. It is not feasible to identify

the particular individuals (or families) benefited and so to charge for the services rendered. There is therefore a significant "neighborhood effect."

What kind of governmental action is justified by this particular neighborhood effect? The most obvious is to require that each child receive a minimum amount of schooling of a specified kind. Such a requirement could be imposed upon the parents without further government action, just as owners of buildings, and frequently of automobiles, are required to adhere to specified standards to protect the safety of others. There is, however, a difference between the two cases. Individuals who cannot pay the costs of meeting the standards required for buildings or automobiles can generally divest themselves of the property by selling it. The requirement can thus generally be enforced without government subsidy. The separation of a child from a parent who cannot pay for the minimum required schooling is clearly inconsistent with our reliance on the family as the basic social unit and our belief in the freedom of the individual. Moreover, it would be very likely to detract from his education for citizenship in a free society.

If possible, parents should pay for the schooling of their own children—again, classical liberalism places the primary onus on markets and civil society. However, in cases of poverty, the government could step in. But just as Friedman and other classical liberals call for state support of education, they do not claim to know the details, which are left to local communities (in a very Hayekian move). Friedman continues:

> The qualitative argument from "neighborhood effects" does not, of course, determine the specific kinds of schooling that should be subsidized or by how much they should be subsidized. The social gain presumably is greatest for the lowest levels of schooling, where there is the nearest approach to unanimity about content, and declines continuously as the level of schooling rises . . . What forms of education have the greatest social advantage and how much of the community's limited resources should be spent on them must be decided by the judgment of the community expressed through its accepted political channels. The aim of this analysis is not to decide these questions for the community but rather to clarify the issues involved in making a choice, in particular

whether it is appropriate to make the choice on a communal rather than individual basis.

In sum, the state can play a supporting role, to fix market failures. But classical liberalism rejects outright government control, such as the current state quasi-monopoly and quasi-nationalization of education:

> As we have seen, both the imposition of a minimum required level of schooling and the financing of this schooling by the state can be justified by the "neighborhood effects" of schooling. A third step, namely the actual administration of educational institutions by the government, the "nationalization," as it were, of the bulk of the "education industry" is much more difficult to justify on these, or, so far as I can see, any other, grounds. The desirability of such nationalization has seldom been faced explicitly. Governments have, in the main, financed schooling by paying directly the costs of running educational institutions. Thus this step seemed required by the decision to subsidize schooling. Yet the two steps could readily be separated. Governments could require a minimum level of schooling financed by giving parents vouchers redeemable for a specified maximum sum per child per year if spent on "approved" educational services. Parents would then be free to spend this sum and any additional sum they themselves provided on purchasing educational services from an "approved" institution of their own choice. The educational services could be rendered by private enterprises operated for profit, or by non-profit institutions. The role of the government would be limited to insuring that the schools met certain minimum standards, such as the inclusion of a minimum common content in their programs, much as it now inspects restaurants to insure that they maintain minimum sanitary standards.

Thus, Milton Friedman, a standard bearer of liberty and limited government, is not associated with purely private education but with school vouchers. This approach epitomizes the classical liberal philosophy of minimal government involvement in a supporting rather than a central role and then only to fix market failures.

By contrast, minarchy and anarcho-capitalism reject any government involvement in education: the former because government is limited to the protection of individual rights and the latter because there is no government. But both approaches reject government involvement and rely instead on markets and civil society. I thus treat them together.

THE RIGHTS-BASED CASE AGAINST STATE INVOLVEMENT IN EDUCATION

The simplest case against state-provided education is rights based. In the most basic terms, forcing A to pay for the education that B is compelled by C to receive (when C also decides what is good for B) is a violation of the rights of both A and B. There is no place for such coercion in a free society (see Rogge and Goodrich 1973); anarcho-capitalism and minarchy thus reject any government involvement in education.

Even apparent defenders of liberty become mysteriously willing to curb liberty when it comes to education, usually based on the argument that education is a public good. That is, the argument goes, (a) the market, left to its own devices, would underprovide education; and (b) education is required for a free society; therefore, (c) the state must support or provide education. In other words, to save liberty, we must coerce people to receive education for liberty. But this is a contradiction and a violation of rights.

ROBUST POLITICAL ECONOMY AND THE CASE AGAINST STATE-SPONSORED EDUCATION

Beyond rights, the case against state involvement in education is practical and based on sound analysis of the world rather than a romantic vision of the state.

Assuming that education is required for the free society, it is still fallacious to conclude that it must, therefore, be provided coercively by the state. Such "Nirvana fallacy" thinking would also have the state provide morality, religion, food, or other goods. But economic theory, along with the weight of historical evidence, clearly shows that state provision of either one of these staples leads to disaster. Fortunately, civil society and the market, respectively, provide these goods more effectively and without the unintended consequences of central planning. The market failure argument for state-sponsored education simply fails—another reason for the minarchist and anarcho-capitalist rejections of state involvement in education.

What is more, coercive governmental provision of education comes laden with unintended consequences. The government does not face a market test. From 1970 to 2009 in the United States, there was a 252 percent increase in the number of public schoolteachers and a 700 percent increase in administrators . . . all for a 96 percent increase in students (Scafidi 2012). In spite of these increases, which have been supported by an inflation-adjusted federal spending jump from $446 per student in 1971 to $1,185 per student in 2009, student scores have remained stagnant.[6] We have gone, in less than a century, from teaching Latin in high school, to teaching English in college. So much for government education!

What, then, of the need for citizenship and the case for civic education? Market failure is possible, but government failure is certain. Interventionists have ceded liberty ab initio. Fortunately, the case for market failure is exaggerated. Having shown what does not work (coercion), I now turn to the positive case for "education in a free society" (generally, see Rogge and Goodrich 1973).

MARKETS, CIVIL SOCIETY, AND LIBERTY: THE LIBERTARIAN ALTERNATIVE

I now make the minarchist and anarcho-capitalist case for liberty in education (in this subsection, I will simply use "libertarian"). The libertarian alternative to state coercion is simple and elegant: Respect liberty, trust the market and civil society, and trust the forces of spontaneous order over the limited minds of social engineers.

Libertarianism recognizes the need for education, from basic skills to civic affection. But a need does not imply a coercive solution. Food and morality are arguably as important for maintaining life and civilization—yet governmental provision of either has historically proven to be disastrous. The same goes for education.

Education under libertarianism begins with freedom as the underlying principle, recognizing the inherent contradiction in forcing people to be educated for freedom. It continues with a faith in markets—those same markets that, when left unhampered, feed us, clothe us, and heal us. Returning to Roy Childs and his cautionary note that he is not a builder of utopias, I cannot offer here a comprehensive blueprint of every aspect of education in a free society (for a more developed, but still very humble, outline, see Rogge and Goodrich 1973). Each individual in a free society would choose the education suitable to him or her, and the market would respond, supported by civil society.

This still leaves three potential problems: children, the poor, and positive externalities.

The case of children is simple, and I will quote from libertarian educators Ben Rogge and Pierre Goodrich to make my case:

> There is a strong presumption among those who would use the state to bring about the good society to distrust the decision-making of the family in many areas, particularly in the rearing and educating of the young. In almost all of the better-known utopian schemes (e.g., those of Plato, Fourier, Robert Owen, and Skinner), the children are to be taken from their parents at an early age so that their upbringing can be under the control of the all-wise agents of the state, rather than of the foolish and primitive family circle.

> Needless to say, while recognizing the serious, and at times tragic, imperfections of the family system of child raising, we reject all arrangements that would substitute for the imperfect family the even less perfect state. It is appropriate for the state to intervene in the family relationship when improper force is used against the child, and it may be necessary at times for the court to resolve questions of legal guardianships for orphan children. But except for the obvious cases, the state has no jurisdiction over the relationship of parent and child, including all questions of the education of the child. (Rogge and Goodrich 1973, 67)

Second, civil society has historically done a better job than government at helping the poor, at a fraction of the cost and without the unintended consequences (see Read 1964, 215; see also Beito 1992). We need only look at the current efforts of academic entrepreneur James Tooley to see that markets, if allowed, educate the poorest of children more effectively than the central planning of charity or education (Tooley 2013; see also Dixon 2013). We need only look at the failure and disastrous consequences of the welfare state to reject state provision of education for the poor.

Finally, what of positive externalities? It seems obvious that most people derive some positive externality from an educated population, from increased productivity to better conversation. The right to tax does not follow from this, however. With a tax, A is forced by C to pay for B's education, because—it is claimed—A derives a benefit from B's education but would attempt to obtain this benefit without paying for it. Beyond the obvious violation of liberty, this argument is fallacious. Any A who wanted such benefits could purchase them directly, by voluntarily supporting B's education. Many symphony orchestras, art galleries, colleges, and the like are supported primarily through charitable and voluntary contributions and not by the state.

Divorcing Marriage from the State:
A Libertarian Case for Freedom of Association

Marriage offers another quintessential case study to reflect the differences between libertarianism and conservatism. More precisely, *government regulation of marriage*, and specifically one version of marriage and its attendant legal privileges, is the point of contention. Marriage, after all, is not per se a political question; it thus falls outside the purview of libertarianism—even if marriage, like so many other institutions, formal and informal, has implications for liberty.

For this case study, I employ a slightly different approach from the other sections, as I start by first describing the communitarian/interventionist/conservative vision of marriage. I then turn in my second subsection to robust political economy and the case for ending government intervention, from a minarchist and anarcho-capitalist perspective. In the third subsection, I address positive externalities and possible classical liberal justifications for support of marriage. I close in my fourth subsection with a rights-based argument, by juxtaposing the libertarian position (which defends individual liberty and freedom of association) with the communitarianism of interventionism and its attempt to impose private preferences through public means.

COMMUNITARIAN INTERVENTIONISM

Communitarian interventionists would impose one vision of marriage on everybody through the political process, as they have so often in the past.

Nevertheless, the understanding of marriage has changed over centuries and civilizations, as contracting individuals seek different things from the union.

In 1864, legal commentator Joel Prentice Bishop wrote of marriage, with characteristic hubris, that it would be "too absurd to require a word of refutation . . . the idea that any government could, consistently with the general well-being, permit [the] institution [of marriage] to become merely a thing of bargain between men and women, and not regulate it" (Cott 2000, 6). In a more recent echo, conservative intellectual Roger Scruton removes individual liberty from marriage, claiming that "the obligations [of marriage] are not contracted between partners, but imposed by the institution" (Clulow 1993, 39). Of course, the philosophical hubris of claiming a unique definition is one thing; the imposition of these preferences through the law is another. Alas, "the US has shown through its national history a commitment to exclusive and faithful monogamy, preferably intraracial. In the name of the public interest and public order, it has furthered this model as a unifying moral standard" (Cott 2000, 5).

ROBUST POLITICAL ECONOMY AND MARRIAGE

The minarchist and anarcho-capitalist perspectives on marriage are essentially the same. The only difference is that minarchy recognizes a role for the state in adjudicating disputes and enforcing contracts whereas anarcho-capitalism relies entirely on civil society and private arbitration. Both, however, reject regulation of marriage by the state.

Through the Middle Ages, marriage was considered as basically a private matter, with no uniform religious or other ceremony required (McSheffrey 2006, 21); marriage was basically an exchange of vows by two consenting adults.[7] The Catholic Council of Trent, in 1563, decreed that a Roman Catholic marriage would be official only if the ceremony were performed by a priest with two witnesses. The Church of England did not obtain a monopoly on weddings until 1753, and civil registration of marriages did not occur until 1836 in England. In continental Europe, the recording of marriages moved from the church to the state with the Reformation, as part of Martin Luther's injunctions. At the time of the American founding, monogamy was the exception, rather than the rule, throughout the world (Cott 2000, 10). U.S. Justice Murphy, in a 1946 dissent, recognized polygamy as one of several historical kinds of marriage and one that "far exceeded that of any other form" (Ibid., 194). As late as 1911, American women were subsumed into their husband's legal identity. Six of the original thirteen U.S. colonies and twenty-three of thirty-three states in 1860 prohibited interracial marriage, a ban that was not struck down throughout the United States until 1967 (Ibid., 40 and 162). No-fault divorce did not become widespread in the United States until the 1970s. And marital rape was not universally recognized until the 1980s (Ibid., 205–220).

Moving from history to economic analysis, economist Steven Horwitz (2007) explains how changing economic conditions (and thus changing needs) have changed the function of marriage over the years—from a primarily economic (and often arranged) partnership in a preindustrial subsistence economy, to the male-breadwinner family of the Victorian era, to today's "companionate" marriage, where love and shared life goals have largely replaced economic need. Working in the Hayekian tradition of spontaneous order and evolving institutions, Horwitz concludes that many conservatives "continue to pay lip service to the great things capitalism provides and often understand correctly the ways in which its economic effects cannot be controlled." At the same time, however, "they complain about the cultural dynamism that is the direct result of the dynamism of the market." He concludes that "the only way to stop the cultural changes that conservatives object to would be to shut down the individual liberty, entrepreneurial market processes, and economic growth that are part and parcel of the market economy" (Horwitz 2007). The knowledge problem thus precludes state definition of marriage.

Moving from knowledge to incentives, we have the public choice problem of state involvement in marriage. The necessary consequences of state involvement are ossification of one particular vision and violation of individual rights. Thus have we seen women lacking legal standing in marriage until well into the twentieth century; laws against interracial marriage that persisted until 1967; and marital rape exemptions that persisted until the 1980s—all things that were later regarded as offensive to liberty. In the reductio ad absurdum of coercive imposition of private preferences through public means, federal troops were deployed against Mormons by Democratic President James Buchanan "in part to show that his party no less than the

Republicans abhorred polygamy" (Cott 2000, 73). Regulation begets regulation; as with so many other forms of interventionism, from education to immigration and from welfare to the war on drugs, the fundamental problem is one of regulation, not the sanctioned behavior. Thus do we see more than 1,000 federal statutes that grant privileges and redistribution to (heterosexual and monogamous) marriage—this, of course, shifts the debate from a question of rights to one of access to the public trough. I should note here the difference between the libertarian approach to same-sex marriage and the progressive approach: The latter would extend privileges to same-sex couples, whereas libertarianism would remove privileges for all. As a libertarian, I hate to look a gift horse in the mouth; I applaud the advance of liberty in the recent *Obergefell v. Hodges* Supreme Court decision, which lifted bans on same-sex marriage. But I also worry about the extension of privileges (rather than an extension of rights).

Likewise, the breakdown of the family can be ascribed more to the perverse incentives of the welfare state than to the individual liberty of no-fault divorce. Finally, in an ironic twist that shows that interventionism is interventionism (whether it comes from conservatism or progressivism), New Deal policies favored the male wage-earner model against the then-emergent two-earner model, subsidizing married couples at the expense of individuals and discriminating against married women in the federal workforce (Ibid., 172–179).

In sum, robust political economy cautions us against a political definition of marriage and the ensuing coercive enforcement by the state.

POSITIVE EXTERNALITIES: JOHN LOCKE'S ARGUMENT AND CLASSICAL LIBERALISM

There is one interventionist argument that should give us pause: positive externalities to marriage, going all the way back to Locke's famous articulation in his *Second Treatise* (Locke 1988, chapter 7). According to this argument, the benefit to society from the kind of children who come from marriage—and only from marriage—is so high that the state has an interest in regulating marriage and supporting it through various privileges. I do not deny that most studies point in the same direction: the benefit to children from having been raised by a married mother and father, over alternate arrangements. For minarchy and anarcho-capitalism, the jump from a good outcome to a need for governmental regulation is a non sequitur, as should be plain from the preceding chapters. Indeed, many things are good, and many things have positive externalities—education, culture, physical exercise, church attendance, or volunteering, just to name a few. But the market and civil society provide them amply and without the unintended consequences of coercive government support. Should the market and civil society not provide these goods, government-forced provision must ipso facto come with violation of liberty and a coterie of unintended consequences.

Classical liberalism, however, is less sanguine about the market's ability to solve the positive externality problem to marriage. To repeat the argument about positive externalities and market failure, the social benefit of marriage exceeds the private benefit, so there is likely to be underproduction. That is, more marriages make for a stronger civil society, less crime, and so on—all benefits that accrue to everybody and not just those who are married. Individuals contemplating marriage will not directly feel the social benefits, so they are apt to undermarry.

Classical liberalism, with its usual blend of prudence and marginal improvement, would thus reject heavy-handed government intervention in marriage, including political definition of marriage. However, classical liberalism is compatible with measures to encourage marriage, such as tax credits or denial of public welfare to the unmarried, as well as light restrictions on divorce, such as mandatory counseling or waiting periods.

MARRIAGE AND LIBERTY: THE RIGHT TO FREE ASSOCIATION

Beyond robust political economy, marriage comes down to a simple basic: the right of free individuals to associate freely.

This libertarian vision will be disappointing to social engineers because it does not attempt to foresee all possible situations. In sum, the libertarian vision recognizes three distinct fields for marriage: the individual, civil society, and the state. Individuals enjoy freedom of association and may engage in whatever contracts they wish, with others who freely sign them. The state neutrally enforces contacts and arbitrates disputes arising thereunder, so as to protect individual rights and prevent coercion. And civil society, from churches to clubs and families, informally enforces the prevalent norms, as they contain the inherited wisdom of the past, so long as those norms do not infringe coercively upon any individual's rights (see, for example, Boaz 1997b on privatizing marriage).

In its call for liberty over coercion, libertarianism does not deny the importance of marriage. Nor does it call for the abolition of marriage, for that would be social engineering and meddling in the affairs of others. Libertarianism does reject the state monopoly on the definition of marriage and the coercive granting of privileges to some through marriage law. Catholicism or Unitarianism or Islam, or any number of other religious or philosophical codes, might very well define marriage for their adherents, but that does not mean there is one real, true definition of marriage. Such a claim would amount to asserting one's individual definition as the truth because one is claiming a privileged access to knowledge, and one is then willing to impose that understanding through secular coercion. Like any other contract between two (or more) parties, marriage is what the contracting parties say it is—within the established contract law that has emerged under minarchy (or the legal arrangements that emerge in anarcho-capitalism).

If marriage has historically involved militarily enforced monogamy, the legal subjugation of women, and bans on interracial marriage—all things that are now abhorrent to friends of liberty—why not allow same-sex marriage or polygamy, if the contracting parties (all consenting adults) so desire?

Civil society is a much more powerful repository and teacher of tradition than the state. And, unlike the state, it does not suffer from stasis, and it cannot serve as a vehicle for imposition of private preferences through public means. In fact, although one cannot predict the specific consequences of moving from the current coercion to a state of liberty, it would not be surprising if the removal of state restrictions, the removal of a one-size-fits-all definition of marriage—and the removal of the parallel morass of regulations, interventions, and privileges—might not actually *strengthen* marriage. After all, liberty yields better results than coercion.

For Further Reading

A representative approach to classical liberal policy proposals can be found in Milton Friedman's *Capitalism and Freedom*, just as Murray Rothbard presents a dozen anarcho-capitalist case studies in *For a New Liberty: The*

Libertarian Manifesto. For the minarchist case on immigration, see Harry Binswanger's essay "Open Immigration." On the minarchist case on education, see the hard-hitting and crystal-clear opening essay by Ben Rogge and Pierre Goodrich in *Education in a Free Society.* For a simple and straightforward liberty-based case for marriage, see David Boaz's article "Privatize Marriage: A Simple Solution to the Gay Marriage Debate," or, more generally, Steven Horwitz's *Hayek's Modern Family: Classical Liberalism and the Evolution of Social Institutions.*

CHAPTER SIX

Conservative Case Studies

NATHAN W. SCHLUETER

AN EXAMINATION OF IMMIGRATION, MARRIAGE, AND EDUCATION helps bring the fundamental issues in the libertarian–conservative debate into focus. To some degree, they highlight once again the central question dividing conservatives and libertarians: Can political and social life be understood in terms of the basic methodological assumptions of economics? Traditionalist conservatives and neoconservatives, each in different ways, answer this question in the negative. Traditionalist conservatives emphasize the cultural and moral conditions that are required for a free society. They also insist that those conditions can grow only from local communities responding to their own particular needs and interests. In general it can be said that traditionalist conservatives oppose liberal immigration policy; support private schools, or local control of schools empowered to reinforce moral, and especially theological, teachings; and favor traditional marriage laws, usually on moral grounds. Unfortunately, traditionalist conservatives have sometimes defended these concerns in ways that are decidedly racist and xenophobic, thus alienating mainstream Americans and making it more difficult to publicly defend the reasonableness of their concerns.

Neoconservatives for their part are more sensitive to the dangers of religious and racial intolerance, especially in local communities, and have been far more cosmopolitan in their policy prescriptions. Neoconservatives oppose the progressive ideologies of multiculturalism, egalitarianism, and identity politics that have come to dominate public institutions and public policy. In general, then, neoconservatives support a liberal immigration policy, the reform (rather than the privatization) of public education, and traditional marriage, though usually on pragmatic rather than moral grounds. Traditionalist conservatives worry that neoconservatives are too suspicious of moral and religious influences, especially among ordinary Americans, and too confident in the ability of government experts to fix and manage complex social orders like education.

American conservatism, as I have defended it here, brings the legitimate concerns of both traditionalist conservatives and neoconservatives to bear on its critique of libertarianism. It looks to the principles of the American founding for guidance on how to bring tradition, reason, and liberty into an equilibrium that promotes human flourishing. Conservatives believe that libertarians ignore the complex conditions required for civil and political liberty and rely instead on a naïve view that political life can be understood, and sustained, on economic grounds alone. Conservatives affirm the justice and value of market forces, but they insist that the market works only within a moral, cultural, legal, and political framework.

I have insisted throughout this book that the attraction of libertarianism is its clarity and simplicity. Ordinarily in market exchanges the subjective values of the parties to the exchange reign supreme. In politics things are not so simple. To cite just one example: The Fourth Amendment to the Constitution protects "the right of the people" against "unreasonable searches and seizures." But what is a "reasonable" search? People will disagree, sometimes vehemently, on how this requirement should be specified and applied, and that specification will always involve a prudential assessment of circumstances and weighing of goods. Certainly it would be much clearer to simply prohibit (or allow) all searches, but this would hardly serve the cause of freedom. Difficult decisions must be made. Life is messy, and so is political life.

The point of these remarks is to make clear here at the outset of my treatment of public policy that although conservatism provides clear principles (like the right to be free from unreasonable searches), it cannot always provide clear determinations of those principles. This requires the virtue of prudence, the only virtue explicitly appealed to in the Declaration of Independence. The appeal to prudence should not count against conservatism, any more than it counts against the Declaration of Independence, one of the most principled documents ever written. Immigration, education, and marriage policy all involve complex and difficult prudential considerations that go well beyond what this brief chapter can traverse, but, without a clear understanding of principles, prudence is impossible. I hope to provide a sketch of these principles in the following three sections.

Immigration

The fundamental disagreement between libertarians and conservatives over immigration is not whether immigration restrictions should be more generous or more strict but whether there should be any restrictions at all. As libertarian Jason Brennan puts it, "Libertarians . . . support free immigration. They believe people have a right to cross borders as they see fit" (Brennan 2012b, 38). Even F. A. Hayek looked forward to "a state of affairs in which national boundaries have ceased to be obstacles to the free movement of men" (Hayek 1976, 58).

Libertarians rely on two different kinds of arguments for their position, one principled and one consequentialist. The principled argument is that restrictions on immigration violate individual natural rights to freedom of movement and to freedom of contract. The consequentialist argument is that immigration is good for America, that there are no objective criteria on which to base immigration restrictions, and that in any case territorial boundaries are impossible to secure. I will deal with the principled objection first.

Conservatives deny that immigration restrictions violate any rights. Just as the negative freedom to leave your house does not entail the positive freedom to enter my house, so the right to leave your country does not entail the right to enter my country. Libertarians, however, may doubt the validity of this analogy by challenging the claim that territorial boundaries are like private property. The common territory that defines the political association, so the argument goes, is nothing more than the sum of the individual property owners, whom the government is instituted to protect. And because it is the natural right of each of those property owners to admit, exclude, or cooperate with whom they will, government sovereignty over territorial borders is nothing less than a violation of the personal and property rights of individuals. Opposition to open borders is motivated by nothing more than tribal, populist, and even racist impulses against the open society.[1]

The objection goes to the heart of the libertarian–conservative debate. Conservatives deny that the political association can be understood, or even exist, as simply a sum of private individuals, without remainder. As I have repeated throughout this book, the political association is characterized by citizenship, a form of public, though not comprehensive, identity that is neither tribal nor cosmopolitan and that provides the social capital that makes the bonds of trust required for human flourishing, if not liberty itself, possible. Citizenship involves not only common legal institutions but also a common territory in which those institutions can effectively operate. An absolute right to immigration would not only place unreasonable demands on those institutions; it would also violate the right of citizens to determine the composition of the political association of which they are members (see West 1997, 157).

One of the greatest achievements of classical liberalism is to break with the comprehensive forms of citizenship found in classical republicanism and to promote a limited form of citizenship aimed at protecting and promoting private individuals and voluntary associations within civil society. But although classical liberals like Adam Smith promoted a liberal form of citizenship, they never imagined that citizenship itself, much less territorial boundaries, could or should ever disappear altogether. The power provided in the U.S. Constitution to "establish a uniform Rule of Naturalization" (see U.S. Constitution 1.7.4) and to prohibit the "Migration or Immigration" of persons into the United States (subject to 1.9.1) is an affirmation of territorial sovereignty that no classical liberal to my knowledge, and no American founder, ever contested.

The restriction of immigration, therefore, does not violate either the personal or property rights of individuals any more than does the power of eminent domain (Fifth Amendment) or the common law of nuisance. But this power, like any political power, is subject to requirements of justice, common defense, and the general welfare (see the preamble to the U.S. Constitution). Thomas G. West suggests two principles that animated the American founders: "First, America should generously welcome as equal citizens people from many nations and religions. Second, the numbers and kinds of immigrants may need to be limited with a view to the qualities of character required for democratic citizenship" (West 1997, 149). In support of his claim, West cites George Washington, Alexander Hamilton, and Thomas Jefferson. Jefferson, the most "libertarian" of the founders, is worth quoting at length:

[Our species of government] is a composition of the freest principles of the English constitution, with others derived from natural right and natural reason. To these nothing can be more opposed than the maxims of absolute monarchies. Yet, from such, we are to expect the greatest number of emigrants. They will bring with them the principles of the governments they leave, imbibed in their early youth; or, if able to throw them off, it will be in exchange for an unbounded licentiousness, passing, as is usual, from one extreme to another. It would be a miracle were they to stop precisely at the point of temperate liberty. These principles, with their language, they will transmit to their children. In proportion to their numbers, they will share with us the legislation. They will infuse into it their spirit, warp and bias its direction, and render it a heterogeneous, incoherent, distracted mass. (Jefferson, *Notes on the State of Virginia*, Query VIII, in 1975, 124–125)

Although these principles are sound, they do not fully address today's immigration problem, which involves many persons who are not interested in citizenship but *work*. Any sound immigration policy should distinguish between these two classes of persons, prospective citizens and guest workers. And here the libertarian consequentialist argument is on firmer ground. For conservatives, border limits are governed by prudence. There may be times and circumstances when the best policy is to leave borders open, as in they were for the first 100 years of our nation's history.[2] And then there are times and circumstances when prudence suggests stricter immigration controls. (Would libertarians be in favor of open immigration if Mexico and Canada were controlled by ISIS or the Taliban?) But once the decision is made to control immigration, enormous logistical problems emerge that to address will require a significant and problematic increase in government power.

In the first place, what are the criteria for limiting immigration? The most obvious reason is security. Americans have good reason to oppose the immigration of criminals and terrorists bent on destroying America. The more problematic reason is economic. Do Americans have a legitimate interest in protecting their jobs from the competition of immigrant workers? In general, the conservative answer must be no, though this will doubtless be a controversial position for some conservatives. But the best economic evidence indicates that immigrant labor is a benefit to Americans overall, even if it sometimes puts a strain on certain classes of American workers. It has been rightly said that America is a nation of immigrants, and it has a long history of welcoming immigrants. In most cases those immigrants have enriched America not only economically but also culturally, bringing labor, skills, creativity, inventions, cuisines, art, and music that have made American lives more secure, prosperous, diverse, and interesting. Conservatives can learn from the libertarian strain of conservatism to have more trust in the spontaneous forces of the market to improve the lives of everyone. Except in cases involving national security, conservatives must always be suspicious of economic protectionism, which corrupts the political process, harms consumers, and, in the long run, hurts the workers themselves.[3]

How many immigrants should be allowed in? A conservative policy would let that number be determined by the market, so long as all immigrants, including prospective citizens (until they achieve citizenship), are denied welfare benefits. Although limiting welfare benefits to citizens might strike some people as unfair because immigrants would be required to pay taxes, this would result in an economically sustainable number of immigrants. Moreover, it is not unjust because immigrants have no *right* to work in the United States and because they themselves are free to judge the value of the trade-off.[4] Moreover, Americans who are skeptical of immigration might be more supportive knowing that those immigrants were supporting, instead of depleting, American social services.[5] But this policy would also require the registration of every eligible worker (American and immigrant) in a national database and harsh penalties for those who employ ineligible workers.[6] Again, these are the costs of gaining a reasonable control over immigration. But this cost is compounded by another one: border control.

The enforcement of immigration restrictions has largely been a failure. According to the Pew Research Center, there were 11.2 million illegal immigrants in the United States in 2012, about half from Mexico (see Krogstad and Passel, 2015). The fact that it is impossible to prevent illegal immigration does not necessarily mean that immigration restrictions should be repealed, any more than laws against theft and murder should be repealed because these crimes cannot be perfectly prevented. But it is also true that neither the public nor politicians have shown a firm willingness to commit the resources necessary to adequately enforce immigration law. If conservatives believe immigration restrictions are for the common good, then they are obliged to pursue serious proposals to secure the borders. This should include the efficient use of unoccupied drones to monitor the long stretches of uninhabited territory, but it will also require an increase in armed staffing.

In sum, conservatives deny that the natural rights to liberty and property require open borders. The political association is a distinctive community whose members have a legitimate interest in living and working with other human beings who are at least not hostile to their pursuit of flourishing, and government has a legitimate role in protecting that interest. But like any other government power, this one is liable to abuse. Conservatives therefore promote a careful weighing of trade-offs and sound institutional design for its immigration policy. As always, this is a complex and difficult process, but one that should not be excluded for this reason a priori.

Education

If it is true that the political association, including the libertarian association, depends on a shared set of opinion, habits, and customs, then it is also true that the members of the political association have a legitimate interest in preserving those opinions, habits, and customs by providing for some kind of education. In some, perhaps many, cases, that interest will be met by voluntary action. This is especially true in smaller and more homogenous communities. In larger and more heterogeneous communities, as we find presently in the United States, the assistance of political authority becomes more pressing.

The sclerotic condition of public education in America today makes public support for education difficult to defend. But like other pathologies in contemporary American politics, this malaise, conservatives believe, is not the result of public education itself but of progressive influences (see Ravitch 2001). Libertarians oppose public support for education in principle. That opposition, however, illustrates the larger flaw in libertarianism more generally: It reflects a misunderstanding of the nature of the political association as a means for human flourishing. The solution to today's problems in education is not the repudiation of public support for education altogether but of the principles on which it is currently based. A return to the more decentralized, privatized, and traditional models of the past would in large part restore the benefits of universal education in America.

For libertarians, education is a purely private affair. Government simply has no business encouraging, requiring, or providing education. Decisions about whether, when, and how to learn should be made by private individuals (or, for children, presumably by their parents, though libertarians rarely make a principled argument as to why this must be so) according to their own value judgments and circumstances. For political authority (or anyone else) to dictate these matters is a gross interference with individual liberty and inevitably leads to indoctrination by "the state."

Libertarians are often surprised to learn that three of their most beloved figures, Adam Smith, Thomas Jefferson, and Alexis de Tocqueville, *all supported public education*. Although each of them understood the value of economic freedom, they never thought politics could be reduced to the terms of business management, contracts, or economics. In short, they were conservatives, not libertarians.

Smith's *An Inquiry into the Nature and Causes of the Wealth of Nations* is perhaps the single most influential defense of the free market ever written. In Book Five of that work, Smith raises the question as to whether education should be a public concern. He answers that although there are some societies in which individuals, "without any attention of government," are able to acquire "almost all the abilities and virtues which that state requires," there are others where "some attention of government is necessary in order to prevent the almost entire corruption and degeneracy of the great body of the people" (Smith 1981 [1776], 2:781). As it turns out, those societies requiring public education are precisely those that are most "civilized," where the free market and division of labor are most developed, and where governments derive their authority from the consent of the governed. Smith's arguments are decidedly *political* in nature:

> Though the state was to derive no advantage from the instruction of the inferior ranks of people, it would still deserve its attention that they should not be altogether uninstructed. The state, however, derives no inconsiderable advantage from their instruction. The more they are instructed the less liable they are to the delusions of enthusiasm and superstition, which, among ignorant nations, frequently occasion the most

dreadful disorders. An instructed and intelligent people, besides, are always more decent and orderly than an ignorant and stupid one. They feel themselves, each individually, more respectable and more likely to obtain the respect of their lawful superiors, and they are therefore more disposed to respect those superiors. They are more disposed to examine, and more capable of seeing through, the interested complaints of faction and sedition, and they are, upon that account, less apt to be misled into any wanton or unnecessary opposition to the measures of government. In free countries, where the safety of government depends very much upon the favourable judgment which the people may form of its conduct, it must surely be of the highest importance that they should not be disposed to judge rashly or capriciously concerning it. (Smith 1981 [1776], 2: 789)

This justification for public provision of education does not mean that the government must deliver that education or cover the full cost of tuition. Even as he defends public education, Smith does not abandon his insights about the motives of human action: The schoolmaster, he writes, should be "partly, but not wholly, paid by the public, because, if he was wholly, or even principally, paid by it, he would soon learn to neglect his business" (Smith 1981 [1776], 2: 785). We might do well to heed his advice.

Libertarians frequently claim Thomas Jefferson as their ally. David Boaz calls the Declaration of Independence, written by Jefferson, "probably the finest piece of libertarian writing in history" (Boaz 1997a, 43). But Boaz completely overlooks those elements in Jefferson's thought that most libertarians would despise. One of these is Jefferson's plan for public education, which, as he himself proudly points out, he introduced to the first Virginia legislature after the Declaration of Independence, along with the proposal to abolish the laws of entail and primogeniture. All three of these proposals, he claimed in a letter to John Adams, were for the purpose of realizing in law the principles of the Declaration, and had all three been adopted, "our work would have been complete" (Jefferson 1975, 537). The plan would have divided every county in Virginia into wards and established a "free school" in each, followed by scholarships for the best students to continue their education at higher levels. Notice again the *political* justification for the proposal: "This [proposal] on Education would have raised the mass of the people to the high ground of moral respectability necessary to their own safety, and to orderly government; and would have compleated the great object of qualifying them to select the veritable aristoi, for the trusts of government, to the exclusion of the Pseudalists [that is, artificial aristocrats]" (537–538). Although Jefferson's plan was not adopted, he still expressed "great hope that some patriotic spirit will, at a favorable moment, call it up, and make it the key-stone of the arch of our government" (538).

Finally, Alexis de Tocqueville, another figure libertarians are fond of quoting, writes in his magisterial *Democracy in America* that "it is by the prescriptions relative to public education that, from the beginning, one sees revealed in the full light of day the original character of American civilization" (Tocqueville 2000, 41). He proceeds to quote the "old deluder, Satan" law from the Massachusetts Code of 1650, which created schools in all of the townships and required the inhabitants "under penalty of heavy fines, to tax themselves to support them" (41). Like Jefferson and Smith, Tocqueville saw an intimate connection between education and the achievement of a free society: "One cannot doubt that in the United States the instruction of the people serves powerfully to maintain a democratic republic" (2000, 291).

Smith, Jefferson, and Tocqueville share a common conviction that politics cannot be understood simply in managerial, contractual, or economic terms. Limited government requires people of a certain character, and therefore people who care about a free society cannot be indifferent to whatever influences the character of citizens for good or ill. At the same time, parents have the right (and the duty) to oversee the education of their children, and there is no substitute for a stable family for the proper rearing of children.

Properly conceived, both of these are legitimate and complementary interests. In the conservative perspective, progressives, placing too much authority on the side of the state, would displace rightful roles of parents with the nanny state; libertarians, placing rights on the side of parents, would surrender children to the utter negligence, and even abuse, of some parents. Better would be a solution that assists parents in their duty to educate without displacing their rightful authority.

The most conservative way to do this corresponds to Smith's suggestion that education be subject in some degree to market forces: Give every parent a fixed voucher per child for education expenses. The voucher scheme furthers the public interest in education, assists parents in their rightful authority and duty, expands the options for parents and children, and places market pressure on educators to succeed. In this scheme, public schools (if they exist) would be subject to competition from private schools. There would be conditions on schools that qualify for vouchers, but those conditions would be determined by local communities, especially parents, and not professional bureaucrats. This is not a libertarian solution; it is a conservative one in that it recognizes that education is part of the common good and that political authority therefore may make provision for it but in a way that relies most on the associations and authorities of civil society.

Marriage

Marriage has recently become a hotly contested political issue in America. Whereas progressives have sought to preserve marriage as a public institution—but to expand it to include homosexual and, in some cases, polygamous relationships—libertarians have sought to eliminate the unique public dimension of marriage altogether, replacing it with ordinary contracts. Although these seem like different goals, they are both animated by a similar commitment to individual autonomy that, consistently followed, must result in the libertarian goal of completely privatizing marriage. In the minds of conservatives, such a goal would strike a blow to limited government.

The conservatism I have been defending seeks to "conserve" the principles of the American founding. The founders were profoundly aware that limited government is not a bare, neutral coordination mechanism that can simply be imposed on a fixed and constant human nature but is a rare and delicate historical, cultural, and political achievement whose conditions must be protected and preserved with vigilance. Arguably the most important of these conditions is marriage. Limited government depends on a robust and virtuous civil society, of which marriage is a foundation.

As we have discussed, conservatives follow Edmund Burke, F. A. Hayek, and Alasdair MacIntyre in regarding traditions of various sorts not as irrational prejudices fostered by unenlightened peoples but as a form of knowledge that can be understood, developed, and corrected by rational inquiry over time. Few traditions are more firmly and uniformly established than the institution of marriage. Despite some cultural and historical differences on the nature of marriage, every known human culture throughout history has agreed on two things: First, marriage is essentially a *public* institution, requiring some kind of formal sanction, recognition, and enforcement of norms by the other members of the community; second, marriage is intrinsically *heterosexual*. In the last fifty years progressives and libertarians have called these beliefs into question.

How far we have traveled from the conservative view of limited government can be gauged by comparing the Supreme Court's treatment of marriage in *Reynolds v. United States* in 1878 to the Court's more recent treatment in *Obergefell v. Hodges* in 2015. At issue in *Reynolds* was a congressional statute prohibiting polygamy in the federal territories—one that George Reynolds, a Mormon convicted under the statute, claimed was a violation of the free exercise clause of the First Amendment. Writing for a unanimous court, Justice Morrison Waite upheld the conviction and the statute. Waite denied that the legal prohibition of polygamy rests on theological grounds. His remarks on the subject are worth quoting:

> Polygamy has always been odious among the northern and western nations of Europe . . . At common law, the second marriage was always void (2 Kent, Com. 79), and from the earliest history of England, polygamy has been treated as an offence against society . . . From that day to this, we think it may safely be said there never has been a time in any State of the Union when polygamy has not been an offence against society, cognizable by the civil courts and punishable with more or less severity . . . Marriage, while from its very nature a sacred obligation, is nevertheless, in most civilized nations, a civil contract, and usually regulated by law. Upon it society may be said to be built, and out of its fruits spring social relations and social obligations and duties with which government is necessarily required to deal.

Justice Waite then highlighted the intimate historical (also anthropological) connection between marital and political principles:

> In fact, according as monogamous or polygamous marriages are allowed, do we find the principles on which the government of the people, to a greater or less extent, rests. Professor Lieber says, polygamy leads to the patriarchal principle, and which, when applied to large communities, fet-

ters the people in stationary despotism, while that principle cannot long exist in connection with monogamy. Chancellor Kent observes that this remark is equally striking and profound. 2 Kent, Com. 81, note (e) . . . There cannot be a doubt that . . . it is within the legitimate scope of the power of every civil government to determine whether polygamy or mo- nogamy shall be the law of social life under its dominion.[7]

The crux of what Justice Waite expresses here is the conservative view that marriage is by its very nature both a private and a political institution with its own objective features and norms.[8] Consider now Justice Kennedy's opinion for the Court in *Obergefell*. Despite Justice Kennedy's many poetic paeans to marriage, the core of his opinion is exemplified in one statement: "A first premise of the Court's relevant precedents is that the right to per- sonal choice regarding marriage is inherent in the concept of individual au- tonomy."[9] This premise underlies Justice Kennedy's conclusion that laws that limit legal marriage to a man and a woman violate both the liberty and the equality of same-sex couples and are, therefore, unconstitutional. This inter- pretation radically transforms the meaning of marriage from a public institu- tion with objective ends, features, and norms to a private contract that can be conceived of differently by autonomous individuals

Because most libertarians (including Wenzel) support the decision in *Obergefell*, it's useful to state the conservative case against it. This will also help highlight the conservative case for legal marriage.

In the first place, conservatives view the Court's decision as striking a blow to democratic self-government by substituting the views of five un- elected judges for the deliberative will of American citizens in their respective states. The legalization of same-sex marriage in American has been facilitated by judges, as opposed to elected officials, beginning with *Goodridge v. De- partment of Public Health* in Massachusetts in 2003. And it is notable that, despite all the shifting opinion polls in favor of same-sex marriage, when left to the deliberative democratic process only eleven states approved same-sex marriage.

Secondly, although conservatives believe in liberty and equality before they law, they point out that discrimination (for example, between victims and criminals) is in the very nature of law. The real question is whether the legal discrimination in question has a rational basis or is merely motivated by prejudice. And conservatives argue that whereas antimiscegenation laws can be explained only by racial prejudice (and so such laws, historically speaking, have been rare and widely condemned), laws limiting marriage to heterosexual couples have a rational basis in the intimate relationship between sexual union and the bearing of children.

Marital sex reverberates in two directions, and this dual structure is the reason for the traditional marital norms of monogamy, exclusivity, and permanence. On the one hand, sexual union is the distinctive ground of real, organic unity of the spouses on the biological level because only in the heterosexual conjugal act can two persons form one reproductive principle (thus the term *conjugal* from the Latin *conjungere*, "to join.") This comprehensive unity, this sharing of hearts, minds, wills, and bodies, is the essential and private good of marriage and remains a good even when that unity does not (or cannot) in fact result in children. (And so infertile heterosexual marriage is still comprehensively unifying.)[10]

On the other hand, sexual union is naturally apt for the bearing and rearing of children. This is the public ground of marriage because how children are reared potentially and profoundly affects everyone else in the social order. Despite loud disagreements over marriage and the family in the public square, there quietly exists a strong consensus among social scientists that children do best when raised by their married biological parents. As one report summarizing the conclusions of the major studies on marriage and the family puts it, "The intact, biological family remains the gold standard for family life in the United States, insofar as children are most likely to thrive—economically, socially, and psychologically—in this family form" (Wilcox 2011, 11). To put the point negatively, children raised outside of families headed by two married biological parents are at significantly greater risk for virtually every social pathology: poverty, illegitimacy, divorce, drug abuse, illness, crime, and low performance in school.[11]

This leads to the third critique from a conservative view. Nonintact families inflict considerable costs on the rest of society that inevitably contribute to the growth of government. As Jennifer Roback Morse puts it, "A society which allows the dissolution of marriage for any reason or no reason will not be a minimal government society for very long" (George and Elshtain 2006, 74). In the language of economics, traditional legal marriage, by privileging the best arrangement for the care and rearing of children, is the most unobtrusive and inexpensive way for a society to treat the inevitable positive and negative externalities of child rearing.

In sum, conservatives believe that there are strong reasons for the legal recognition of the conjugal view of marriage. The law cannot make marriage, any more than it can make the natural rights of persons. Just as the law ought to recognize and protect the natural rights of persons, so the law ought to recognize and protect marriage, structuring our government (tax policies, property law, visitation and inheritance rights, and so on) in ways appropriate to the nature of that union.[12]

To the progressive or libertarian who objects to the account of marriage given here, the conservative asks: What is marriage, if not a uniquely comprehensive (and thus bodily) union of one man and one woman? It is precisely the inability of progressives to respond adequately to this question that leads to the libertarian conclusion. For if marriage is not intrinsically heterosexual, if it must include whatever romantic or loving bond autonomous individuals want it to be, then it is difficult to see how it could have any other intrinsic features (twoness, for example) that could defeat the objection of those who have been excluded from it. Opponents of same-sex marriage are not making ad hominem or slippery slope arguments when they point out that the principal arguments for extending legal marriage to same-sex couples, by their own inner logic, also apply to virtually any consensual adult relationship (see Girgis, George, and Anderson 2011, 250).[13] But, if marriage is whatever autonomous individuals want it to be, then the justification for legal marriage has evaporated.[14] In this case, libertarian David Boaz is perfectly right to ask, "Why should the government be in the business of decreeing who can and cannot be married?" (Boaz 1997b). Boaz would treat marriage like an ordinary contract:

> If they wanted to contract for a traditional breadwinner/homemaker setup, with specified rules for property and alimony in the event of divorce, they could do so. Less traditional couples could keep their assets separate and agree to share specified expenses. Those with assets to protect could sign prenuptial agreements that courts would respect. Marriage contracts could be as individually tailored as other contracts are

in our diverse capitalist world. For those who wanted a standard one-size-fits-all contract, that would still be easy to obtain. Wal-Mart could sell books of marriage forms next to the standard rental forms. Couples would then be spared the surprise discovery that outsiders had changed their contract without warning. Individual churches, synagogues, and temples could make their own rules about which marriages they would bless. (Boaz 1997b)

Boaz's proposal to treat marriage as an ordinary contract corresponds best to the logic of libertarianism. But Boaz does not attend to the rights or needs of children. And it is far from clear how the availability and proliferation of "throuples," "wedleases," and "monogamish" marriages (all ideas coming from mainstream publications) will promote this end.[15] That children would suffer from the complete privatization of marriage cannot, of course, be proved because it has never been tried. However, the precedent of no-fault divorce, which resulted in a doubling of the divorce rate (nearly always to the detriment of women and children) is not promising (see Wilcox 2009 and Murray 2012).

Despite its apparent neutrality, the change Boaz proposes replaces one definition of marriage (a comprehensive union of a man and a woman, actualized in reproductive-type acts that are apt to produce children and are governed by norms of exclusivity and permanence) with another (marriage is whatever private individuals want it to be). In either case the law will have an expressive effect on the social understanding of marriage and on practices that follow on that meaning. As Martin Luther King Jr. claimed, "The law itself is a form of education" (*Stride* 199) even when it is silent.

Finally, conservatives argue that proposals from libertarians such as Boaz do not expand freedom but reduce it. There is nothing today that prevents individuals from contracting in the way Boaz suggests. But the elimination of legal marriage (as historically understood) prevents those who believe in that longstanding institution from living according to their beliefs.

Marriage is a fitting subject on which to conclude this debate, for it serves to illustrate the core issues that divide conservatives and libertarians. If the human body is the ground of individuality, liberty, and natural rights, the sexual complementary inscribed on the body points to the human incompleteness, neediness, and dependence that make marriage and the family a necessary foundation for human flourishing. Libertarians acknowledge the individual dignity that is rooted in human subjectivity and in the incommunicable singularity of the body, but they are less ready to acknowledge the internal and dynamic ordering of this dignity to another kind of dignity, the fulfillment of persons in communities rooted in an order of truth and goodness. It is precisely here where spiritual qualities like love, justice, duty, generosity, gratitude, and caregiving are born and sustained and without which no human association, and certainly no limited and free government, can ultimately survive.

For Further Reading

In *Vindicating the Founders: Race, Sex, Class, and Justice in the Origins of America*, Thomas G. West offers a brief but compelling summary and defense of the founders' principled positions on immigration, education, and marriage, among other things. For a more detailed articulation of a conservative position on immigration, see *The Immigration Solution: A Better Plan Than Today's*, by Heather MacDonald, Victor Davis Hanson, and Steven Malanga. For the best arguments in defense of traditional marriage, see Sherif Girgis, Ryan T. Anderson, and Robert P. George, *What Is Marriage? Man and Woman: A Defense*. (See also Ryan Anderson's most recent book, written in light of *Obergefell v. Hodges*, *Truth Overruled: The Future of Marriage and Religious Freedom*.

CHAPTER SEVEN

A Conservative's Conclusion

NATHAN W. SCHLUETER

IN OUR PREFACE, WENZEL AND I EXPRESSED our agreement that there is no silver bullet deductive argument that can conclusively determine the debate between libertarians and conservatives. Wenzel's arguments against natural law liberalism illustrate why this is so. Wenzel presents three formidable challenges to natural law liberalism. First, how can "fallible human beings with limited cognitive capacities" have confidence that they know the "objective moral order"? Second, how can a good be called "common" that is not voluntarily agreed to by each and all of the parties but that coercively imposes on some of the parties the "interests, desires, and preferences" of others? Finally, does it make any sense to speak of a "single philosophy of the American founding," rather than seeing America as a history of conflict between the advocates of libertarian ideals, as expressed in the Declaration of Independence, and the advocates of strong government, as expressed in the U.S. Constitution?

These are indeed pressing questions, and I have attempted to account for each of them in my defense of conservatism in the preceding pages. (A fully adequate response would require a separate book on each.) But it is worth repeating here, if only briefly, some of what I have said previously, to make clearer what is at stake in the disagreement between libertarians and conservatives. Above all, the reader should notice that Wenzel's arguments, if they pose challenges for conservatism, also undermine his own case for libertarianism. If this is true, the real question is whether conservatism or libertarianism overall has the better resources to deal with the problems that concern libertarians.

Begin with Wenzel's arguments about moral knowledge. Wenzel frets about changes in belief concerning the requirements of the natural law, but he does not point out that one can observe a similar pattern in scientific discovery: Aristotle is replaced by Newton; Newton is revised and augmented by Einstein. Cosmology, physics, chemistry, biology have all been subject to change, development, and fundamental revision. Yet it is not reasonable to conclude from this fact that scientific knowledge does not exist or to deny that some scientific claims are better than others. And this is true, even if some portion of the world's population repudiates the premises and conclusions of modern science (as they do). Why should we expect moral inquiry to be exempt from the same kinds of change, development, and revision that we find in the natural sciences?

As philosophers like Michael Polanyi, Thomas Kuhn, and Alasdair MacIntyre have made clear, scientific, philosophical, and moral inquiry do not ground human experience; they grow from human experience. They necessarily exist as historical traditions, requiring for their success and development a shared language, shared standards of achievement, a shared acquisition of knowledge already gained and of outstanding problems or questions that demand further inquiry. These traditions of inquiry involve elements of continuity and rupture, consensus, and conflict. (For a more extensive treatment of these issues, see MacIntyre 1999 and 2006).

If this account of knowledge is accurate, as I think it is, then Wenzel is simply unreasonable to make the truth of moral principles depend on simple clarity, immunity to change over time, and the universal consensus of human beings. This expectation reflects a Cartesian rationalism that no human knowledge, including knowledge of economics, can successfully meet and that can only end in skepticism about all knowledge, including the knowledge of libertarianism.

And so, not surprisingly, Wenzel's own arguments against the natural law subtly rely on natural law reasoning. "How do we explain the awful things that have been done to promote the good forcefully," Wenzel asks, "from slavery to execution of those who did not attend weekly services, and from denial of basic rights to women or racial minorities, to arbitrary deprivation of property or life by an absolute monarch?" Wenzel exaggerates when he claims that "all of these things were justified, at some point, by the contemporary understanding of natural law" (and I am not sure what he means by "contemporary"). But how does Wenzel know that these "awful things" are wrong, except by reasoning from the natural law? Indeed, how does Wenzel know that violating the rights of others is wrong?

Wenzel's confusing combination of skepticism about moral knowledge and conviction about libertarianism is intimately related to his reservations about the conservative conception of the common good. Wenzel seems to conclude that because human beings disagree about moral principles, that the government ought to be neutral with respect to those claims. I have already pointed out that this argument involves a logical fallacy, that one cannot derive a conclusion of moral obligation from a premise of moral skepticism.

Moreover, it is notable that Wenzel continues to describe moral claims in the economic language of "interests, desires, and preferences." I have argued in the preceding chapters why this substitution of economic for moral language fundamentally distorts the natural meaning of language users. Moral judgments, at least implicitly, are impersonal and universal truth claims and are thus subject to reasons and arguments in a way that preferences are not. This fact is illustrated in our case studies. The reader will notice that Wenzel and I do not merely assert our preferences for and against open borders, education, and marriage; we use arguments and evidence in support of our assertions, convinced that there is a truth of the matter about which the reader might be convinced, even if neither of our positions has the simple clarity, historical immunity to change, and universal assent that Wenzel requires of moral knowledge.

Our disagreement in the case studies further shows that the libertarian principle of government neutrality with respect to competing conceptions of the good is impossible. No position on the issue of open borders is in fact a position in favor of open borders. Political authority therefore *must* come down one way or another on these issues, and however it comes down, whether in the libertarian or conservative direction, it will favor some conceptions of the good over others. Despite its claims to the contrary, libertarianism, like conservatism, is informed by a positive view of the good society that it seeks to realize through coercive law. Thus Wenzel's objections to the conservative conception of the common good apply equally to libertarianism.

The fact that politics necessarily involves disagreement over competing conceptions of the good relates to the third part of Wenzel's criticism. Here, as with his account of moral knowledge, Wenzel seems to require for an adequate account of political identity that the political principles be clear, immune from historical change, and subject to unanimous agreement. And here again, I submit, such expectations are unreasonable, given what we know about human nature and knowledge.

Like scientific and moral knowledge, political knowledge is inevitably historical and subject to its own processes and pressures. This is true not only for the general features of political life but especially for the particular identities that characterize diverse political associations. The singularity of the American political identity, exemplified in the principles of the American founding, is to ground its particularity in principles open to the universal claims of nature and reason. Every American founder acknowledged the precarious nature of this experiment, both its promises and its dangers. They knew that politics is a permanent feature of human existence and that a free society and a free government are rare and difficult achievements that must be won anew by each generation. Not only did they bestow on Americans better, freer political institutions than the world had seen, and has yet to see; they exemplified for future generations the kind of prudence, courage, moderation, and wisdom required to defend, and improve, those institutions.

Libertarians and conservatives agree that we live in a time when that inheritance is deeply threatened. Whether the best response to that threat lies in a libertarian philosophy that, like progressivism, repudiates the American founding and denies the necessity of political life or in the steadfast defense of the American inheritance through the messiness of political life, the reader must decide.

In sum, Wenzel seems to commit two Nirvana fallacies in his arguments against conservatism, one epistemological, the other political. First, Wenzel questions the best standards of human knowledge because they do not offer the simplicity and clarity that only angelic beings could have. Second, Wenzel assumes that, because governments often fail by abusing power or becoming tyrannous, one therefore must embrace a form of government that has never existed in the whole of human history.

Conservatism, on the other hand, refuses to measure human knowledge or political life by anything other than the nature we have been given, as it has been discovered through human history and experience. Conservatism does not offer human beings the firm confidence of a demonstrative proof or the heady excitement of a neatly unified system. But it does provide the best guide to reality and the best hope for the preservation of political liberty and human flourishing.

CHAPTER EIGHT

A Libertarian's Conclusion

NIKOLAI G. WENZEL

I THANK MY FRIEND NATHAN SCHLUETER for engaging with me in a civil, productive, and constructive debate. Even after we have both carefully laid out our assumptions and foundations, there will linger some disagreement between our two positions. That is to be expected and is even welcome. In these concluding remarks, I will not seek to address and rebut every one of Schlueter's points. I invite the reader to judge and to dig more deeply into these questions. My purpose here is merely to tie things together.

Conservatism: Good Aspiration, Bad Outcome

I should start by pointing out that there are many strengths and noble aspirations in conservatism.

Conservatism's emphasis on an objective moral order is a useful foil against oppression, torture, and the tyranny of the majority.

Conservatism rightly points out that virtue and good character are necessary foundations for a free society.

Conservatism is naïve about politics, public service, and the common good, but its romantic vision, if properly constrained by libertarianism's realistic analysis, might serve to inspire us and to demand better behavior from our elected officials. Perhaps conservatism can be the heart, and libertarianism the mind, of public life.

Conservatism's emphasis on human flourishing offers a laudable and refreshing aspiration in an often crass and materialistic world.

Conservatism's prudent emphasis on the subsidiary role of the state and its espousal of somewhat limited government are a welcome change from today's rampant interventionism. (Note that this applies only to the principled conservatism presented by Schlueter and not to the vast majority of today's political conservatives, who suffer from what Ayn Rand decried as "metooism" vis-à-vis their alleged political enemies.)

Finally, conservatism's emphasis on community and a communal spirit offers a call to action against the anomic and atomistic tendencies of radical individualism and the contemporary American proclivity for "bowling alone" (Putnam 2000).

Unfortunately, the means by which conservatism would advance these noble aspirations are coercive and self-defeating. Each of conservatism's virtues becomes a vice when it is imposed coercively and through central planning.

Without clear epistemological foundations, the "objective" moral order becomes merely an imposition of private preferences through public means.

Just as virtue is important, government imposition of virtue will lead to tyranny and unintended consequences.

Just as a romantic vision of politics can lift our hearts, a naïve understanding of politics provides a convenient shield for naked power and rampant redistribution.

Just as human flourishing is a noble aspiration for civilization, any attempt to advance it through government—beyond providing a basic framework of rights within which individuals can pursue their happiness and flourish—is doomed ab initio.

Just as subsidiarity is more prudent than wholesale interventionism, it still uses the coercion of a flawed and ignorant political process. In its rejection of principle, it will lead to government failure.

The conservative emphasis on community reminds us, in the words of poet John Donne, that "no man is an island / entire of itself" but that "any man's death diminishes me / Because I am involved in mankind." However, conservatism's communitarianism is not grounded in the rights of individuals freely associating but in the alleged right of an abstract "community." Although conservatism would endow that community with powers to curb individual choice, robust political economy reminds us that a "community" is typically only a majority, or a vocal minority that has captured the political process.

Conservatism is self-defeating, as it naively deploys the coercive apparatus of the state to advance private preferences through public means while disregarding human nature and the constraints of robust political economy. Conservatism is also arbitrary in the preferences it seeks to advance, as evinced by the multitude of different conservatisms and different immoral behaviors that different flavors of conservatism would ban.

In sum, conservatism has many strengths and many valuable lessons. But it is ultimately inimical to liberty—and to human flourishing.

The Libertarian Alternative

Libertarianism is subject to ridicule from critics of both the left and the right. "So, you're a libertarian, eh? How many babies did you throw out in the snow so the rich could get another tax break?" To his credit, Schlueter does not engage in such attacks. He does, however, express misplaced worries about libertarianism. Libertarianism does not erode public spirit by proclaiming that the emperor has no clothes—instead, it places constraints on our romantic aspirations. Libertarianism has most certainly not allied with modern liberals to undermine the moral fabric of America—instead, libertarianism decries both moral decay and the interventionism that fosters it.

Libertarianism, through its emphasis on markets, civil society, and a government limited to the defense of rights, promotes human material and nonmaterial flourishing. It provides a space where people can pursue their happiness and cooperate with others to flourish. Markets provide goods, and civil society provides virtue. Rendering unto Caesar, the state limits itself to defending individual rights, lest it destroy markets and civil society in its attempts to impose preferences.

I will close by responding to two of Schlueter's objections because they are so central to the libertarian–conservative debate.

Schlueter rightly points out the distinction between moral judgments and preferences. It bears repeating that libertarianism is not moral relativism; it is merely humble about knowledge and cautious about imposing that knowledge. A Chinese proverb says that "there are three truths: my truth, your truth, and the truth." Although libertarianism rejects the moral relativism that claims that there is no truth, it is also very cautious about imposing what is (most likely) a flawed understanding of the truth as *the* truth—especially through a flawed political process and especially by the sword. Conservatives should be doubly leery of imposing their understanding of the truth as *the* truth through coercion. They should remember that natural law has historically been used to justify such awful things as slavery, the absolute right of monarchs, torture, and death of dissenters—all of which natural law somehow now rejects. Conservatives would impose their understanding of the truth, and their moral judgments, through the political process and through state coercion; they are thus attempting to impose their private preference (a world that conforms to their understanding of the truth and their moral judgments) through public means. Libertarianism rejects this on grounds of epistemology and justice and seeks instead to persuade, except in the very limited case of protection of individual rights.

Consider a thought exercise. Take any disputed policy, whether drugs or same-sex marriage or education, and suppose a conservative policy is imposed by some on everybody. If conservatives are right, we may indeed have a good outcome (assuming that government has the means to reach the desired ends, which is, of course, a heroic assumption). If conservatives are wrong, we will have a disaster on our hands, with awful outcomes, unintended policies, and destroyed lives. On the other hand, suppose libertarians are able to protect individual rights and oppose the conservative imposition. If they are right that the policy in question is not wrong, time will vindicate them, with good outcomes along the way. If libertarians are wrong, the problem can still be addressed through persuasion, civil society, and markets (and without the unintended consequences of government). In sum, conservatism would do well to practice a bit of humility before it imposes its preferences coercively.

Second, Schlueter rightly points out that the libertarian promotion of government neutrality rests on a particular conception of knowledge and the human good and is thus not neutral. Indeed, libertarianism rests on the defense of individual rights and the rejection of imposition of knowledge of some on others. That is, after all, the very premise of libertarianism! Freedom and individual rights are good; coercion and imposition are bad. This is admittedly a nonneutral foundation. However, libertarianism shows that any further government activity will violate individual rights (and lead to undesirable and unintended consequences), so the government should remain otherwise neutral, beyond the defense of individual rights. Schlueter further worries that libertarianism compels those who disagree with libertarianism to live in a social order they reasonably believe to interfere with their pursuit of the good and that libertarianism prohibits others from seeking to promote their moral judgments through law with reasoned arguments. This is correct: Libertarianism compels everybody to respect the individual rights of others, and it indeed prohibits anybody from imposing ends (including moral judgments) on others through the coercive apparatus of the state. A communist village, or a commune without property rights, or a religious community that bans sinful activity and rewards virtue can all exist within a libertarian system; the opposite does not hold.

Conclusion

Libertarianism is not perfect—nor, aware of the Nirvana fallacy and the limitations of fallible human beings, does it claim to be. However, libertarianism, with its defense of individual rights, private property, voluntary exchange and cooperation, civil society, and market incentives and its realistic assessment of human ignorance and nonbenevolence provides the system that is most likely to allow for human flourishing and that most minimizes the opportunity for humanity's uglier proclivities from lapsing into harm and disaster.

To be sure, tensions exist within libertarianism. There is honest discussion among the classical liberals (who claim that minarchy and anarchy do not address isolated cases of market failure), the anarcho-capitalists (who claim that minarchy is still coercive, as the minimal state will be financed by taxes), and the minarchists (who claim to have found a happy medium). I disagree with the ultimate conclusions of the two thinkers, F. A. Hayek and James M. Buchanan, who have most influenced me. They blazed glorious trails on the road to freedom but didn't go quite far enough. Plenty of ink has already been spilled on these subtleties, and it is not my purpose to add here to an already rich conversation.

For all these lingering and difficult questions, libertarianism is still a philosophy of human liberty and human flourishing. The same cannot be said of conservatism.

I close with an excerpt from F. A. Hayek's explanation, "Why I Am Not a Conservative" (Hayek 1960). Although Hayek was writing primarily about European conservatism, his critique also applies to American conservatism and Schlueter's natural law liberalism:

> Let me return, however, to the main point, which is the characteristic complacency of the conservative toward the action of established authority and his prime concern that this authority be not weakened rather than that its power be kept within bounds. This is difficult to reconcile with the preservation of liberty. In general, it can probably be said that the conservative does not object to coercion or arbitrary power so long as it is used for what he regards as the right purposes. He believes that if government is in the hands of decent men, it ought not to be too much restricted by rigid rules. Since he is essentially opportunist and lacks principles, his main hope must be that the wise and the good will rule— not merely by example, as we all must wish, but by authority given to them and enforced by them. Like the socialist, he is less concerned with the problem of how the powers of government should be limited than with that of who wields them; and, like the socialist, he regards himself as entitled to force the value he holds on other people. (Hayek 1960, 401; notes omitted)

There lurks a deep contradiction within conservatism. Indeed, conservatism decries excessive or inefficient government, progressivism, venal politicians, and social engineering. But it will not take the final step of recognizing that interventionism itself is the problem. Instead, conservatism seems to think that the right kind of government, and the right kind of intervention, and the right people in power will somehow overcome the inherent flaws of the political process and robust political economy. Alas, "the right kind of interventionism" will not solve the problems inherent to interventionism. Instead of adopting conservatism's tortured and romantic use of state power, physiologists of the body politic would do better to adopt libertarianism's Hippocratic oath.[1]

Primum non nocere: First, do no harm. *There* is a maxim for good government. Translated into political economy, this medical maxim is best reflected in the writings of the Marquis d'Argenson, who gives a simple answer to what government can really do to help:

> *Laissez faire!* That should be the motto of all public powers, since the beginning of civilization . . . What a detestable notion to claim that we cannot flourish, except at the expense of our neighbors! Only wickedness and malice of the heart is satisfied with such a principle and human interest is opposed to it. *Laissez faire,* for heaven's sake! *Laissez faire!* (Argenson 1858, 362).

Laissez faire, laissez passer! Let us live peacefully; do not hinder us. Protect our rights, then stop. Such is the libertarian vision for human liberty and human flourishing.

Notes

Introduction

1. Technically, we should refer to "left-liberalism" to distinguish it from classical liberalism, a point we explain in the following discussion.

2. As Murray Rothbard points out in his essay, "Frank S. Meyer: The Fusionist as Libertarian *Manqué*" (Carey 2004 [1984], 135–162), fusionism is really libertarianism. It is too early to judge the success of conservatarianism, but Charles Cooke's objections to libertarianism in *The Conservatarian Manifesto* are not likely to win over libertarians.

3. Carey 2004 [1984] offers a rich collection of essays on libertarianism versus conservatism. Although the individual essays are (mostly) insightful, there is no cohesive thread, and they often talk past each other. We nonetheless owe a debt of intellectual gratitude to the late Dr. Carey.

Chapter One: What Is Conservatism?

1. Not all narratives of historical development are subject to Butterfield's critique of Whig history, which focuses on nineteenth-century progressive historians. See Butterfield 1965. Indeed, as Alasdair MacIntyre argues, all knowledge (including scientific knowledge) depends on an account of historical development. See MacIntyre 2006, especially "Epistemological Crises, Dramatic Narrative and the Philosophy of Science" (3–23) and "Moral Relativism, Truth and Justification" (52–85).

2. Of course, this is a simplified picture. There are "liberaltarian" libertarians who positively repudiate conservatism and seek alliances with progressivism (see, for example, Lindsey 2010), and the Christian right and Tea Party movements don't fit neatly into any of these categories. But the Christian right and Tea Party can to some extent be characterized as grassroots populist movements in search of clarification about their own identity.

3. I am reminded here of C. S. Lewis's remark on love, bettering Emerson's quip that when love ceases to be a god, he ceases to be a demon: "Only when love ceases to be a God, can . . ." See also his similar remark on nature in miracles.

4. See Meyer, "The Twisted Tree of Liberty," and Rothbard, "Frank S. Meyer: The Fusionist as Libertarian *Manqué*" in Carey 2004 [1984], 13–19 and 135–162, respectively.

5. This is especially true in the free market, whose price system allows for the best coordination and uses widely dispersed information. See Hayek's essay, "The Use of Knowledge in Society," in Hayek 1996, 77–91. But it also applies to noncommercial activities and associations.

6. For the most comprehensive and insightful account of this strategy, see Rahe 1994.

7. For an overview of this argument, see Hannan 2013.

8. Hayek is quoting a sermon by Joseph Butler.

9. Although this phrase is commonly attributed to Irving Kristol, I have not been able to track down its source.

10. By "American founding," I mean both the revolutionary and constitutional periods (roughly 1765–1790), and especially the most important documents of that period, the state constitutions, the Declaration of Independence, and the U.S. Constitution. My use of the word "founders" refers to the primary leaders during this period, especially George Washington, Thomas Jefferson, and the writers of the *Federalist Papers* (James Madison, Alexander Hamilton, and John Jay).

11. They would have agreed with Franklin's guarded optimism on the last day of the constitutional convention. The most evident conflict between principle and practice was the constitutional protection of slavery, but the founders were well aware of this conflict, and their actions with respect to slavery can be understood as a prudential compromise in the service of principle. For an elaboration of this argument, see Herbert Storing's "Slavery and the Moral Foundations of the American Republic" in Storing 1995, 131–150, and West 1997, 1–36.

12. Hayek 1996, 4, citing R. Bisset in *The Life of Edmund Burke*.

13. See, for example, Skinner 1978, Tierney 1997, and Chafuen 2003. As yet there is no comprehensive monograph that carefully distinguishes the lines of argument and influence among these thinkers, but the similarities among them are striking and notable.

14. Of course it would take centuries for these ideas to work themselves out (and indeed they are still being worked out), and there are differences among Christians (especially between Catholics and Protestants) over how that history is told, but there can be little doubt that Christianity fundamentally changes the meaning of politics. On the ancient unity of theology and politics, see Coulanges 1980. On the liberal influence of Christianity, see Tocqueville 2000. For a more recent elaboration of the argument, see Siedentop 2014.

15. In my judgment, the best works on this subject to date are by Lutz 1988 and Rahe 1994. But for other influential works, see also Bailyn 1967, Wood 1969, and McDonald 1985.

16. Wolfe's book is largely critical in nature. He promises a second volume in which he lays out the positive requirements of natural law liberalism. Unfortunately that volume has not yet appeared. He may or may not agree with my account here.

17. Natural law reasoning began in ancient Greece, developed through Roman stoicism, early Christianity, the Middle Ages, and the early modern era; it languished in the nineteenth century and then experienced an energetic renewal in the twentieth century that continues today. The most influential thinker of this particular tradition is of course Thomas Aquinas, although it includes thinkers before him, such as Aristotle, Cicero, and Augustine, and thinkers after him, such as Suarez, Cajetan, Jacques Maritain, and, most recently, John Finnis (Finnis 2011). For a helpful summary of this tradition and an evaluation of the competing arguments, see Douglas Kries (2008). In calling the natural law a tradition, I am taking sides with Alasdair MacIntyre (2009) on the point that moral reasoning has a history and cannot be articulated a priori.

18. See Arkes 1986, Budziszewski 1997, George 1999, Finnis 2011, and, most recently, Snell 2014.

19. According to Thomas Aquinas this is the first precept of the natural law: "The good is to be done and pursued, and evil is to be avoided" (Aquinas 1981, I–II, q. 94, a. 2).

20. See Hayek 2011 [1960], Polanyi 1962, and MacIntyre 2006, especially "Epistemological Crises, Dramatic Narrative and the Philosophy of Science" (3–23) and "Moral Relativism, Truth and Justification" (52–85).

21. This historical or developmental view of the natural law is supported by Lewis 1974. See especially the discussion at 44–51, in which Lewis compares the natural law to poetry and contrasts true development from within and innovation from without.

22. Although Finnis would not likely describe himself as a "conservative," his thought corresponds closely to the kind of conservatism I am defending here.

23. For a development of this argument, see Finnis 2011, especially chapters 3 and 4. Finnis's departure from Aquinas's famous threefold order of goods (94–95) and his account of practical reason operating independently of speculative and metaphysical judgments have been challenged by a number of Thomists. See, for example, Hittinger 1989 and Long 2007. It would be fruitful to compare Finnis with John Locke, who also maintains in his *An Essay Concerning Human Understanding* that happiness is the greatest object of human desire (Locke 1959, II.XXI.42–43) and also acknowledges the diversity of ways in which happiness is achieved (ibid., II.XXI.56). But, as Fraser's annotations repeatedly point out (Locke 1959), Locke's theory of human action, which reduces happiness to pleasure and pleasure to the relief of "uneasiness" (II.XXI.31), makes it very difficult to see how he avoids determinism.

24. Locke begins the third book of his *Essay Concerning Human Understanding* with the following claim: "God, having designed man for a sociable creature, made him not only with an inclination, and under a necessity to have fellowship with those of his own kind, but furnished him also with language, which was to be the great instrument and common tie of society" (Locke 1959, 3). He repeats this almost verbatim in the first sentence of chapter 6 of *The Second Treatise*. In linking human social life to language, Locke is similar to Aristotle in *The Politics* I.2. See also Thomas Jefferson in a letter to Thomas Law: "The Creator indeed would have been

a bungling artist, had he intended man for a social animal, without planting in him social dispositions" (Jefferson 1975, 542). Whether this means that for Locke and Jefferson human beings are *political* animals by nature is a much more difficult question to answer. If by *political* is meant coercive authority, then both Augustine and Thomas Aquinas would deny with Locke and Jefferson that human beings are political (that is, under coercive authority) by nature. See Thomas Aquinas's treatment of human equality and mastership in the state of innocence, in which he appeals approvingly to Augustine, in *Summa Theologiae* (1981, 1.96.3–4).

25. Libertarians sometimes appeal to Crusoe as a model of individualism and self-sufficiency. Indeed, anarchist Murray Rothbard refers to his theory as "a Crusoe social philosophy" (see Rothbard 2003, 29–34). *The Swiss Family Robinson*, published in 1812 by Johann David Wyss, is sometimes regarded as a communal response to DeFoe's individualism.

26. Aquinas 1981, II–II, q. 10, a. 11. See also his response to the question, "Should human law repress all vices?" (ibid., I–II, q. 96, a. 2).

27. See Leo Strauss (1965).

28. For an argument that the idea of natural rights originates in canonical disputes during the Middle Ages, see Brian Tierney (1997).

29. John Locke made clear in one of the most famous liberal defenses of property rights that the right to private property cannot be absolute, and he added to his labor theory of acquisition the proviso that there be "enough and as good left in common for others" (*Second Treatise on Government*, section 27). For a critique of Locke's arguments, see Nozick 1974, 174–182. There is not space here for a critique of Nozick's alternative theory of property rights, what he calls the "entitlement theory." Suffice to say here that the theory is connected to his larger arguments for libertarianism, which I will criticize in my next chapter.

30. The natural law does not, like progressivism, begin from a presumption of equality in property rights and then demand a justification for any inequalities. As Finnis puts it, "The objective of justice is not equality but the common good, the flourishing of all members of the community, and there is no reason to suppose that this flourishing of all is enhanced by treating everyone equally when distributing roles, opportunities, and resources" (Finnis 2011, 174). For a powerful defense of private property that is sympathetic to the concerns of progressivism, see Tomasi 2012.

31. For a very helpful philosophical treatment of why there cannot be a moral right to a wrong, see Robert George 1995, 110–128.

32. The state constitutions are Virginia (1776), Pennsylvania (1776), Maryland (1776), North Carolina (1776), New York (1777), and Massachusetts (1780).

33. See David Hume's critique in his essay "On the Social Contract" (Hume 1985, 465–487).

34. See chapter XIX of the *Second Treatise* and also Pitkin 1965 and 1966.

35. Locke 1988, 348. More generally, see Locke's *Second Treatise*, chapter VIII, especially 118–122.

36. See Randy Barnett's critique of tacit consent in Barnett 2004. See also Hannah Pitkin, 1965 and 1966.

37. Is it the need of the child? If so, why doesn't every adult have the same authority over children? Is it the biological connection between parent and child? But how can biology entail moral rights to coerce, and what does this mean for the authority of adoptive parents? The right answer seems to be some combination of both of these arguments: The needs of children for care and direction and the suitability of biological parents for providing it. For an excellent treatment of this subject, see Moschella 2012.

38. I appeal to *The Federalist Papers* here not only as one important source for interpreting the Constitution but also as an independent source of political wisdom.

39. For an overview of colonial and revolutionary police power legislation, see McDonald 1985.

40. See especially *Federalist 68* and *70*. For the most comprehensive and insightful account of this strategy, see Rahe 1994.

41. On the significance of the difference between "contracts" and "compacts" and on the American development of the compact theory of government, see Lutz 1988, especially 13–34.

42. Although a larger proportion of Americans were enfranchised than anywhere else in the world (and perhaps in human history), this still only included between 50 and 65 percent of white males. See Lutz 1988, 10. Notably free black citizens and (in New Jersey) women were allowed to, and did, vote at the time of the ratification of the Constitution. See West 1997, 75–79.

43. See Thomas Aquinas 1981, I–I, q. 105, a. 1.

Chapter Two: What Is Libertarianism?

1. Competitive Enterprise Institute, "Ten Thousand Commandments 2015: An Annual Snapshot of the Federal Regulatory State."

2. I thank Peter Boettke for this phrasing.

3. Thanks to reviewer Chris Coyne for help with phrasing this. For a thorough and accessible overview of intellectual history, see the opening chapters of Leighton and Lopez 2012; for a basic primer on public choice theory, see Buchanan and Tullock 1999.

4. I thank Geoffrey Lea for his help with phrasing these problems.

5. See National Taxpayers Union Foundation, "Who Pays Income Taxes 2013."

6. See Perry 2013.

7. For such inspiration, see, for example, Lewis 2009. Much as Lewis is beautiful on aesthetics, I take issue with his epistemological assertions.

8. This quotation, although widely attributed to George Washington, is likely apocryphal.

9. I thank Geoffrey Lea for his phrasing of a Misesian synthesis.

10. It is also associated with Virginia political economy, which can be grossly summarized as a synthesis of Chicago public choice theory and the Austrian knowledge problem; see Lea and Martin 2014.

11. In the tradition of John Stuart Mill, Hayek confines himself to adults of sound mind for his general argument (as do I, and as do almost all libertarians, with the notable exception of Murray Rothbard).

12. Hayek calls this "the fatal conceit," using the eponymous title of his last book (Hayek 1988).

13. I note that Schlueter adds a fourth category, morals legislation, to these three. He also makes the claim that morals legislation is compatible with classical liberalism. I am not convinced, but we have left this question to further research.

14. See Hayek 1944, 120–121; Hayek 1976, 87; and Hayek 1979b, 44–59 and chapter 9.

15. I should emphasize that all forms of libertarianism reject slavery (obviously). However, the philosophical case for humanitarian intervention in a foreign country is not clear. What is clear, however, is the lack of constitutional authority for the federal government to prevent a state from seceding from the Union, or to invade a foreign country to preserve liberty. It is also clear that, for Lincoln, ending slavery was secondary to preserving the Union; in a letter of 1862, he wrote: "My paramount object in this struggle is to save the Union, and is not to save or destroy slavery. If I could save the Union without freeing ANY slave I would do it, and if I could save it by freeing ALL the slaves I would do it; and if I could save it by freeing some and leaving others alone I would also do that. What I do about slavery and the colored race, I do because I believe it helps to save the Union; and what I forbear, because I do NOT believe it would help save the Union" (Lincoln 1862). Finally, it is also clear that Lincoln's wartime measures killed not only federalism, but also constitutional restraints on the federal government, thus paving the way for progressivism (see Hummel 1996).

16. Frédéric Bastiat makes a similar argument but then adds rights (see Bastiat 1995a [1848]).

17. See LeGuin 1975 for a chilling fictional example.

18. Especially contrasted with Pigou 1932, who proposed taxation as a remedy.

19. See Rosenberg and Birdzell 1987; McCloskey 2007, 1–54; or Wenzel 2008.

20. See Gwartney, Lawson, and Hall 2015.

21. Ayn Rand did not call herself a libertarian; nevertheless, I quote her here because she offers one of the strongest defenses of a system of individual liberty that I have found. See Rand 1967a,b,c.

22. Mises 1985 [1929] makes such a jump.

Chapter Three: What's Wrong with Conservatism

1. "Up to the point of laughter," per Aquinas's enjoiner (see Dailey 2012).

2. This expression was coined by Grover Norquist, president of Americans for Tax Reform.

3. See, for example, Edward H. Crane's question, "Is Hillary Clinton a Neocon?," posed after she complained on the campaign trail that the American nation (as a whole) lacked goals (Crane 2007).

4. The consumer price index has jumped from 9.9 to 233 since the Federal Reserve was created in 1913, indicating that the value of the dollar—one of the Federal Reserve's main responsibilities—has fallen dramatically (controlling for technological changes, a bundle of goods that would have cost $9.90 in 1913 now costs about $233; as a reference, consider the drop in real prices of food, computers, travel, and the like over the past two generations). Alternatively, in 1913, an ounce of gold sold for $18.93 (where it had been since 1833); today, an ounce of gold runs roughly $1,200 (after a peak of $1,900 during the writing of this book). In other words, the dollar, which was once worth roughly 1/20 ounce of gold, has fallen to roughly 1/1,200 ounce of gold, under the Federal Reserve's watch. To be fair, the Fed got help from a few presidents along the way.

5. I thank Chris Coyne for help with this distinction.

6. This was, in fact, the very question posed by a panel at the September 2001 meeting of the American Political Science Association. I thank the Claremont Institute and Dr. R. J. Pestritto for inviting me to be the lone libertarian voice, the lone affirmative (if tepid) on the panel. I also thank my fellow panelists for pushing my thinking.

7. To be sure, the Declaration contains other interesting material, from prudential considerations about the right time to alter government, consent of the governed, and a list of grievances, to the appropriateness of expressing the reasons for severing ties. But the crux of the Declaration lies in its expression of rights, and the purpose of government, viz. securing those rights.

8. Beyond Lincoln's suspension of habeas corpus and detention of thousands of political prisoners (see Hummel 1996), we are still haunted by this clause. For example, the 2010 National Defense Authorization Act grants the power of detaining American citizens indefinitely, without trial, and without habeas corpus to the executive branch. Then again, in our contemporary environment, it is not clear that constitutional considerations even entered the mind of the legislative drafters or President Obama, who signed the Act into law.

9. For an introduction to Austrian business cycle theory, see Ebeling 1996 or Callahan 2004.

10. See also Hummel and Marina 1981 for a libertarian debate on this question.

Chapter Four: What's Wrong with Libertarianism

1. Capitalism is not neutral with respect to economic transactions but favors a particular legal structuring of economic relations that privileges impersonal, large-scale, and profit-driven economic arrangements over personal, small-scale, and humane economies. Micklethwait and Wooldridge 2005 trace the revolutionary nature of corporate capitalism, though their judgment of corporations is overall positive. For a good illustration of some negative consequences, see Robert Miller 2012. It seems to me that there is something to the traditionalist opinion and that a good conservative debate on the rightful scope and limits of corporations would be very useful.

2. See, for example, Bruce Frohnen's entry on Conservatism in Frohnen et al., 2006: "Ideological defenses of economic freedom are unconservative because they posit one universal spring of human action—the desire for material gain" (182). This claim is not only patently false; it has a nefarious origin. See McGurn 2011.

3. For an argument that public choice theory does not accurately predict political behavior, see Pressman 2004. A "revisionist" public choice explanation for the apparent divergence of economic assumptions about human behavior and actual practice in voting is the "expressive theory of voting." According to that theory, people vote merely to express a preference, not to achieve an outcome. (See especially Brennan and Lomasky 1997 and also Brennan and Hamlin 2008). This theory, however, is subject to a number of important objections. In the first place, it still does not accurately describe why people *say* they vote. In the next place, voting that does not determine the outcome of an election can be pivotal in signaling mandates. Third, voters can have reasonable moral objections to free riding. Finally, the expressive theory cannot explain strategic voting. (For a critique of the expressive theory of voting, see Mackie 2011.)

4. For an outstanding account of the role of hypocrisy in politics, see Grant 1999.

5. Notably Hayek did not require that government action benefit *every citizen* for it to be justified: "But though the existence of an apparatus capable of providing for such collective needs is clearly in the general interest, this does not mean that it is in the interest of society as a whole that all collective interests should be satisfied. A collective interest will become a general interest only in so far as all find that the satisfaction of collective interests of particular groups on the basis of some principle of reciprocity will mean for them a gain in excess of the burden they will have to bear" (Hayek 1976, 6).

6. "Neither moral nor religious ideals are proper objects of coercion" (2011 [1960], 524). If Hayek acknowledges something like moral harm, coercion might be justified under these principles, but Hayek does not likely have this in mind. On libertarian antiperfectionism, see Brennan 2012b and Boaz 1997a. On progressive antiperfectionism, see Rawls 2005 [1993].

7. Hayek refers to the "empiricist evolutionary tradition" in Hayek 2011 [1960], 122. Hayek expresses his indebtedness to David Hume's epistemological skepticism, metaphysical nominalism, and moral emotivism. On skepticism, Hayek writes that "it has to be admitted that in some respects the liberal is fundamentally a skeptic" (Hayek 2011 [1960], 528). On nominalism, see Hayek's essay "Individualism True and False" in Hayek 1996, 1–32, especially footnote 6, in which he states, following Karl Pribram, that "philosophical nominalism" is the root of individualism, "while collectivist theories have their roots in the 'realist' . . . or 'essentialist' tradition." Finally, on emotivism, see Hayek 2011 [1960], 124.

8. Hayek insists that the rules or norms of behavior that make spontaneous orders possible are discovered, not made, by human beings (see especially Hayek 1973, 72–123), and he expresses agreement with Lord Acton that "the notion of a higher

law above municipal codes, with which Whiggism began, is the supreme achievement of Englishmen and their bequest to the nation" (Hayek 2011 [1960], 531).

9. See Archbold 2004, first published in 1822, and the definitive lawyer's guide on criminal law in the common law jurisdictions of the United Kingdom.

10. On the significance of strong evaluations, see Taylor 1976. The strange division of humanity into political regimes has preoccupied the greatest minds since Plato, including Aristotle, Augustine, Thomas Aquinas, Thomas Hobbes, John Calvin, John Locke, Jean Jacques Rousseau, G. W. F. Hegel, and many others.

Chapter Five: Libertarian Case Studies

1. Letter to the *London Times*, February 11, 1978.

2. Email to Henryk A. Kowalczyk, October 16, 2006.

3. In fact, I wrote my doctoral dissertation and a dozen subsequent articles on the importance of "constitutional culture" for constitutionally limited government. See Wenzel 2010a or 2013.

4. By *unrestricted*, I mean legally unrestricted. In a free society, immigration will still be restricted by market considerations.

5. Or parents, in the case of children.

6. McCluskey 2012.

7. Clulow (1993, 12–13) explains this was the case through the thirteenth century; McSheffrey 2006 places this as late as the sixteenth century.

Chapter Six: Conservative Case Studies

1. We have already seen Hayek's claim. Libertarian literature on immigration frequently asserts that opponents of open immigration are simply racist. Although this is doubtless true in some cases, libertarians should at least consider the possibility of legitimate nonracist interests in closed borders. An excellent example is Jason 2012.

2. Although citizenship restrictions limited the number and nationality of immigrants to white Europeans, in principle the borders were open to all immigrants. The first legal exclusion of immigrants came in 1882, with the Chinese Exclusion Act.

3. There is a strong case to be made for ensuring that America avoids a dependence on forms of technology or manufacturing that would be necessary in a time of war. On this, see none other than Adam Smith 1981 [1776], Vol. 1, Book IV. On the injustice and futility of economic protectionism, see Hayek 1979b, 65–97.

4. Currently only illegal immigrants are denied welfare benefits, except for emergency medical care and primary and secondary education. According to Nick Gillespie, already "about two thirds of illegals pay Medicare, Security, and income taxes [with fake or stolen Social Security numbers]" as well as sales and property taxes. See Gillespie 2006, 33.

5. This would add some of the advantages, without the disadvantages, of Gary Becker's proposal that immigrants pay a fee, say $50,000, to immigrate; see Becker

2011. Whereas every working immigrant could pay taxes, Becker's fee would exclude many immigrants who would benefit America.

6. Currently employers are required to verify the legal status of their workers, but there is no way to verify the verification, that is, to ensure the authenticity of the documentation. A national database like the Basic Pilot program could take care of this problem.

7. *Reynolds v. United States* U.S. 145, 164, 165, 166 (1878).

8. For a more comprehensive and detailed account of the founders' views on marriage and family, see West, forthcoming).

9. *Obergefell v. Hodges*, 135 S. Ct. 2599 (2015).

10. And so it would be both unreasonable and utterly impractical to limit marriage to only those couples who can in fact have children. Childless marriages are still marriages, and they can still model for others the marital norms of exclusivity and permanence.

11. See the summary of the data in Wilcox 2011. The data show significant differences in outcomes even between families with *married* biological parents and families with *nonmarried* cohabiting biological parents. Marriage matters.

12. Maggie Gallagher describes some of these mechanisms in "(How) Does Marriage Protect Child Well-Being?" in George and Elshtain 2006, 197–212.

13. For a more complete elaboration of their defense of marriage, see Girgis, George, and Anderson 2012: "Rigorously pursued, the logic of rejecting the conjugal [that is, traditional] conception of marriage . . . leads, by way of formlessness, toward pointlessness: It proposes a policy of which, having removed the principled ground for any restrictions, it can hardly explain the benefit" (21). Hadley Arkes (2006) makes the same point: "This is of course the most serious charge that the proponents of same-sex marriage have to meet: that by extending the notion of marriage to cover couples of the same sex we will set in train the changes in principle that will undermine marriage itself."

14. Same-sex marriage therefore is really only a halfway house to the elimination of legal marriage altogether, a point that is celebrated by some advocates of same-sex marriage. See the citations in Girgis, George, and Anderson 2011, 31–35.

15. These ideas are treated (respectively) in *New York Magazine, The Washington Post,* and *The New York Times.* See Anderson, 2013.

Chapter Eight: A Libertarian's Conclusion

1. I thank Jon Fennell for drawing my attention to the concept of political physiology; even if our conclusions differ, I am grateful for our conversations.

Bibliography

Acton, John Emerich Edward Dalton, Lord. 1907 [1877]. *The History of Freedom in Antiquity*. London: Macmillan.

Allen, William. 2000. Why Liberty? In *Why Liberty? A Collection of Liberty Fund Essays*. Indianapolis: Liberty Fund.

Anderson, Ryan. 2013. "The Social Costs of Abandoning the Meaning of Marriage." The Heritage Foundation. Issue Brief No. 4038, September 9. Available at http://thf_media.s3.amazonaws.com/2013/pdf/ib4038.pdf.

———. 2015. *Truth Overruled: The Future of Marriage and Religious Freedom*. Washington, DC: Regnery Publishing.

Anderson, Terry, and Donald Leal. 2001. *Free-Market Environmentalism*. New York: Palgrave Macmillan.

Aquinas, Thomas. 1947. *Summa Theologica. First Complete Edition in Three Volumes*. Trans. by the Fathers of the English Dominican Province. New York: Benziger Brothers.

Archbold, John Frederick. 2004. *Criminal Pleading: Evidence and Practice*, revised edition, James Richardson and David A. Thomas (eds.). London: Sweet & Maxwell.

Argenson, René-Louis de Voyer de Paulmy, Marquis d'. 1858. *Mémoires et Journal Inédit du Marquis d'Argenson, Ministre des Affaires Etrangères sous Louis XV*. Paris: Jannet.

Aristotle. 1996. The Politics and The Constitution of Athens. Stephen Everson (ed.). Cambridge, UK: Cambridge University Press.

Arkes, Hadley. 2006. "The Family and the Law," In Robert P. George and Jean Bethke Elshtain (eds.), *The Meaning of Marriage: Family, State, Market and Morals*. Dallas: Spence Publishing Company, 127.

———. 1986. *First Things*. Princeton, NJ: Princeton University Press.

Auster, Lawrence. 2002. Immigration is Harming American Culture. Reprinted in Mary Williams (ed.), 2004. *Immigration: Opposing Viewpoints*. Farmington Hills, MI: Greenhaven Press.

Bailyn, Bernard. 1967. *The Ideological Origins of the American Revolution*. Cambridge, MA: Belknap Press of Harvard University.

Barnett, Randy. 2004. *Restoring the Lost Constitution: The Presumption of Liberty.* Princeton, NJ: Princeton University Press.

Bastiat, Frédéric. 1995a [1848]. Property and Law. In *Selected Essays on Political Economy.* Irvington-on-Hudson, NY: Foundation for Economic Education.

———. 1995b [1848]. What Is Seen and What Is Not Seen. In *Selected Essays on Political Economy.* Irvington-on-Hudson: Foundation for Economic Education.

———. 2012 [1850]. *The Law.* New York: Tribeca Books.

Beard, Charles. 2004 [1913]. *An Economic Interpretation of the Constitution of the United States.* Mineola, NY: Dover Publications.

Becker, Gary. 2011. *The Challenge of Immigration.* London: The Institute of Economic Affairs.

Beito, David. 1992. *From Mutual Aid to the Welfare State: Fraternal Societies and Social Services.* Chapel Hill: University of North Carolina Press.

Benson, Bruce. 1998. *To Serve and Protect: Privatization and Community in Criminal Justice.* New York: New York University Press.

Binswanger, Harry. 2014. Open Immigration. Available at www.hblist.com/immigr.htm.

Boaz, David. 1997a. *Libertarianism: A Primer.* New York: The Free Press.

———. 1997b. Privatize Marriage: A Simple Solution to the Gay Marriage Debate. *Slate.* April 25. Available at www.slate.com/articles/briefing/articles/1997/04/privatize_marriage.html.

Borjas, George. 2008. Immigration. In David Henderson (ed.), *The Concise Encyclopedia of Economics.* Indianapolis: Liberty Fund.

Brennan, Geoffrey, and James Buchanan. 1988. Is Public Choice Immoral? The Case for the Noble Lie. *Virginia Law Review.* 74(2): 179–189.

Brennan, Geoffrey, and Alan Hamlin. 2000. *Democratic Devises and Desires.* Cambridge, UK: Cambridge University Press.

———. 2008. Revisionist Public Choice Theory. *New Political Economy.* 13(1): 77–88.

Brennan, Geoffrey, and Loren Lomasky. 1997. *Democracy and Decision: The Pure Theory of Electoral Preference.* Cambridge, UK: Cambridge University Press.

Brennan, Jason. 2012a. *The Ethics of Voting.* Princeton, NJ: Princeton University Press.

———. 2012b. *Libertarianism: What Everyone Needs to Know.* Oxford, UK: Oxford University Press.

Buchanan, James. 1964. What Should Economists Do? *The Southern Economic Journal,* XXX (January): 3.

———. 2000a [1975]. The Limits of Liberty: Between Anarchy and Leviathan, in *The Collected Works of James M. Buchanan,* volume 7. Indianapolis: Liberty Fund.

———. 2000b. Political and Meddlesome Preferences. In *Politics as Public Choice, The Collected Works of James M. Buchanan,* volume 13. Indianapolis: Liberty Fund.

———. 2003. Public Choice: Politics without Romance. *Imprimis,* 32(3): 1–8.

Buchanan, James, and Gordon Tullock. 1999. *The Calculus of Consent*. Indianapolis: Liberty Fund.

Budziszewski, J. 1997. *Written on the Heart: The Case for Natural Law*. Westmont, IL: Intervarsity Press.

Burke, Edmund. 1987. *Reflections on the Revolution in France*. Indianpaolis: Hackett.

Butterfield, Herbert. 1965. *The Whig Interpretation of History*. New York: W. W. Norton.

Callahan, Gene. 2004. *Economics for Real People: An Introduction to the Austrian School*. Auburn, AL: Ludwig von Mises Institute.

Caplan, Bryan. 2008. *The Myth of the Rational Voter: Why Democracies Choose Bad Policies*. Princeton, NJ: Princeton University Press.

Carey, George (ed.). 2004 [1984]. *Freedom and Virtue: The Conservative/Libertarian Debate*. Wilmington, DE: Intercollegiate Studies Institute.

Catholic Church. 1995. *The Catechism of the Catholic Church*, second edition. New York: Doubleday.

Chafuen, Alejandro. 2003. *Faith and Liberty: The Economic Thought of the Late Scholastics*, second edition. Lanham, MD: Lexington Books.

Childs, Roy. 1969. Objectivism and the State: An Open Letter to Ayn Rand. *The Rational Individualist*, August.

Clark, J. R., Robert Lawson, Alex Nowrasteh, Benjamin Powell, and Ryan Murphy. 2014. Does Immigration Impact Economic Freedom? Washington, DC: Cato Working Paper.

Clulow, Christopher (ed.). 1993. *Rethinking Marriage: Public and Private Perspectives*. London: Kamac Books.

Coase, Ronald. 1960. The Problem of Social Cost. *Journal of Law & Economics*, III (October).

Cooke, Charles C. 2015. *The Conservatarian Manifesto*. New York: Crown Forum.

Cott, Nancy. 2000. *Public Vows: A History of Marriage and the Nation*. Cambridge, MA: Harvard University Press.

Coulanges, Fustel De. 1980. *The Ancient City*. Baltimore: The Johns Hopkins University Press.

Courtois, Stéphane, and Mark Kramer (eds.). 1999. *The Black Book of Communism: Crimes, Terror, Repression*. Cambridge, MA: Harvard University Press.

Crane, Edward. 2007. Is Hillary Clinton a Neocon? *Financial Times*, July 11.

Dailey, Sean. 2012. The Lost Art of Catholic Drinking. *Crisis Magazine*. April 13. Available at www.catholicity.com/commentary/dailey/00968.html.

Demsetz, Harold. 1969. Information and Efficiency: Another Viewpoint. *Journal of Law and Economics*, 12 (April).

Deneen, Patrick. 2012a. Beyond Wishful Thinking: A Reply to Schlueter. *Public Discourse*, December 14. Available at www.thepublicdiscourse.com/2012/12/7411.

Deneen, Patrick. 2012b. Unsustainable Liberalism. *First Things*. August.

Dershowitz, Alan. 2004. *Rights from Wrongs: A Secular Theory of the Origin of Rights*. New York: Basic Books.

Dixon, Pauline. 2013. *International Aid and Private Schools for the Poor: Smiles, Miracles and Markets*. Cheltenham, UK, and Northampton, MA: Edward Elgar.

Duncan, Marion Moncure. 1964. National Origins Quotas Should Be Retained. Reprinted in Mary Williams (ed.), 2004. *Immigration: Opposing Viewpoints*. Farmington Hills, MI: Greenhaven Press.

Ebeling, Richard (ed.). 1996. *The Austrian Theory of the Trade Cycle and Other Essays*. Auburn, AL: Ludwig von Mises Institute.

Ebenstein, A. 2003. *Friedrich Hayek: A Biography*. Chicago: University of Chicago Press.

Eldredge, Dirk Chase. 2004. Immigration Should Be Restricted. In Mary Williams (ed.), *Immigration: Opposing Viewpoints*. Farmington Hills, MI: Greenhaven Press.

Epstein, Richard. 1999. Hayekian Socialism. *Maryland Law Review*, 58: 271–299.

———. 2011. *Design for Liberty: Private Property, Public Administration, and the Rule of Law*. Cambridge, MA: Harvard University Press.

Farrand, Max, ed. 1967. *The Records of the Federal Convention of 1787, Volume II*. New Haven, CT: Yale University Press.

Finnis, John. 2011. *Natural Law and Natural Rights*, second edition. Oxford, UK: Oxford University Press.

Fischer, David Hackett. 1989. *Albion's Seed: Four British Folkways in America*. Oxford, UK: Oxford University Press.

Frey, Bruno S., and Reto Jegen. 2001. Motivation Crowding Theory. *Journal of Economic Survey*, 15(5): 589–611.

Friedman, Milton. 1962. *Capitalism and Freedom*. Chicago: University of Chicago Press.

Frisch, Morton J., ed. 1985. *Selected Writings and Speeches of Alexander Hamilton*. Washington, DC: American Enterprise Institute.

Frohnen, Bruce, Jeremy Beer, and Jeffrey O. Nelson. 2006. *American Conservatism: An Encyclopedia*. Wilmington, DE: ISI Books.

Fukuyama, Francis. 2006 [1992]. *The End of History and the Last Man*. New York: The Free Press.

George, Robert. 1995. *Making Men Moral: Civil Liberties and Public Morality*. Oxford, UK: Oxford University Press.

———. 1999. *In Defense of Natural Law*. Oxford, UK: Oxford University Press.

———. 2002. *Clash of Orthodoxies: Law, Religion and Morality in Crisis*. Wilmington, DE: ISI Books.

George, Robert P., and Jean Bethke Elshtain, eds. 2006. *The Meaning of Marriage: Family, State, Markets and Morals*. Dallas, TX: Spence Publishing.

Gillespie, Nick. 2006. Bush's Border Bravado. *Reason*. August/September: 31–33.

Girgis, Sherif, Robert P. George, and Ryan Anderson. 2011. What Is Marriage? *Harvard Journal of Law and Public Policy*, 34:1 (Winter): 245–287.

———. 2012. *What Is Marriage? Man and Woman: A Defense.* New York: Encounter Books.

Glendon, Mary Ann. 1993. *Rights Talk: The Impoverishment of Political Discourse,* reprint edition. New York: The Free Press.

Gordon, Scott. 1999. *Controlling the State: A History of Constitutionalism from Ancient Athens to Today.* Cambridge, MA: Harvard University Press.

Grant, Ruth. 1999. *Hypocrisy and Integrity: Machiavelli, Rousseau, and the Ethics of Politics.* Chicago: University of Chicago Press, 1999.

Gwartney, James, Richard Stroup, Russel Sobel, and David Macpherson. 2005. *Economics: Private and Public Choice,* eleventh edition.. Mason, OH: Thomson Higher Education.

Gwartney, James, Robert Lawson, and Joshua Hall, 2015. Economic Freedom of the World 2015, www.freetheworld.com

Hamilton, Alexander, John Jay, and James Madison. 2001. *The Federalist.* Indianapolis: Liberty Fund.

Hannan, Daniel. 2013. *Inventing Freedom: How the English-Speaking Peoples Made the Modern World.* New York: Broadside Books.

Hasnas, John. 2005. Towards a Theory of Empirical Natural Rights. *Social Philosophy and Policy,* 22(1), 111–147.

———. 2008. The Obviousness of Anarchy. In Roderick Long and Tibor Machan (eds.), *Anarchism/Minarchism: Is a Government Part of a Free Country?* Burlington, VT: Ashgate Press, 2008: 111–131.

Hardin, Russell. 1999. Liberalism, Constitutionalism, and Democracy. Oxford, UK: Oxford University Press.

Hayek, F. A. 1944. *The Road to Serfdom.* Chicago: University of Chicago Press.

———.1945. The Use of Knowledge in Society. *The American Economic Review.* 35(4): 519–530.

———. 1960. *The Constitution of Liberty.* Chicago: The University of Chicago Press.

———. 1973. *Law Legislation and Liberty, Vol. 1: Rules and Order.* Chicago: The University of Chicago Press.

———. 1976. *Law, Legislation and Liberty, Vol. 2: The Mirage of Social Justice.* Chicago: The University of Chicago Press.

———. 1979a [1952]. *The Counter-Revolution of Science: Studies on the Abuse of Reason.* Indianapolis: Liberty Fund.

———. 1979b. *Law, Legislation and Liberty, Volume 3: The Political Order of a Free People.* Chicago: The University of Chicago Press.

———. 1988. *The Fatal Conceit: The Errors of Socialism.* Chicago: University of Chicago Press.

———. 1996. *Individualism and Economic Order.* Chicago: University of Chicago Press.

———. 2011 [1960]. *The Constitution of Liberty: The Definitive Edition.* Edited by Ronald Hamowy. Chicago: The University of Chicago Press.

Hittinger, Russell. 1989. *A Critique of the New Natural Law Theory*. Notre Dame, IN: University of Notre Dame Press.

Hobbes, Thomas. 2002. *Leviathan*. Cambridge, UK: Cambridge University Press.

Hornberger, Jacob. 2004. Immigration Should Not Be Restricted. In Mary Williams (ed.), *Immigration: Opposing Viewpoints*. Farmington Hills, MI: Greenhaven Press.

Horwitz, Steven. 2007. Capitalism and the Family. *The Freeman: Ideas on Liberty*, 57(6, July/August).

———. 2015. *Hayek's Modern Family: Classical Liberal and the Evolution of Social Institutions*. London: Palgrave Macmillan.

Horwitz, Steven, and Peter Boettke. 2010. *The House That Uncle Sam Built: The Untold Story of the Great Recession of 2008*. Irvington-on-Hudson, NY: Foundation for Economic Education.

Hume, David. 1985. *Essays Moral, Political and Literary*, revised edition. Edited by Eugene F. Miller. Indianapolis: Liberty Fund.

Hummel, Jeffrey Rogers. 1996. *Emancipating Slaves, Enslaving Free Men: A History of the American Civil War*. Peru, IL: Open Court.

Hummel, Jeffrey Rogers, and William Marina. 1981. Did the Constitution Betray the Revolution? The Independent Institute, January 1, 1981. Available at www.independent.org/newsroom/article.asp?id=1400.

Ikeda, Sanford. 2003. How Compatible Are Public Choice and Austrian Political Economy? *Review of Austrian Economics* 16:1, 63–75.

Janssen, Maarten C. W., and Ewa Mendys-Kamphorst. 2004. The Price of a Price: On the Crowding Out and In of Social Norms. *Journal of Economic Behavior and Organizations* 55: 377–395.

Jason, Gary. 2012. *A Classical Liberal Case for Immigration Reform*. Liberty Unbound. December 7. Available at www.libertyunbound.com/node/952.

Jefferson, Thomas. 1787. "Thomas Jefferson to James Madison, 20 December 1787," Chapter 18, Document 21, in Philip B. Kurland and Ralph Lerner, eds., 1986, *The Founders' Constitution*. Chicago: University of Chicago Press, and Indianapolis: Liberty Fund.

———. 1798. "Resolutions Relative to the Alien and Sedition Acts, 10 November 1798," Chapter 8, Document 41, in Philip B. Kurland and Ralph Lerner, eds., 1986, *The Founders' Constitution*. Chicago: University of Chicago Press, and Indianapolis: Liberty Fund.

———. 1801. "First Inaugural Address, March 4, 1801." New Haven, CT: The Avalon Project at Yale Law School. Available at http://avalon.law.yale.edu/19th_century/jefinau1.asp.

———. 1975. *The Portable Thomas Jefferson*, Edited by Merill D. Peterson. New York: Penguin Books.

———. 1979. *Thomas Jefferson Selected Writings*. Edited by Harvey Mansfield Jr. Arlington Heights, IL: Harlan Davidson.

John Paul II. 1991. *On the Hundredth Anniversary of Rerum Novarum*. Boston: Pauline Books & Media.

Kant, Immanuel. (1970) 1992. *Political Writings*. Edited by Hans Reiss and translated by H. B. Nisbet. Cambridge, UK: Cambridge University Press.

———. 1997. *Lectures on Ethics*. Cambridge, UK: Cambridge University Press.

Kessler, Charles. "Introduction." *The Federalist Papers*. New York: A Mentor Book, 1999.

King, Martin Luther Jr. 1958. *Stride Toward Freedom: The Montgomery Story*. San Franciso: HarperSanFrancisco.

Kirk, Russell. 1982. Introduction. In Russell Kirk (ed.), *The Portable Conservative Reader*. New York: Viking Penguin.

———. 1986 [1953]. *The Conservative Mind: From Burke to Eliot*, 7th revised edition. Washington, DC: Regnery Books.

Klein, Daniel. 2005.The People's Romance: Why People Love Government (as Much as They Do). *The Independent Review*, X(1), Summer.

Kries, Douglas. 2008 *The Problem of Natural Law*. Lanham, MD: Lexington Books.

Krogstad, Jens Manuel and Jeffrey S. Passel. 2015. "Five Facts about Illegal Immigration in the U.S." Available at www.pewresearch.org/fact-tank/2014/11/18/5-facts-about-illegal-immigration-in-the-u-s/.

LaRochefoucauld, François duc de. 1959. *Maxims*. Trans. Leondard Tanock. New York: Penguin Books.

Lawson, Gary. 1994. The Rise and Rise of the Administrative State. *Harvard Law Review*, 107(6): 1231–1254.

Lea, Geoffrey, and Adam Martin. 2014. From Vienna to Virginia. Review of Austrian Economics: Exchange, Rules and Social Cooperation. An Introduction to the Symposium. *Review of Austrian Economics*, 27(1): 1–9.

Leeson, Peter, and J. Robert Subrick. 2006. Robust Political Economy. *Review of Austrian Economics*, 19: 107–111.

LeGuin, Ursula. 1975. The Ones Who Walk Away from Omelas. In *The Wind's Twelve Quarters*. London: Orion Books.

Leighton, Wayne, and Edward Lopez. 2012. *Madmen, Intellectuals and Academic Scribblers: The Economic Engine of Political Change*. Palo Alto, CA: Stanford Economics and Finance.

Leonard, Thomas. 2004. The Price is Wrong: Causes and Consequences of Ethical Restraint of Trade. *Journal des Economistes et des Etudes Humaines* 14(4): 1–18.

Levy, Robert, and William Mellor. 2008. *The Dirty Dozen: How Twelve Supreme Court Cases Radically Expanded Government and Eroded Freedom*. New York: Sentinel.

Lewis, C. S. 1972 [1948]. God in the Dock. In *God in the Dock: Essays on Theology and Ethics*. Grand Rapids, MI: Wm. B. Eerdmans Publishing Co.

———. 1974. *The Abolition of Man*. New York: HarperOne.

———. 1944. *The Abolition of Man*. New York: HarperOne.

Lincoln, Abraham. 1989. *Speeches and Writings, 1832–1858*. New York: The Library of America.

———. 1862. "Letter to Horace Greeley, August 22. Washington, DC: The Abraham Lincoln Papers at the Library of Congress, General Correspondence, 1858–1864.

Lindsey, Brink. 2010. Where Do Libertarians Belong? *Reason.com*. July 12.

Locke, John. 1959. *An Essay Concerning Human Understanding (in Two Volumes)*. Edited by Alexander Campbell Fraser. New York: Dover Books.

———. 1988. *Two Treatises of Government*. Edited by Peter Laslett. Cambridge, UK: Cambridge University Press.

Long Steven. 2007. *The Teleological Grammar of the Moral Act*. Washington, DC: Sapientia Press.

Lutz, Donald S. 1988. *The Origins of American Constitutionalism*. Baton Rouge: Louisiana State University Press.

MacDonald, Heather, Victor Davis Hanson, and Steven Malanga. 2007. *The Immigration Solution: A Better Plan Than Today's*. Lanham, MD: Ivan R. Dee.

MacIntyre, Alasdair. 1999. *Dependent Rational Animals: Why Human Beings Need the Virtues*. Chicago: Open Court.

———. 2006. *The Tasks of Philosophy, Selected Essays, Vol. 1*. Cambridge, UK: Cambridge University Press.

———. 2007. *After Virtue*, third edition. Notre Dame, IN: University of Notre Dame Press.

———. 2009. *Intractable Disputes about the Natural Law*. Edited by Lawrence S. Cunningham. Notre Dame, IN: University of Notre Dame Press.

Mackie, Gerry. 2011. "An Examination of the Expressive Theory of Voting." Unpublished. Available at http://pages.ucsd.edu/~gmackie/documents/Expressive%20Voting.pdf.

Maloberti, Nicolas. 2011. Government by Choice: Classical Liberalism and the Moral Status of Immigration Barriers. *The Independent Review*, 15(4, Spring): 541–562.

McCloskey, Deirdre. May/June 2006. The Bourgeois Virtues? *Cato Policy Report* (May/June).

———. 2007. *The Bourgeois Virtues: Ethics for an Age of Commerce*. Chicago: University of Chicago Press.

McCluskey, Neal. 2012."Education Spending Doesn't Deliver." Cato Institute. Available at www.cato.org/publications/commentary/education-spending-doesnt-deliver.

McDonald, Forest. 1985. *Novus Ordo Seclorum: The Intellectual Origins of the Constitution*. Lawrence: University of Kansas Press.

McGurn, William. 2011. The Not So Dismal Science: Humanitarians versus Economists. *Imprimis*, 40 (3).

McSheffrey, Shannon. 2006. *Marriage, Sex and Civic Culture in Late Medieval London*. Philadelphia: University of Pennsylvania Press.

Mencken, H. L. 1996. Sham Battle. In Malcolm Moos (ed.), *On Politics: A Carnival of Buncombe*. Baltimore: The Johns Hopkins University Press.

Meyer, Frank S. 1996. *In Defense of Freedom*. Edited by William C. Dennis. Indianapolis: Liberty Fund.

Micklethwait, John, and Adrian Woodrbridge. 2005. *The Company: A Short History of a Revolutionary Idea*. Reprint edition. New York: Modern Library.

Miller, Robert. 2012. Hotel Pornography and the Market of Morality. *Public Discourse*, July 13. Available at www.thepublicdiscourse.com/2012/07/5936.

Mill, John Stuart. 1978 [1959]. *On Liberty*. Indianapolis: Hackett Publishing Co.

Mises, Ludwig von. 1985 [1929]. *Liberalism: The Classical Tradition*. Irvington-on-Hudson, NY: Foundation for Economic Education.

———. 1990 [1920]. *Economic Calculation in the Socialist Commonwealth*. Auburn, AL: Ludwig von Mises Institute.

———. 1999 [1949]. *Human Action: A Treatise on Economics*. Auburn, AL: Ludwig von Mises Institute.

———. 2007 [1955]. *Economic Policy: Thoughts for Today and for Tomorrow*. Auburn, AL: Ludwig von Mises Institute.

Moschella, Melissa. 2012. "Parental Rights in Education." PhD dissertation, Princeton University, Princeton, NJ.

Murray, Charles. 2012. *Coming Apart: The State of White America, 1960–2010*. New York: Crown Forum.

Nash, George. 2006 [1996]. *The Conservative Intellectual Movement in America since 1945*. Wilmington, DE: Intercollegiate Studies Institute.

National Taxpayers Union Foundation, "Who Pays Income Taxes 2013." Retrieved on May 3, 2016, from www.ntu.org/tax-basics/who-pays-income-taxes.html.

Neily, Clark M. III. 2013. *Terms of Engagement: How Our Courts Should Enforce the Constitution's Promise of Limited Government*. New York: Encounter Books.

Neily, Clark M. III, and Robert J. McNamara. 2010. Getting Beyond Guns: Context for the Coming Debate over Privileges or Immunities. *Texas Review of Law & Politics*, 14 (1).

Newman, John Henry. 1989. *An Essay on the Development of Christian Doctrine*. Notre Dame, IN: University of Notre Dame Press.

Nozick, Robert. 1974. *Anarchy, State, and Utopia*. New York: Basic Books.

Ostrom, Vincent. 1984. Why Governments Fail: An Inquiry into the Use of Instruments of Evil to Do Good. In James M. Buchanan and Robert D. Tollison (eds.), *The Theory of Public Choice: II*. Ann Arbor: University of Michigan Press.

Pennington, Mark. 2011. *Robust Political Economy: Classical Liberalism and the Future of Public Policy*. Cheltenham, UK, and Northampton, MA: Edward Elgar.

Perry, Mark. 2013. "Protectionist Sugar Policy Cost Americans $3 billion in 2012." Available at www.aei-ideas.org/2013/02/protectionist-sugar-policy-cost-americans-3-billion-in-2012/February 14, 2013.

Pestritto, Ronald J., and Thomas G. West, eds. 2005. *Challenges to the American Founding*. Lanham, MD: Lexington Books.

Pigou, A. C. 1932. *The Economics of Welfare*, fourth edition. London: Macmillan.

Pitkin, Hanna. 1965. Obligation and Consent—I. *The American Political Science Review.* 59(4): 990–999.

———. 1966. Obligation and Consent—II. *The American Political Science Review.* 60(1): 39–52.

Polanyi, Michael. 1962. *Personal Knowledge.* Chicago: The University of Chicago Press.

Powell, Benjamin. 2012. Coyote Ugly: The Deadweight Cost of Rent Seeking for Immigration Policy. *Public Choice* 150: 195–208.

Pressman, Steven. 2004. What Is Wrong with Public Choice. *Journal of Post-Keynesian Economics.* 27(1): 3–18.

Putnam, Robert. 2000. *Bowling Alone: The Collapse and Revival of American Community.* New York: Simon and Schuster.

Rahe, Paul. 1994. *Republics Ancient & Modern, Volume III: Inventions of Prudence: Constituting the American Regime.* Chapel Hill: University of North Carolina Press.

Raico, Ralph. 2006. "What Is Classical Liberalism?" in Bruce Frohnen, Jeremy Beer, and Jeffrey O. Nelson, *American Conservatism: An Encyclopedia.* Wilmington, DE: ISI Books.

Rand, Ayn. 1957. *Atlas Shrugged.* New York: Signet Books.

———. 1964. Government Financing in a Free Society. In *The Virtue of Selfishness: A New Concept of Egoism.* New York: Signet Books.

———. 1967a. Man's Rights. In *Capitalism: The Unknown Ideal.* New York: Signet Books.

———. 1967b. The Nature of Government. In *Capitalism: The Unknown Ideal.* New York: Signet Books.

———. 1967c. What Is Capitalism? In *Capitalism: The Unknown Ideal.* New York: Signet Books.

Ravitch, Diane. 2001. *Left Back: A Century of Battles over School Reform.* New York: Simon & Schuster.

Rawls, John. 1971. *A Theory of Justice.* Cambridge, MA: The Belknap Press of Harvard University.

———. 2005 [1993]. *Political Liberalism.* Expanded edition. New York: Columbia University Press.

Read, Leonard. 1958. *I, Pencil: My Family Tree as Told to Leonard Read.* Irvington-on-Hudson, NY: Foundation for Economic Education.

———. 1964. *Anything That's Peaceful.* Irvington-on-Hudson, NY: Foundation for Economic Education.

Rogge, Benjamin, and Pierre Goodrich. 1973. Position Paper: Education in a Free Society. In Anne Husted Burleigh (ed.), *Education in a Free Society.* Indianapolis: Liberty Fund.

Rosenberg, Nathan, and L. E. Birdzell Jr. 1987. *How The West Grew Rich: The Economic Transformation of the Industrial World.* New York: Basic Books.

Ross, Alf. 1959. *On Law and Justice*. London: The Lawbook Exchange.

Rothbard, Murray. 1977. Robert Nozick and the Immaculate Conception of the State. *Journal of Libertarian Studies*. 1(1): 45–57.

———. 2003. *The Ethics of Liberty*. New York: NYU Press.

———. 2006. *For a New Liberty: The Libertarian Manifesto*, second edition. Auburn, AL: Ludwig von Mises Institute.

Samuelson, Paul. 1954. The Pure Theory of Public Expenditure. *Review of Economics and Statistics* 36(4): 387–389.

Sandel, Michael. 1998. *Liberalism and the Limits of Justice*. Cambridge, UK: Cambridge University Press.

———. 2012. *What Money Can't Buy: The Moral Limits of Markets*. New York: Farrar, Straus and Giroux.

Scafidi, Benjamin. 2012. *The School Staffing Surge: Decades of Employment Growth in America's Public Schools*. The Friedman Foundation for Educational Choice.

Schlueter, Nathan. 2012. Sustainable Liberalism. *Public Discourse*, December 7.. Available at www.thepublicdiscourse.com/2012/12/7322/.

———. 2013. Natural Law Liberalism beyond Romanticism. *Public Discourse*. Available at www.thepublicdiscourse.com/2013/03/7511/ March 4.

Scruton, Roger. 2006. *A Political Philosophy: Arguments for Conservatism*. New York, Continuum.

Scully, Gerald. 1992. *Constitutional Environments and Economic Growth*. Princeton, NJ: Princeton University Press.

———. 1998. The Institutional Framework and Economic Development. *Journal of Political Economy*, 96 (3, June): 652–662

Siedentop, Larry. 2014. *Inventing the Individual: The Origins of Western Liberalism*. Cambridge, MA: Belknap Press.

Silvergate, Harvey. 2011. *Three Felonies a Day: How the Feds Target the Innocent*. New York: Encounter Books

Skinner, Quentin. 1978. *The Foundations of Modern Political Thought* (two volumes). Cambridge, UK: Cambridge University Press.

Smith, Adam. 1981 [1776]. *An Inquiry into the Nature and Causes of the Wealth of Nations*. Two volumes. Indianapolis: Liberty Fund.

Smith, Adam, and Bruce Yandle. 2014. *Bootleggers and Baptists: How Economic Forces and Moral Persuasion Interact to Shape Regulatory Politics*. Washington, DC: Cato Institute.

Snell, R. J. 2014. *The Perspective of Love: Natural Law in a New Mode*. Eugene, OR: Pickwick Publications.

Sowell, Thomas. 1980. *Knowledge and Decisions*. New York: Basic Books.

———. 1996. *The Vision of the Anointed: Self-Congratulation as a Basis for Public Policy*. New York: Basic Books.

Storing, Herbert. 1995. *Toward a More Perfect Union*. Joseph M. Bessette, editor. Washington, DC: AEI Press.

Strauss, Leo. 1965. *Natural Right and History*. Chicago: University of Chicago Press.

Taylor, Charles. 1976. Responsibility for Self. In Amelie Oskenburg Rorty (ed.), *The Identities of Persons*. Oakland: University of California Press.

Tierney, Brian. 1997. *The Idea of Natural Rights*. Grand Rapids, MI: Eerdmans Publishing Company.

Titmuss, Richard. 1971. *The Gift Relationship: From Human Blood to Social Policy*. New York: Pantheon Books.

Tocqueville, Alexis de. 2000. *Democracy in America*. Edited and translated by Harvey C. Mansfield and Delba Winthrop. Chicago: University of Chicago Press.

Tomasi, John. 2012. *Free Market Fairness*. Princeton, NJ: Princeton University Press.

Tooley, James. 2013. *The Beautiful Tree: A Personal Journey into How the World's Poorest People Are Educating Themselves*. Washington, DC: Cato Institute.

Tullock, Gordon. 2005. Legitimacy and Ethics. In *The Social Dilemma of Autocracy, Revolution and Coup d'Etat: The Selected Works of Gordon Tullock*, volume 8. Indianapolis: Liberty Fund.

Voltaire. 1733. "Letter on the Presbyterians," in Voltaire's Philosophical Letters, Letter 6. Indianapolis: Liberty Fund. Available at www.oll.libertyfund.org/titles/Voltaire-the-works-of-Voltaire-vol-xix-philosophical letters.

Wattenberg, Ben. 2002. Immigration Is Good for American Culture. Reprinted in Mary Williams (ed.), 2004. *Immigration: Opposing Viewpoints*. Farmington Hills, MI: Greenhaven Press.

Waugh, Evelyn. 1983. *The Essays, Articles and Reviews of Evelyn Waugh*. Boston: Little, Brown & Co.

Weaver, Richard. 1984. *Ideas Have Consequences*. Chicago: University of Chicago Press.

Wenzel, Nikolai. 2008. Postmodernism and Religion. In Peter Clarke (ed.), *Oxford Handbook of the Sociology of Religion*. Oxford, UK: Oxford University Press.

———. 2010a. From Contract to Mental Model: Constitutional Culture as a Fact of the Social Sciences. *Review of Austrian Economics*, 23(1).

———. 2010b. An Institutional Solution for a Cognitive Problem: Hayek's Sensory Order as Foundation for Hayek's Institutional Order. In William N. Butos (ed.), *The Social Science of Hayek's "The Sensory Order," Advances in Austrian Economics*, volume 13. Bingley, UK: Emerald Group Publishing Limited.

———. 2013. Judicial Review and Constitutional Maintenance: John Marshall, Hans Kelsen and the Popular Will. *PS: Political Science and Politics*, 46 (July): 3.

West, Thomas G. (forthcoming) *The Political Theory of the American Founding*. New York: Cambridge University Press.

———. 1997. *Vindicating the Founders: Race, Sex, Class, and Justice in the Origins of America*. Lanham, MD: Rowman & Littlefield Publishers.

Wilcox, Bradford. 2009. The Evolution of Divorce. *Public Affairs*, I (Fall): 81–94.

———. 2011. *Why Marriage Matters: Thirty Conclusions from the Social Sciences*, third edition. West Chester, PA: Broadway Publications.

Wolfe, Christopher. 2009. *Natural Law Liberalism*. Cambridge, UK: Cambridge University Press.

Wood, Gordon. 1969. *The Creation of the American Republic: 1776–1787*. Chapel Hill: University of North Carolina Press.

Zywicki, Todd. 2013. Libertarianism, Law and Economics, and the Common Law. *Chapman Law Review*, 16(2): 309–324.

Index

CPSIA information can be obtained
at www.ICGtesting.com
Printed in the USA
LVOW12s0008081217
559043LV00003B/3/P